T0381493

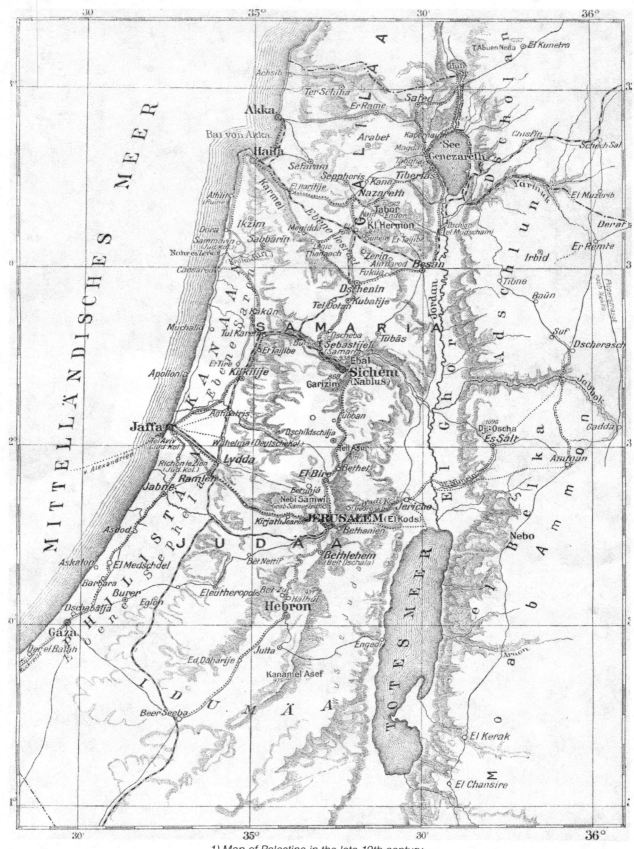

1) Map of Palestine in the late 19th century
Note: Saron plain (Ebene Saron)

ii

FROM DESERT SANDS TO GOLDEN ORANGES

WRITTEN BY HELMUT GLENK

IN CONJUNCTION WITH HORST BLAICH AND MANFRED HAERING

Order this book online at www.trafford.com
or email orders@trafford.com

Most Trafford titles are also available at major online book retailers.

The book's cover design and page layout was created by Horst Blaich with technical assistance by Trevor Evans from Tree of Life Publishing, Ringwood East, Victoria, Australia—email familybookste@optushome.com.au

Printed in the United States of America.

ISBN: 978-1-4120-3506-4 (sc)
ISBN: 978-1-4122-2670-7 (e)

Trafford rev. 05/15/2014

www.trafford.com
North America & international
toll-free: 1 888 232 4444 (USA & Canada)
fax: 812 355 4082

FROM DESERT SANDS TO GOLDEN ORANGES

THE HISTORY OF THE GERMAN TEMPLER SETTLEMENT OF SARONA IN PALESTINE 1871-1947

SARONA IS KNOWN TODAY AS HAKIRYA
IN THE HEART OF TEL AVIV, ISRAEL

WRITTEN BY HELMUT GLENK
IN CONJUNCTION WITH HORST BLAICH AND MANFRED HAERING

INTRODUCTION

THIS BOOK IS AN IMPORTANT episode in the history of the development and modernisation of Palestine in the latter 19th and early 20th Centuries. It portrays the significant contribution made by a small group of German settlers from Wuerttemberg in southern Germany during their 80 years in Palestine. These settlers from the Temple Society first started settlements in the Holy Land in 1869. This book focuses on the settlement of Sarona which was established as an agricultural settlement on the outskirts of Jaffa in 1871.

"From Desert Sands to Golden Oranges" is an authentic historical account of the Sarona settlement. The achievements of the German settlers, before the first significant Jewish immigration in the 1880s, demonstrated that European settlement was possible in the Holy Land. The achievements of the Sarona settlers were regarded by some Jewish pioneers as a "model" similar to what the Jewish immigrants should aspire to. It is the first such detailed account of an individual German Templer settlement in the Holy Land and Palestine.

The book was written after several years of extensive research. It details the settlement's foundation; the extreme hardships endured by the early settlers; the innovations in agriculture (plants and cultivation) and introduction of motorised irrigation systems; the trade skills brought and developed; orderly settlement planning and new styles of architecture and building; the traumas and internment of World War I; the rebuilding after the war; life generally in the settlement; the many and varied business enterprises; sporting, social and cultural activities during the British Mandate period; the settlers' internment during World War II and their forced departure from Palestine.

"From Desert Sands to Golden Oranges" is a timely publication considering the recent historical interest within Israel relating to the pioneering work of the Germans in Palestine. One chapter deals with the issues of preservation and restoration of significant buildings and structures built by the settlers. That restoration work is now in the care of the City Council of Tel Aviv and its Preservation Team.

The settlers of Sarona left a proud heritage in the Holy Land, Palestine and Israel. Their buildings, their enterprises and their agricultural ventures will forever be remembered as having contributed significantly to the modernisation of Palestine and ultimately Israel.

TABLE OF CONTENTS

TABLE OF CONTENTS

TABLE OF CONTENTS

The plan of Sarona at the rear of the book, shows the streets and buildings. Each building has been numbered and if the building is referred to in the text its number is shown in brackets.

PREFACE

THIS BOOK SPANS ONLY 77 YEARS in the history of the Holy Land (Palestine and Israel). It is a story of severe hardship and sorrow. It is a story of hope and aspirations and what can be achieved by human endeavour. It is a story of joy, happiness and pride. It is also a story which we, Helmut Glenk, Manfred Haering and Horst Blaich, are proud to be associated with, in memory of our ancestors. The book provides a record for our descendants and other descendants of those persons who built, lived and died in the German Templer Sarona Settlement and their achievements. Today the area where Sarona was is known as Hakirya in the heart of Tel Aviv, Israel.

This book project began in late 2001 when the Tel Aviv City Council, following representations by a number of persons, the Gottlieb-Schumacher Institute (University of Haifa) and other groups, agreed to allow a sector of former Sarona to be preserved and restored.

The Tempelgesellschaft in Deutschland (TGD) (Temple Society in Germany) was advised that this could only proceed if plans and photographs of the houses could be provided. This seemed improbable because so much had been lost and destroyed. Time was of the essence and Dr. Jakob Eisler, Architect Danny Goldman and the Tel Aviv Municipal Office together with the Sarona Restoration team lead by Peera Goldman were pressing for details.

The archives of the TGD, under the qualified leadership of Brigitte Kneher, could help only superficially. A plan of Sarona was prepared and all owners of the homes were recorded. A request for support was sent to the Temple Society in Australia (TSA) in regard to the restoration and preservation of a number of buildings in Hakirya. The TSA published the request for assistance in its monthly publication "Templer Record", and expressed interest, but could not offer any financial support nor commit other resources to the project.

In Australia, Manfred Haering wrote an article in the Templer Record in March 2002 indicating that the project should be supported and that he was prepared to undertake some work to obtain photographs, plans and any other details of the buildings in question. Manfred, who was born in Jaffa, Palestine, visited Israel in 1999 with the TGD—the tour leaders were Dieter Lange and Karin Klingbeil from the

TGD. Jakob Eisler from the University of Haifa, Israel, provided detailed information during the actual visits to the former settlements. Manfred's visit to Sarona, especially to his former family home, left a deep personal impression with him. He felt a desire to preserve the history and heritage of the buildings of our forefathers so that future generations could look back proudly on what had been achieved.

There was a poor response to Manfred's written request for assistance. He therefore approached some persons individually. Helmut Glenk agreed to work with Manfred on the project. Helmut, a descendant of a family that had lived in Sarona for several generations, saw a much broader need to record the life and times, that is, the history and achievements of the Templers in Sarona. Both Manfred and Helmut agreed that unless their generation did this, much of the information gleaned from the personal recollections from people who had lived in Sarona would be forever lost. Already many of these persons had passed away.

Thus the project began. Initially, the emphasis was on locating information on the buildings designated for preservation. The scope of the project soon grew from just concentrating on buildings to include life generally in the former settlement. Former residents of Sarona were contacted and interviewed, photographs were borrowed and copied, archives examined, ongoing articles were published in the Templer Record to maintain interest within the Templer community and gradually more and more information was forthcoming. During a visit to Australia by Peter Lange, President of the Temple Society, in 2002, Manfred and Helmut were both personally encouraged to continue with the project as he recognised the importance of the valuable information that was being gathered and documented. In an article in the Templer Record of April 2002 he encouraged the Templer community as a whole to give support to the work Manfred and Helmut were doing. Manfred also started a dialogue with interested persons in Israel, namely Architect Dr Danny Goldman and the Tel Aviv Preservation Team. Their contribution was significant.

Horst Blaich was born in the German Templer settlement of Haifa and lived there until the outbreak of World War II when he was interned in Waldheim, Palestine until 1942. His family was then part of an internee exchange program with Germany. He came to Australia in 1951.

His wife Irene, nee Eppinger, was born in Jaffa, and lived there in the German Templer settlement. Interned during the war she left Palestine in 1948 and came to Australia via Cyprus in 1949. She is a descendent of Martin Wennagel, the pioneer builder, who built most of the houses in Sarona. Irene is deeply involved in family history research. Together, Horst and Irene, had already developed a comprehensive data base of photographs and images of the former German Templer Settlements in Palestine. Images of Sarona were of course amongst them. Their photographic library of images of Sarona has increased dramatically since this project began. Many of these images and photographs are published in this book. Irene's and Horst's contribution was enormous in putting together all the photographic data and the detailed plans of Sarona.

Any information gathered which was relevant to the homes and buildings to be restored and preserved, was forwarded to the Sarona Preservation Team in Tel Aviv, Israel, and to the TGD, Degerloch, Germany. This was important to ensure the work that needed to be undertaken in Israel could proceed. In the meantime the fact finding on other aspects of life in the Sarona settlement continued.

The information in this book was researched by interviewing people who actually grew up in Sarona, written recollections of previous Sarona residents and by interviewing descendants of those families who had lived in Sarona. The verbal information was corroborated wherever possible to ensure its correctness. Many families gave us photographic material. Personal family records and archival material and records were examined, as well as archival material from the Temple Society. Reference was made to several Temple Society publications including *Damals in Palaestina (Memories of Palestine)*, *100 Jahre Tempelgesellschaft (100 Years Temple Society)* and *Denen, die uns vorangegangen sind, zum Gedenken (In Memory of Those Who Have Gone Before Us)*. Reference was also made to the book *The Holy Land Called*, by Paul Sauer, and numerous other texts and publications, as well as unpublished private manuscripts. A full bibliography is listed at the end of this book.

The compilation of the book was a team effort. Without each other's input the "Sarona Story" book may not have been put together. We used each others' skills and contacts to gather information, old photographs and other historical material, especially amongst the Templer community in Australia. Helmut interviewed people, researched books and historical records and wrote the text. Horst and Irene compiled the photographs and graphic material and, together with Manfred, who worked tirelessly, continued to interview people and gather information and maintained contacts in Australia, Germany and Israel.

We wish to thank the many persons in Australia and overseas who provided us with so much information and material because without their input this publication would not have been possible. We thank them for the time they so freely and willingly gave us when we interviewed them—for their recollections, their stories, their anecdotes, photographs and letters we received and **their encouragement** to document the history which they had been part of.

Our appreciation goes to Peter Lange, President, Temple Society, for writing the Foreword and for his support, deep interest and advice from the very beginning of the project, and to Mark Herrmann, Office Manager, TSA, for his assistance and friendship whenever we were researching material in the TSA archives and office.

We are appreciative of the late Professor Dr Alex Carmel's pioneering research work on Templer history in Palestine. Without his great personal endeavours and diligence, as well as his well documented works, much of the Templer history would have been lost. He has inspired further young historians to build on his works. He was the founder and head of the Gottlieb-Schumacher Institute, established at the University of Haifa as a faculty for research and study of Christian contributions to the development of Palestine in the 19th century. Professor Dr Carmel passed away in December 2002.

We are grateful to Dr Ejal Jakob Eisler, a noted historian and one of Professor Dr Carmel's successors, for his authoritative comments. His expert knowledge of the Templers and the Temple Society's history in Palestine is greatly respected worldwide. Despite his wide ranging academic and research commitments, he checked the text. He provided us with material from his own personal archives, as well as informed comment. His contribution is highly valued.

A special mention of Dr Charlotte Laemmle, Victoria, Australia and Martin Higgins, England, for their dedicated ongoing interest, access to their personal archives, proof reading and comment. To Dieter Glenk for his wise counsel and comment during the preparation of the text. A special thanks to Lorraine Glenk and Peter Hornung for their dedicated proof reading of the final text.

We also thank Brigitte Kneher, the archivist from the TGD, Degerloch, Germany. Brigitte is the grand-daughter of the former Head of the Temple Society (Tempelvorsteher) Christian Rohrer. Her great knowledge of existing archival material and personal acquaintance with Israeli historians was vital in our research of material and our requests for information. The time she spent extracting archival material, providing information and comment was greatly appreciated.

PREFACE

We are grateful for the valuable technical advice and assistance from Trevor Evans of Tree of Life Publishing in arranging the illustrations and text layout throughout this book. We also recognize the special effort of Michael Ramsden in meticulously indexing the contents which was appreciated.

We thank Dr Danny Goldman, an architect and student of Templer architecture in Israel, for his enthusiastic ongoing contribution and interest in this project. Also Dr Yaron Perry, University of Haifa for his thoughful evaluation and valuable comments.

We also sincerely thank our wives, Lorraine Glenk, Irene Blaich and Minnie Haering, for their patience, encouragement and humour which were needed at times during this long exercise. They were just fantastic!

Once we started, there was no turning back nor were there any thoughts of giving up. Analysing all the material we gathered over two years was a lengthy and tedious process but nevertheless a fascinating and enjoyable task—so rewarding! We hope you all get as much enjoyment from reading this book as we did in compiling it.

We have listed the "helpers" in the "Acknowledgements".

Helmut Glenk
Melbourne, Victoria, Australia
February 2004

FOREWORD

AN IMPORTANT CHAPTER IN THE HISTORY of the Temple Society has now been documented. Helmut Glenk, with the assistance of Manfred Haering and Horst Blaich, has completed an outstanding literary work. His publication on Sarona is a detailed description of the third Templer settlement in Palestine, founded only two years after the Templer work started in Haifa in 1869. I am pleased that the Sarona settlement now receives the attention and appreciation which it so highly deserves and which in the past had not been adequately covered by the Temple Society's narrative publication of 1990 *Damals in Palaestina*. I extend my sincere thanks to Helmut and his team for their initiative and unfailing commitment.

The struggle of the early Sarona Templers to establish an exemplary Christian community; their trust in God's guidance to overcome their initial difficulties; and their strong faith when malaria took its heavy toll of lives are of great significance for all present-day Templers. The settlers' multifarious achievements in later years have already been mentioned and described by several modern historians. It is with admiration that we look back and see how they created flourishing gardens and fields out of a neglected, mostly uncultivated area; how they introduced new methods of agriculture and established cooperatives and other public services which proved to be of vital importance in the further development of the country.

I am grateful to the authors for giving me the opportunity of writing this Foreword. I am a "Saroner" myself having spent seven years of my life in this settlement, three years of which were within the barbed-wire enclosed internment camp during World War II. I left Sarona in the middle of the war for Germany. The quiet streets of Sarona were the playground of my childhood, the old community house and "Saal" building my wartime school rooms, the eucalypts and pines of the "Waeldle" (little forest) as well as Lippmann's Bassin (swimming pool) represented my favourite areas of fun and adventure. All inhabitants of our village were regarded and treated as neighbours, at birthdays of classmates all boys and girls of the same age group were invited by the respective parents. I never had the impression in those years that I was missing out on anything in life.

Foreword

It was fateful for Sarona to be located so close to the fast growing city of Tel-Aviv. In my youth, we could spot the buildings of Tel-Aviv in the distance. Since then, the rural setting of the Sarona village has turned into a bustling inner district of the metropolis. It no longer reflects its original agricultural structure, but some of its characteristic features are still visible: the shade trees planted by the early settlers, some of the homes built in different architectural styles over a period of 76 years and the communal buildings reflecting the settlers' efforts as they strove to achieve good relations amongst all members of the community.

My generation has accepted the loss of "our Sarona Colony". We know that we are now challenged to spread the Templer faith in other parts of the world. We try to keep our tradition, our religious and spiritual heritage alive wherever we are. On the other hand, we appreciate very much what is being done in Israel for the protection of the remaining parts of our former settlements, in particular the characteristic features of Sarona which I have mentioned above. We know that many difficulties are encountered in this endeavour and that many obstacles have to be removed by people engaged in conservation and preservation activities. It is my conviction that the result of this work will be in the interest of not only the Templers in Australia and Germany but also of all people in Israel who want to become aware of the history and of the influences on the development of their country in the past.

The historical research presently being done in Israel with respect to the pioneering work of the Germans and all the activities of conservation and preservation undertaken by Israelis are going a long way towards more tolerance, better understanding and friendship. Templers should therefore co-operate as much as possible. As one of our friends in Israel said—it is our common historical research which has created a bridge between Templers and Israelis; almost 60 years after World War II we do things together and have respect for each other; it is now our duty to widen the bridge.

Peter Lange
President of the Temple Society
February 2004

KEY DATES AND EVENTS[1]

1845—Founding of the journal *SueddeutscheWarte* (Southern German Sentinel), after 1877 called *Warte des Tempels* (Templer Sentinel), for a while also named *Jerusalem Warte,* (Jerusalem Sentinel)

24 August 1854—The compilation of a petition for establishing Christian congregations in the Holy Land, with 439 signatures, at a meeting of "The Friends of Jerusalem". It is directed to the 'Hohe' Deutsche Bundesversammlung (German Federal Assembly) in Frankfurt and was signed "Society for the Gathering of the Children of God in Jerusalem".

14 March 1858—A commission is sent to the Holy Land to investigate conditions for possible settlements. Members of the commission were: Christoph Hoffmann, Georg David Hardegg (1812-1879) and Joseph Bubeck (1795-1871).

8 September 1858—The commission reports their findings in the Kursaal at Cannstatt, Wuerttemberg, Germany. In the commission's report mention is made of a possible settlement site in the Plain of Saron where the Audsche River flows.[2]

1860—Karl Heuschele (1832-1894), from Osweil near Ludwigsburg; Christian Fr. Eppinger (1833-1918), from Kornwestheim; Hieronymus Sonderegger (1826-1878), from Aldingen; and Philipp Hochstetter (1820-1860), from Grossaltdorf near Schwaebisch Hall, are sent to the Holy Land as missionaries by the Friends of Jerusalem to proselytise the Templer cause. They had been trained at the Kirschenhardthof Templer Missionary School.[3]

19/20 June 1861—A conference is held at Kirschenhardhof to discuss secession from the State Church. About 60 men are present from Wuerttemberg, Baden and Bavaria. The **Temple Society** is founded under its original name **Deutscher Tempel**—as an independent religious community. Christoph Hoffmann is elected Bishop and twelve others as elders.

1867—The first Templer groups emigrate, unauthorised, to Palestine to establish agricultural settlements. The first houses are built at Chnefiss and Samunieh on the western slopes of the hills of Nazareth. They encounter great difficulties in relation to climate and disease as well as thefts of their belongings.

6 October 1868—Christoph Hoffmann and Georg David Hardegg, Temple Society Directors, leave for Haifa in the Holy Land to work out a plan for co-ordinated communities.

March 1869—Land is bought at Jaffa for a settlement. A discontinued American settlement is taken over and newly arrived German Templer settlers are placed there.

27 August 1871—Approximately 60 hectares of land are purchased near Jaffa for the purpose of establishing an agricultural settlement.

Key Dates and Events

18 October 1871—Sarona is officially named and foundation stones for the first two houses are laid. Hardship and many deaths are endured during the first three years. Nearby swamps are drained and eucalyptus trees are planted to absorb water from marshy areas to stop the breeding of malaria carrying mosquitoes.

February 1873—School and community house consecrated

1876—the Hoffmann Foundation is created. Its purpose is to provide loans for the education of young people. Templer communities become active in North America, Russia and Saxony.

1882—The German Reichstag (parliament) grants a small annual subsidy for German schools in the Holy Land

10 July 1887—"Zentralkasse des Tempels" (Temple Society Central Fund) is registered as a partnership at the Imperial German Consulate in Jerusalem.

1893—"Freie Tempelgemeinde" (Free Templer Community) is formed and splits from the Temple Society

1897—Free Templer Community rejoins the Temple Society

1898—Kaiser Wilhelm II and Kaiserin Auguste Victoria visit the Holy Land (including Sarona)
—Long term credit, of 250,000 Marks, is offered by the German Government for colonial enterprises by the Society for the Advancement of German Settlements in the Holy Land

1904—The Temple Society Central Fund, operating as a partnership, is changed into a corporate body known as "Verein der Tempelgesellschaft" and obtains the status of a legal entity by resolution of the German Federal Council

April 1910—Prince Eitel Friedrich and Princess Sophie Charlotte visit Sarona.

October 1911—second school and community house consecrated

August 1914—World War I starts

Nov 1917—British troops (including many Australian troops) occupy the German settlements in the Holy Land.

1918—In July, 850 inhabitants of the southern settlements (Jerusalem, Jaffa, **Sarona,** and Wilhelma) are interned in Egypt at Helouan near Cairo
—In November World War I ends. Turkish Ottoman Rule ceases in the Holy Land.

1919—300 of the persons in the Egyptian internment camps are deported to Bad Mergentheim in Germany via Hamburg

KEY DATES AND EVENTS

25 July 1920—A Reconstruction Commission (29 persons) travels from Egypt to the Palestine.

9 September 1920—460 interned persons arrive from Egypt at the Railway Station in Lydda, Palestine.

January 1921—Return of the Templer contingent from Bad Mergentheim.

20 September 1923—Great Britain receives a mandate and takes over control of the newly established country of Palestine.

1924—Establishment of the Bank der Tempelgesellschaft Ltd. (Templer Bank).

1925—Sarona water tower is built to provide a good water supply to all homes.

2 September 1929—Amalgamation with the Jaffa Templer community.

1931—Opening of the new school and community building.

3 September 1939—World War II begins and German settlers in Palestine are interned in perimeter settlements. Able-bodied men are taken to separate camps.

July 1941—665 interned Germans in Palestine are deported to Tatura, Victoria, Australia. This included 198 from Sarona.

1941/44—Some Templers who remained in Palestine are exchanged for Jewish persons in Germany. They are taken overland by rail to Germany via Turkey.

1944-45—All remaining German internees from Sarona are taken to the Templer settlement in Wilhelma.

1947—Sarona properties are sold (expropriated) by the British authorities.

1948—Great unrest in Palestine. Nearly all remaining Templers have to leave in haste as the mandate ends and the territory is partitioned. They are taken to Cyprus. The State of Israel is created.

1950—The last Templers leave Israel from Jerusalem.

THE TEMPLERS AND THEIR SETTLEMENTS IN PALESTINE

2) Christoph Hoffmann I—founder of the Temple Society

3) Aerial view of Kirschenhardthof—located in Wuerttemberg, southern Germany, where the Temple Society was formed

THE FORMER SETTLEMENTS of the Temple Society in Palestine resulted from a religious movement that began in the Kingdom of Wuerttemberg in the mid 19th century.

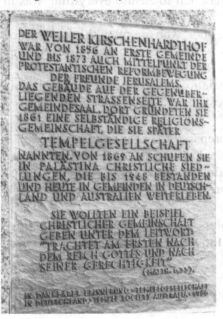

4) Plaque at Kirschenhardthof to commemorate founding of Temple Society in 1861

The Temple Society was founded by Christoph Hoffmann (1815-1885), son of a lawyer. He became a German Protestant Church teacher and lecturer and for a time served in the first democratically elected German Federal Assembly. He was a person devoted to God and religious principles. He believed that the intrusion of the State into religion had corrupted it and that the many rituals, dogmas and sacraments that had grown up in Christianity were obscuring the simple message of the Scriptures. He believed that the two principles of Christianity were—love of God (a personal, inner belief expressing itself in worship, trust and obedience) and love of one's neighbour as of oneself. God's kingdom on earth, Hoffmann believed, could be achieved by the formation of Christian communities adhering to the above principles.

In 1861, Hoffmann and some 60 followers seceded from the Wuerttembergische Landeskirche (Wuerttemberg State Church) and formed the Temple Society at a meeting in Kirschenhardthof (near Stuttgart in southern Germany).

5) Building in Kirschenhardthof where Temple Society was founded

6) Gravestone of Christoph Hoffman I in Jerusalem

Hoffmann was convinced that Templers should begin their work (building Christian communities) in the Holy Land. In 1867 a group of 25 young Templers took the initiative and emigrated from Germany to the Holy Land to begin a settlement in the Plain of Jezreel. This group's initiative was not supported by Hoffmann nor Hardegg (the leaders of the Temple Society at that time). The group planned to join up with Ludwig Hipp, who had migrated to the Holy Land in 1865. The group initially settled at Medjedel and Chnefiss. Unfortunately, the venture failed and most of the settlers died from malaria. The remaining settlers then moved to Samunieh near Nazareth. Belatedly, in 1868, the Temple Society in Germany finally recognised the misery and plight of these pioneering settlers and provided them with some financial assistance.

Hoffmann and Hardegg went to the Holy Land in October 1868 to plan the establishment of the Haifa Templer Settlement.[4]

There were a number of principles which the Temple Society formulated in regard to its settlements in the Holy Land. These included:—

1. That any settlement there be a community undertaking;
2. That each settlement be a centre of spiritual activity and include as many families as necessary to sustain it;
3. That the emigration could not be left to an individual but would ultimately be decided by the leaders of the Temple Society;
4. That personal wealth or means would not be the only factor for selection, but personal skills and commitment to the Templer cause would also be taken into consideration;
5. That emigration to the Holy Land would be negotiated by the Temple Society council to ensure everything was in order;
6. That in regards to the poor, who are often the most skilled and best qualified, they would be supported providing they had financial support (ie. are sponsored) by someone else;
7. That not every Christian would be given approval, only those who felt themselves called by God to do his work.

The Temple Society was also prepared to accept interest free loans from those who, if selected, wished to migrate at a later stage. These loans (shares) would give the individuals preference to purchase land in the Holy Land under conditions set by the Temple Society.[5]

In the Holy Land the Templers initially founded community settlements—Haifa 1869, Jaffa 1869, Sarona 1871 and Rephaim near Jerusalem 1873.

THE TEMPLERS AND THEIR SETTLEMENTS IN PALESTINE -
CHAPTER ONE

The Templers who emigrated to the Holy Land in the 19th century should not be confused with the Knights Templars from the Crusader period 700 years previously.

7) The Plain of Jezreel near Nazareth where the first group of young Templers "unofficially" tried to start a settlement.

The Templers differed from other religious movements in that they did not go to the Holy Land and attempt to convert the local inhabitants to their religious beliefs. They went there out of a religious conviction believing that by setting an example with their family lives, community living and interactions with fellow beings they would be able to demonstrate a Christian society of true ideals. The example set by the Templers was admired by the population at large and many of their agricultural and industrial innovations were adopted by others. For decades the Templers were a major force in the development of the Holy Land and Palestine.[6]

In many ways the Templer settlements, especially Sarona which was an agricultural settlement, could be regarded as one of the first attempts by Europeans, after several hundred years, to start

3

permanent agricultural enterprises in the Holy Land. The successful achievements of these early German settlers contributed significantly to the development of the Holy Land and subsequently Palestine and eventually Israel.

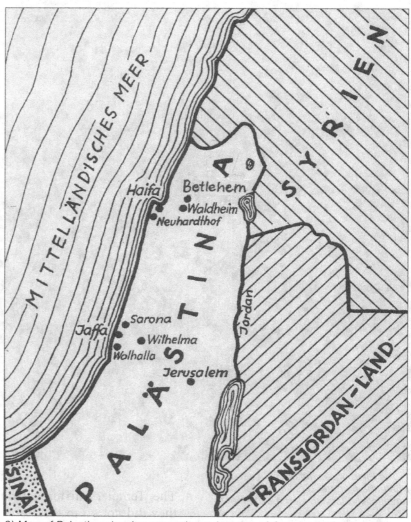

8) Map of Palestine showing approximate location of German settlements. The German Templer settlements were Haifa (1869), Jaffa (1869), Sarona (1871), Jerusalem (1873), Wilhelma (1902), and Betlehem (1906). The settlement of Waldheim was founded by the German Protestant Community (Kirchler) supported by the Jerusalemsverein Berlin in 1907. Neuhardthof (1892) was an off-shoot of the Haifa settlement and Walhalla (1888) an off-shoot of the Jaffa settlement.

THE BEGINNING TO 1900

THE HOLY LAND IN THE LATTER NINETEENTH CENTURY

For nearly 400 years, since December 1516, the area of the Holy Land had been part of the Turkish Ottoman Empire. There had been many skirmishes between Arabs (various sheiks) and the Turks during this period. Even Napoleon Bonaparte invaded the Holy Land from Egypt for a short period in 1799. In 1831 the Holy Land was still largely under the "control" of Mohamed Ali the Great, Pasha of Egypt. In 1840 an uprising was put down when the Turkish army advanced from the north and the Egyptians fled.[7]

The inhabitants of the small towns made their living by trading and a few had small agricultural holdings. In the main they tended to plant and grow only for their and their family's needs.

Wherever there was water or springs very small villages could be found with the occupants living in mud brick huts. The larger land owners owned areas which they leased out at high rates.

9) Arab village scene with typical mud brick huts

The countryside itself was in poor condition

The whole area was run down and neglected

The countryside itself was in poor condition—there were a few sparsely timbered stony areas, a few scattered palm trees, some very old olive trees, a few fig trees and mulberry bushes. Most of the land was desolate. It had been overgrazed over many years by goat herds; the soil had been exhausted through lack of proper care; thistles and other thorny bushes were prevalent. Hardly any new buildings were being built and no trees planted. The whole area was run down and neglected.[8]

This was about to change. During the last half of the nineteenth century a number of missionaries and settlers from foreign countries came to the Holy Land. These were mainly religious groups from Prussia, England, France, America (USA) and Russia establishing monastic type settlements and institutions as well as some Jews who established agricultural settlements.[9]

Land Acquisition and Allocation— the Founding of Sarona

After the arrival in the Holy Land of the first Templers in the late 1860s the first settlement was established in Haifa in 1869 and the second settlement in Jaffa 1869 when an American settlement was purchased. With further Templer settlers arriving from Germany, many of whom had some agricultural and farming background, pressure grew within the Templers in the Holy Land for an agricultural settlement to be started. In the beginning of 1870 a proposal to purchase land on the outskirts of Jaffa to start an agricultural settlement was rejected by Christoph Hoffmann.

The reason for Hoffmann's rejection was that he did not wish to build another settlement at that time because most of the settlers were farmers and could only work in agriculture. Already five families had started buying land for "Landwirtschaftliche Gueter" (agricultural estates). The first person to buy a run down farming property known as Mt Hope was Michael Lutz. The property had originally been established in the 1850s by the Grossteinbeck family who had sold it to Arab interests. When Lutz bought the property, which had a small brick house, barn, stables and a well, it was very run down and neglected.[10]

10) 1869 French 20 francs coin

Later a second property known as "Modelfarm", only one and a half kilometres from Jaffa was leased by some Templers. More land was leased adjacent to the "Modelfarm" by Templers including the garden of Moses Montefiore. Shortly after the Guenthner and Roehm families acquired properties next to the "Modelfarm". The "Modelfarm" was originally established by the Industrial Mission for Jewish Converts as an agricultural school. The project was not a success and the property was entrusted to Martin Metzler, who had previously taken over the property in Jaffa that belonged to the American sect "The Church of the Messiah" and which became the basis for the Templer settlement in Jaffa. When Metzler left to go to Russia the Templers acquired the property.[11]

These pioneering Templer settlers started cultivating German vegetables including lettuces, radishes, beans, peas, lentils, carrots, potatoes, spinach, cabbage and cauliflowers. They also planted citrus trees and other fruit trees.[12]

Notwithstanding Hoffmann's rejection, pressure for the establishment of an agricultural settlement continued to mount. He also became concerned that if he did not agree to build a new settlement the number of families living outside the Templer Jaffa settlement would increase and the community life that he was fostering might well be destroyed.[13]

In early 1871 the Templer Council in Jaffa decided on an application from G Edelmaier from Aldingen, W Besserer from Nussdorf, F Laemmle from Leutenbach, G Stiefel from Fornsbach, as well as representations from Aberle from Stuttgart, to provide land to 10-12 families to start a new settlement as well as to strengthen (increase the size of) the local Templer Jaffa community. Vice-consul Simeon Serapion Murad (1822-1894) had already had some discussions with the owner from Selame (an Arab village) to purchase a parcel of land for this purpose.[14] The German Vice-consul was an educated Armenian and had been in this official position for many years.[15]

11) Old Turkish coin

In August 1871 after some negotiation, a sizeable parcel of land (approx. 60 hectares) was acquired by Christoph Hoffmann

In the next six months applications by interested parties were considered by the Templer Council in Jaffa. It appears that both written and personal applications were considered, with preference being given to those who applied in person.

In August 1871 after negotiation, a sizeable parcel of land (Approx. 60 hectares) was acquired by Christoph Hoffmann in collaboration with the Council of the Templer settlement in Jaffa. Prior to purchase, the land had been owned by a Greek religious order (monastery). The land was on a small rise (approximately 20 metres above the surrounding countryside) in the Plain of Saron near the River Audsche (Yarqon) (nahr al'Audschah) and Wadi Musrara, approximately three to four kilometres (one hour walk) from the Jaffa settlement.

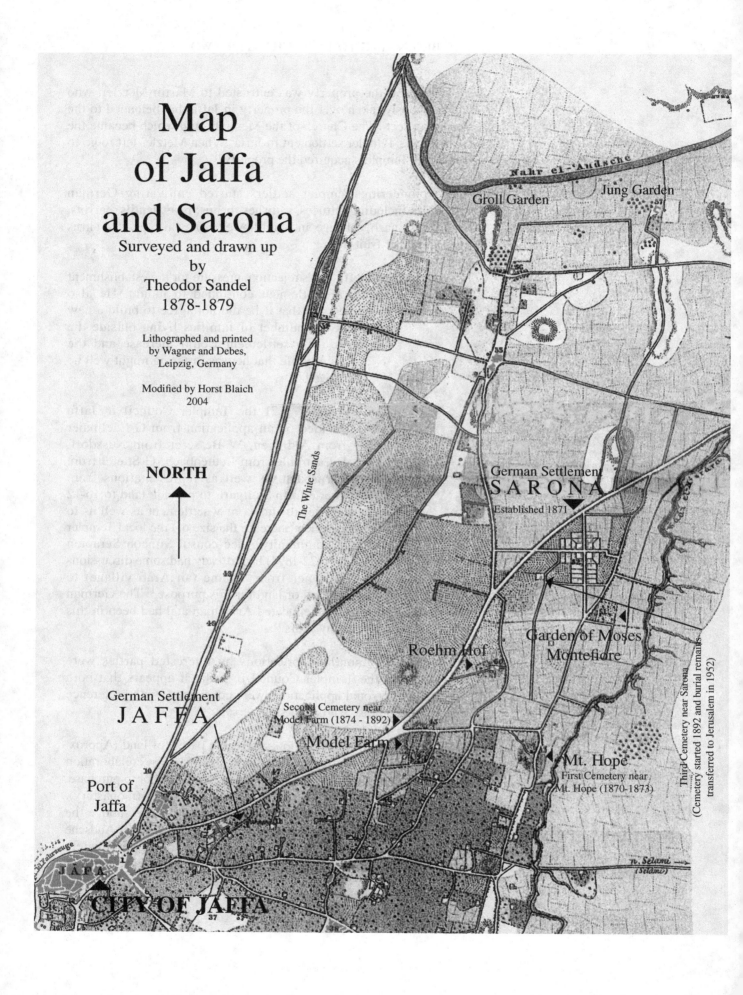

Map
of Jaffa
and Sarona

Surveyed and drawn up
by
Theodor Sandel
1878-1879

Lithographed and printed
by Wagner and Debes,
Leipzig, Germany

Modified by Horst Blaich
2004

NORTH

The White Sands

Nahr el-'Audsche

Groll Garden

Jung Garden

German Settlement
S A R O N A
Established 1871

Roehm Hof

Garden of Moses
Montefiore

Third Cemetery near Sarona
(Cemetery started 1892 and burial remains
transferred to Jerusalem in 1952)

German Settlement
J A F F A

Second Cemetery near
Model Farm (1874 - 1892)

Model Farm

Mt. Hope
First Cemetery near
Mt. Hope (1870-1873)

Port of
Jaffa

n. Selâmi
(Selâmi)

JAFFA

CITY OF JAFFA

13) Theodor Sandel—designer of the Sarona settlement. Sandel was also the architect of many early homes and buildings including the original Sarona wine cellar

The land was barren, no trees, in fact there was no greenery at all. In the whole plain from the sea to the Audsche River there was not one house except the very small Arab village of Sumeil which was half an hour away.[16] It appears that the sale was quickly settled in accordance with oriental practices.

The land had been surveyed by Theodor Sandel (1845-1902). Sandel was the son of the Jaffa's colony physician, Gottlob David Sandel (1817-1879) who lived in Jaffa until 1878.[17]

The following is a vivid description of how the settlers trekked to the site where Sarona was founded. It is based on a speech given by Nikolai Schmidt, the head of the remaining Templers in Palestine in 1946 to mark the 75th anniversary of Sarona.

"On Sunday 27 August 1871 at three in the afternoon, a group of happy and excited persons from the Templer settlement in Jaffa called Amelikan set out to journey on foot to a newly acquired property not far from Jaffa. The difficult sandy path northward had never been used by horse-drawn vehicles. The sand was a hindrance and progress was slow. On the way the group was joined by other settlers who were living in partly completed houses along this sandy track and the unmade Nablus road. This was the beginning of agricultural activity by Templers in the Plain of Saron. Some Templers had settled here on either bought or leased land. (Author: Model Farm and Roehmshof) A few bucket elevators (Paternosterwerke) irrigated the gardens of the German people. When the group's walk came to a halt they all looked around and surveyed the bare and neglected area.

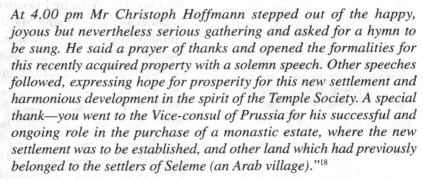

At 4.00 pm Mr Christoph Hoffmann stepped out of the happy, joyous but nevertheless serious gathering and asked for a hymn to be sung. He said a prayer of thanks and opened the formalities for this recently acquired property with a solemn speech. Other speeches followed, expressing hope for prosperity for this new settlement and harmonious development in the spirit of the Temple Society. A special thank—you went to the Vice-consul of Prussia for his successful and ongoing role in the purchase of a monastic estate, where the new settlement was to be established, and other land which had previously belonged to the settlers of Seleme (an Arab village)."[18]

14) Old Arab water well

Theodor Sandel had drawn up the initial plan for the new settlement. Since there were three different types of soil in the area, an attempt was made to include land of each type in every individual allotment. The soil varied from light sandy soil on sandstone, to orange coloured flood sediment to dark, black clay. Around the Wadi and in the flood plain of the Audsche River there were areas of swampy ground. Some preliminary work had been done to dig a well.[19]

Left—12) Map of old Jaffa and Sarona surveyed and drawn up by Architect Theodor Sandel 1878-1879 in Palestine, modified for this book by Horst Blaich, 2004

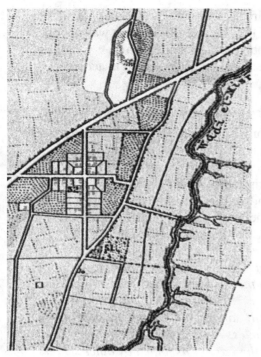

15) Original plan of Sarona. The plan shows Sarona's distinctive cross roads design. The four corner allotments at the crossroads were reserved for community purposes

The above listed settlers were not obliged to accept the allotment they had drawn. They were given the opportunity to either accept or decline it

The plan for the new settlement was based around two roads—one running north south and the other east west. There were 22 initial lots of land—the four allotments at the cross roads were reserved for community purposes and the remaining ones for the first settlers. The land was on a small rise from which adjoining fields could be observed.[20]

Dr Goldman writes in *Sarona-Settlement Design* that:—
"Such rigorous planning of settlements as appeared in the Templer colonies, was an innovation in Palestine, whose settlements thus far were agglomerated Middle-Eastern towns and villages, with random geometry, narrow and winding alleys. Templer planners, Sandel included, brought with them an attitude of ordered and systematic design, with clear geometry such as Sarona. [. . .] The land-use scheme and type of structures are evidence of the intentions of the colony's founders: a rural settlement par excellence. Land-uses include only residences, service structures, farming fields, and few public structures."[21]

Allocation of the lots for the settlers was done by ballot. Two children drew the name of the settler from one small box and the lot number from another box. The name and lot number were then called out to the gathered settlers.[22] The successful original settlers were[23]:—

Number 5 ....Gottlieb Stiefel from Fornsbach
Number 6 .... Karl Wilhelm Besserer from Nussdorf
Number 7 ....J G Weinmann from Sielmingen
Number 8 .... Johann Adam Dreher from Maegerkingen
Number 9 .... Wilhelm Friedrich Bernhardt already in the Holy Land
Number 10..........Johann Martin Wennagel already in the Holy Land
Number 11 .... Johann Daniel Jenner from Erdmannhausen
Number 12...........................Johann Georg Edelmaier from Aldingen
Number 13................ Christian Friedrich Laemmle from Leutenbach
Number 14...Johannes Wurst from Fornsbach
Number 15.............................Sebastian Seitz for Friends in America
Number 16............................Jakob Friedrich Mann from Weiler z St
Number 17............................... Andreas Fickel for Friends in Russia
Number 18............................ Gottfried Pflugfelder from Moeglingen
Number 19.........................Johann Georg Weller from Neustetten
Number 20 .... Johannes Laemmle from Leutenbach
Number 21 ....Karl Wilhelm Kuebler from Waltersberg
Number 22........................ Karl Gottlob Kuebler from Waltersberg

Each lot, allowing for a house and garden, had an area of approx ¼ha.[24] The above listed settlers were not obliged to accept the allotment they had drawn. They were given the opportunity to either accept or decline it. Before accepting they were again reminded of the two matters that they would need to consider:

1. That they had the means to build a house and barn/shed, be able to purchase additional land and be able to live off their means for a few years. A budget of at least 5000fr. was required for these purposes

2. That they (whether family or single person) abide by the conditions for settlement in Palestine as previously published in the Warte (conditions set out previously above).[25]

In Germany, when it became known that the land for the new settlement had been acquired, the families and individuals who planned to settle in the Holy Land were ready to leave. They departed by train and travelled via Vienna to Trieste, Italy, then by ship to Alexandria, Egypt before moving on to the Holy Land. The first train left on 28 August 1871 with G Edelmaier from Aldingen and his wife and seven children aged between 5 and 24; and J G Weinmann's wife from Sielmingen with five children (her husband was already in the Holy Land) and several single persons. The second train left on 11 September 1871 with four families: F. Laemmle from Leutenbach with his wife and two children; G Stiefel with his wife together with S Wieland and two adult children from Fornsbach; Karl Kuebler from Waltersberg with two children and his sister. There were also several single persons with this group.[26] Twelve of the first fourteen families to settle in Sarona came from Germany.[27]

On 18 October 1871 the settlers gathered once more for the laying of foundation stones for the first two houses and for the naming of the new settlement. They formed a semicircle and Mr Wennagel, one of the new home owners, spoke about his feelings and praised and thanked God. This was followed by a religious service conducted by Christhoph Hoffmann, Johann Georg Kappus and Theodor Sandel also made speeches.

The gathering then voted on the future name for the settlement. Two names were put forward—Ebenezer and Sarona. The majority cast their vote for Sarona and that was then the official name for the new Templer settlement

The gathering then voted on the future name for the settlement. Two names were put forward—Ebenezer and Sarona. The majority vote was for Sarona and that then became the official name for the new Templer settlement.[28]

After the vote the two foundation stones were consecrated for the Johann MartinWennagel and Wilhelm Friedrich Bernhardt houses.

EARLY PROGRESS

The building of homes in Sarona was impeded in late 1871 by wet and rainy conditions. On 28 December 1871, a third foundation stone was consecrated for the Stiefel house. During the consecration service a beautiful rainbow appeared and this was taken as a sign of God's satisfaction![29]

By April 1872 good progress was being made with the construction of houses—in several homes the roofs were being constructed. There was, however, still a dispute with the Bedouins regarding ownership of a small parcel of land.

On the agricultural front the *Sueddeutsche Warte* of 11 April 1872 (Southern German Sentinel) reports:—". . . . *the fields are looking good, and if, with God's help, no locust plague comes, we can expect an abundant harvest. Over the past four days during the month of March we have had unusually hot sirocco (Author.—hot desert winds), with 25 to 27 degree temperatures during the day and 14C in the morning. Until now, no locusts have been seen, maybe the heavy winter rains drowned them. Last Wednesday a huge flock of storks, several hundreds, flew over us heading northwards towards our former homeland—it was probably too hot for them here.*"[30]

In May 1872 more land was bought

In May 1872 more land was bought for 3000 Napoleons from Menas, Abu Kabach (both Arab landowners) and a peasant farmer. Mr Hardegg also bought some land. The land was subdivided and sold to the following settlers:—Carl Stiefel, Andreas Schmidt, Ernst Hardegg, Adam Dreher, Friedrich Haecker, Heinrich Harkins, Friedrich Dieterle and Sebastian Seitz. This allocation and sale completed the early land purchases of Sarona.[31]

This allocation and sale completed the early land purchases of Sarona

By June 1872 seven houses had been built and occupied. The families living in Sarona at that time were—Wennagel, Bernhardt, Kappus, Edelmaier, Stiefel, Laemmle, and Pflugfelder.[32]

Construction of the community house had commenced.

Representatives from the new settlers of Sarona were incorporated into the Jaffa Committee in October 1872. The representatives from Sarona were Kappus, Stiefel and Edelmaier.[33]

As more land was acquired and additional settlers sought to come to Sarona a building committee was established and set prices for building blocks and other lots.[34]

First Teacher and School

In April 1872, Philipp Dreher was accepted by the Sarona community as their teacher and representative to the Templer Mission. He had previously been elected by the Mission's committee for this purpose. Unfortunately, Mr Dreher was the teacher for only a short time as he passed away on 31 August 1874.[35]

16) Sketch of the first community house and school

A school was built to which every family made a financial contribution. The school and community building (No 25) were consecrated on 2 February 1873.[36]

It should be noted that even at this time in the development of the Holy Land Templer settlements, Christoph Hoffmann, especially, saw the need to provide educational development for the youth of the settlements. At the beginning of the Jaffa settlement a boys' school for higher education was planned and established with boarding facilities. The school was known as the Institute. An Arab teacher was also employed to teach Arabic. In 1877, the school was moved to Rephaim outside the city walls of Jerusalem and was named "Lyzeum Tempelstift". Rephaim was the location of the German Templer settlement Jerusalem. Thus some boys were able to continue their education after completing their basic three/four years in the settlement school.[37]

DEATH, DISEASE AND EXTREME HARDSHIPS

It is difficult to imagine the hardship that befell the Sarona community during its early years of existence

In the early years Sarona suffered more human losses than any of the other settlements in Palestine

It is difficult to imagine the hardship that befell the Sarona community during its early years of existence. It is even harder to comprehend the endurance and faith of the settlers during this time. They were on their own without State or government assistance—truly a remarkable period. In the early years, Sarona suffered more human losses than any of the other settlements in Palestine—more than 10% of the settlers died. In 1872 alone 28 of 125 settlers perished.[38] Again a description of these times is as recorded in the Nikolai Schmidt speech:

"Without warning, terrible things began to occur. No one could have predicted this. In 1872, 28 persons died in this small Sarona community. The settlers stood helplessly before their fever-stricken family members and friends who, in addition to the raging fever were also suffering from the effects of dysentery. People recalled the 20 dead from Medjedel, Knefis and Samunieh near Nazareth, who had died from this hot fever in the period 1865-68. There were only three survivors from that group! Should Sarona end the same way? Instinctively, they saw the heat of the summer sun as the cause for the illness. They had trees sent from Beirut and other places; the Community Council imposed severe financial fines on anyone working in the middle of the day between 10.00am and 2.00pm. These penalties could be offset by doing community work. For example, a man could offset 2.5 fr. per day community work and for two horses with a driver 8fr per day. Roads were improved, bogs were drained and many trees planted. The Jaffa/Sarona community council was forced to devote much time and effort to deal with the effects of the many deaths.

This involved dealing with the sale or exchange of land from the estates of the deceased as well as looking after the welfare of the orphans. A special "orphans tribunal" was established for this purpose.

An unspeakable amount of sorrow engulfed the living, most of whom were racked by fever themselves. No one knew whether they would be alive the next day. Some left the area but others continued on. Some families were virtually destroyed and everyone mourned the loss of someone.

It needed all the power of faith of Chr. Hoffmann and a belief in God that through this sad ordeal the Templers would not fail in their task, and that the reasons behind these deaths would be discovered and overcome. Their belief in the righteousness of the task to make something of this desolate land, gave the community the strength to overcome the enormous losses of these hard years. By looking at the list of deaths we are able to get an idea of the suffering in those early years."[39]

The loss of so many children was extremely painful for the families. The constant fear of infecting others led to stringent measures being taken, including the requirement that parents take their deceased children to a special room and place them into coffins.[40] The deaths of four family heads (breadwinners) put enormous pressure on the remaining struggling families and the community.

The cause of the sickness (malaria) was baffling the settlers as well as the Temple Society's leaders in the Holy Land and Germany. In the mid 1870s, scientific and medical knowledge had not established that the malaria parasite was carried and spread by the anopheles mosquito. The name "malaria" itself means bad air. It originated from the belief that the disease was caused by vapours in the air near swampy areas.

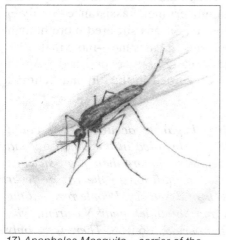

17) Anopheles Mosquito—carrier of the malaria parasite

Some of the reports in the *Sueddeutsche Warte* (SDW) (Southern German Sentinel) appear to "downplay" the extent of the disease amongst the Sarona settlers as reference is made to deaths of the elderly and of a woman shortly after childbirth.[41] This may well have been done so as not to frighten nor deter prospective settlers in Germany from migrating to the Holy Land.

Various other reports in the SDW clearly show that in many ways, the deaths at Sarona were regarded as a challenge by God, as no other cause could be proven. For example; in November 1872 the *SDW* reported:—

"It is understandable that the current situation in Sarona is considered to be unhealthy. It should, however, not be overlooked that there are matters other than the location of the settlement, which could contribute to sickness. Firstly, the unusual autumn heat which occurred in Palestine this year, and then the first ploughing of land that had lain fallow for a long period [. . .].The location of Sarona should not be unhealthy. The settlement is located on a rise not far from the sea, which can be seen from their homes, also the settlers have a direct sea breeze. It is true that the surrounding country is barren, the trees and greenery are missing. One should not forget that this place, like others, has been ordained by God[. . .], in my own personal view, I regard the sickness plight as a test (challenge) of God, through which the settlers will be cleansed and qualify to become people of God"[42]

In January 1873, another article raises the possibility of the sickness being caused by the flooding of the Nile River in Egypt and the release of vapours and sickness into the air.[43]

In July 1873, an article speculates as to the causes of the disease— perhaps the heat of the day or maybe the release of toxic vapours into the air by ploughing the soil could be contributing factors. It had been observed that the highest incidence of the disease seemed to occur during sowing time.[44]

Christoph Hoffmann writes in the *SDW* of 7 August 1873 that he regrets the comments by those persons who claim Sarona is located in an unhealthy location, as no-one has been able to offer a better alternate site. He goes on:—*"The decision whether Sarona will "fail" or whether success can be brought about by faith and patience, despite malaria, rests in the hands of God."*[45]

A contributing factor as to why so many of the early settlers contracted malaria and dysentery was that they came direct from Europe unprepared for the hotter climate and conditions they encountered in the Holy Land

A contributing factor as to why so many of the early settlers contracted malaria and dysentery was that they came direct from Europe unprepared for the hotter climate and conditions they encountered in the Holy Land. In Sarona a number of families lived in only partly completed houses and were exposed to the elements.

In 1871 (October to December) two persons died, in 1872 there were 35 deaths (28 in Sarona proper, out of a population of 125; and seven at Roehmshof and Model Farm), in 1873 seven deaths and in 1874 another 13—a total of 57 in just over three years.[46] As a tribute to the pioneers, all those who died during this period are recorded in Appendix 2.

The tragic deaths in Sarona were probably one of the greatest challenges the Templers faced in the Holy Land in the 19th Century. It may well have raised serious doubts as to whether the settlement program there should continue.

Gradually, with more knowledge and step-by-step adjustment to their new environment, the settlers' hopes and aspirations began to be realized.

It is just amazing how strong people's aspirations and faith in God and the Templer ideals really were. People began to adjust their customary way of life to the climate and conditions of the Holy Land.

COMBATING DISEASE

In July 1873, the SDW made reference to findings from a Mr Colin who specifically states that the cultivation of the ground and particularly the dense planting of tree varieties was the best method to combat malaria.[47] Another method to fight this disease was to take quinine.

18) Eucalyptus trees were planted to dry out swamps

Another interesting article appeared in the *SDW* (26 April 1874) referring to the "fever dissipating tree"—the Eucalypt. It was based on a report in the "Daheim" periodical in Germany. The article made mention that eucalypts had been planted in many parts of the world with some astounding results. Research had also been carried out by the Paris Academy of Science. It had been found that in areas where eucalypts had been planted that the fever was driven away. Furthermore, the eucalyptus tree had the capacity to take up ten times its own weight of water from the soil and emit vapours. If these trees were planted in swampy areas they soon dried up the ground. An example is provided from a fever-infested area in Algeria where people were dying like flies. 1300 eucalypts were planted and, within a few years, although the trees were only nine feet tall, the mortality rate had dropped to virtually zero. Another example refers to an area in Turkey, near Constantinople where the planting of eucalypts produced similar results.[48]

Eucalyptus seeds or seedlings may have been available in the Holy Land as an article in Cathera 59 indicates that the British Consul James Finn brought eucalyptus seeds to the Holy Land in 1862.[49]

In 1874, some eucalypts had already been planted in Sarona. Whether eucalypts were brought to Sarona from Australia, the Holy Land, Algeria or even Turkey, is not known.

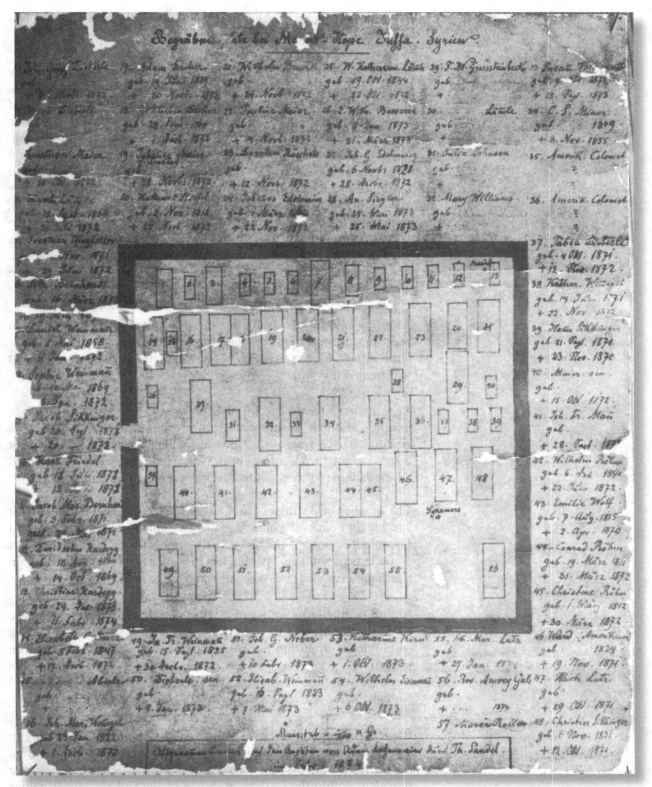

19) Layout of graves in the old Sarona/Jaffa cemetery near Mt Hope in the 1870s. Hand written records of the deceased in background

However, the Sarona settlers were most likely the first ones to plant eucalypts on a large scale in the Holy Land.

When it became known how malaria was transmitted the settlers did their utmost to prevent mosquitoes from breeding

During the latter part of the 1880s when it became known how malaria was transmitted, the settlers did their utmost to prevent mosquitoes from breeding. Swamps were drained if possible, and eucalypts planted to absorb the stagnant waters. However, one of the main breeding areas for the mosquitoes was the flood plain of the wadi. The wadi was east of the settlement and flowed in a northerly direction through the Sarona settlers' land where it joined the Audsche River. In summer and autumn the wadi was a dry watercourse; in winter it would fill and become a flowing creek, sometimes even flooding surrounding country. In springtime after the rainy season, it would dry out and leave pools of stagnant water—an ideal mosquito breeding environment. Compulsory work rosters were drawn up for the settlers to fill these pools with soil. This was an annual chore for many years.[50]

Another method of combating the mosquitoes was to stop them breeding, by pouring kerosene on any remaining stagnant water pools around Sarona. An area of one kilometre around the settlement was treated this way.[51]

20) Larva of the anopheles mosquito. Kerosene was poured onto stagnant water pools to prevent the larva from developing into mosquitos

The medical treatment for dysentery and black water fever (a manifestation of severe malaria), which often affected people simultaneously, improved. However, malaria remained a prevalent disease right through to World War I. All the settlers continued taking quinine to combat this debilitating and often fatal disease.

The number of deaths in Sarona was frightening and depressing. It was higher than in the other Templer settlements of Haifa, Jaffa, and Jerusalem. These deaths had a lasting impact over the first 20 years of settlement and some people left the country to build new lives in Germany, America (USA) or Australia.[52]

Not all people left because of disease and death, some left because of disillusionment. Life in Sarona was harsh, incomes were low, employment opportunities very limited and all items had to be bought. This created a sense of despondency and unhappiness for some who just packed up and left to try their luck elsewhere.[53] Nobody had to leave Sarona due to hunger or food shortages.

Rabies was another disease that caused concern. It is interesting to note that in the early years, hyenas were sighted in Sarona; they were normally shy and usually moved away. However, jackals were more prevalent within the settlement. Some of the jackals carried rabies and would bite other animals or even attack humans. A number of people were bitten and had to be taken to Egypt for treatment, several died from rabies. Jackals were still sighted within Sarona as late as the 1930s and their howling could be heard at night.[54]

Despite all of this Sarona still grew.

CONSOLIDATION

By 1874, fourteen stone homes had been built along the two main roads and another two were under construction in the infant settlement. Some houses were single story and others double story and surrounded by a garden. Several water wells up to 20 metres deep had also been constructed. The open area behind the community house had been reserved for a small forest—wooded area, known as the "Waeldle" (little woods). In later times, many community outdoor functions were held there. 1200 trees were planted— including eucalypts, acacias and mulberry trees. The purpose of this initial planting was to provide shade from the dangerous rays of the sun, cleanse the air and act as a windbreak.[55] The settlers were planning further similar wooded areas. Many of the surrounding fields were already starting to become productive with the assistance of irrigation.[56] Some orange and lemon trees had been planted, as well as apricot, almond, peach, quince, olive, fig and walnut trees. In the vegetable gardens cabbage, cauliflowers, lettuce, onions, carrots, melons and "Arabic" vegetable varieties were planted. Sugar cane was a prevalent crop plant.[57]

21) Overview of Sarona showing extent of orchards, vineyards and other agricultural ventures

Over the next few years other vegetables and plants were grown—these included tomatoes, potatoes, celery, cucumbers, cress, capsicums, mustard, parsley, peppermint, garlic, radishes, lentils, beans, sugar peas and poppy seed.[58]

Some European (German) seeds were not suitable for the hotter conditions of the Holy Land and local seeds and seeds from other areas were being experimented with.[59]

Within a few years, the settlers were already exporting some oranges and lemons as well as selling watermelons and vegetables.

The Sarona settlers are credited with being the pioneers in applying modern agricultural practices in the Holy Land—use of fertilisers and modern farming tools to increase production. They focussed on crops that were in demand and which they could readily sell. This "agriculture-for-profit" was an "economic" innovation compared to the existing practice of "self-sustained agriculture" in the Holy Land.[60]

The Sarona settlers are accredited with being the pioneers in applying modern agricultural practices in the Holy Land

Although not yet at a productive stage, the settlers realised quickly that the sandy soil with its limestone base would be suitable for vineyards. They were looking to wine production as becoming an important product for the future. A variety of vines were imported from Europe. One reason the settlers turned to vineyards was due to the volume of theft that was occurring to other crops. It was estimated a third of the crops of the Sarona farmers were stolen at that time. The wine-making grapes that were planted were not palatable to the Arabs (nor to the jackals).[61]

Some grain crops had been planted and harvested. The dairy industry was also in its infancy. A problem for the owners of cows was to provide proper feed. Fields needed to be fertilised to produce feed for the stock. Arabic shepherds were engaged to look after the stock when it was let out of the cowsheds.[62]

In the publication *Die deutschen Siedlungen in Palaestina, (The German Settlements in Palestine), by Hans Brugger,* reports that after the initial settlement was expanded through land purchases, the diligent and hardworking Sarona farmers really made the settlement "blossom". The well maintained and properly fertilised fields yielded abundant crops. For the animals the farmers cut hay, and clover and lupins were grown for special feed.[63] Vineyards were started and 160 "oil" (presumably olive) trees planted. These trees were brought by camel from the mountains and each one cost one franc.

The trees were root tubers which had been broken from the roots of an established "oil" tree. They were approximately 3-5 centimetres in diameter and young saplings had started to grow from them.[64]

In 1875 Joel Moshe Salomon, the famous Jewish "redeemer of land" visited Sarona and noted that:—"*the heart of Israel is both saddened and filled with joy by this beautiful sight. The heart is happy when it sees how our Holy Land can be changed into God's paradise, however we should be ashamed when we see persons here, who are not our people, but were the first ones to bring our land to blossom, whilst we lazily stand about*"[65]

Gradually the situation improved—the water supply improved, the eucalypts that had been planted grew and absorbed most of the water in the marshy areas, and the water flows in Wadi Musrara were better able to be regulated. The fields, vineyards and orchards started to provide some form of income for the settlers. Life, however, was still spartan—hard work six days a week. Sunday was a day of rest with a regular religious service.

During 1881, ten years after its founding, the settlement experienced a very dry year (no late spring rains) with a resultant drop in the yields of the grain crops. Hot desert winds and a vine disease—"Reblaus" (phylloxera) destroyed many grapevines with a detrimental effect on wine production. New root stock was imported from America to restart the vineyards.[66] Several of the settlers resorted to use their horse and carts to ferry persons (tourists) to and from Jaffa

Life however was spartan—hard work six days a week

22) Main road from the south into the Sarona settlement in approx. 1890. Laemmle's house and barn is on the left and wine cellar buildings and other homes on the right

to Jerusalem to supplement their meagre incomes. Sarona's original plan of 26 dwellings was revised and expanded during that year so as to cope with increasing numbers of new settlers.[67]

During the latter 1880s, Sarona, like the other Templer settlements, was faced with an overall shortage of financial resources for infrastructure development. The building of roads, development of land, and community facilities were a big burden on the struggling settlers. The community council introduced Frondienst (a form of compulsory labour) for the male settlers to help with the construction of roads, drainage and other community related projects. Settlers were required to do a certain number of hours of community work. If they personally could not do it they were permitted to send someone else in their place. This practice of community work continued into the 20th century.[68] Employment opportunities for tradesmen and anyone seeking a profession were very limited.[69]

In an endeavour to overcome the financial problems of the Templer settlements in Palestine, the Temple Society Central Fund was registered as a partnership with the Imperial German Consulate in Jerusalem on 10 July 1887. The purpose of the Fund was to further German colonization in the Orient and, in particular, the interests of agriculture, trade and commerce, by establishing credit facilities.[70]

A separate Sarona community council with a mayor was established in 1879 to deal with local community issues. The council comprised Johannes Dreher (Mayor), Andreas Fickel and Karl Kuebler.[71] The "mayor" was elected for four years and the "councillors" for two. The community council had introduced a levy called "der Zehnte" (one tenth) on all income. This form of levy/tax could be paid in cash or in kind. If it was paid in the latter, the goods or products would be sold. The Central Council of the Temple Society dealt with religious, health and some educational matters as well as support for the poor.[72]

In March 1883, Johannes Dreher, Mayor of Sarona, reported in his Annual Report that nine boys and one girl were born in Sarona during 1882. There were 219 residents in Sarona, including 35 school children and 43 children under six years of age. Three new homes with sheds and barns had been built and more land (small holdings) had been purchased from the Arabs. The irrigation system around Sarona had been extended. Mr Dreher also commented on the narrow, dusty roadways/paths between the orange groves that were bordered by cactus hedges (prickly pear) on both sides.[73]

The building of roads, development of land, and community facilities were a big burden on the struggling settlers

A description of Sarona by Yehiel Brill, a Jewish community leader in the 1880s, states that the Sarona settlement was designed and built *". . . with knowledge and intelligence, in the hands of the diligent and with much effort [. . .] in the colony we sat, also drank beer, and after we saw and studied the houses and the fields, the beauty and the order, the life of tranquillity and quietness in the colony, we remarked, if a Templer congregation, composed of persons low in means, and rich only with a determination to make the Holy Land inhabited as in past days [. . .] if they could aspire and work it out, to erect such a colony not to be found even in Germany, so should we [. . .].*[74]

A further description of a visit to Sarona in 1884 is given by Pastor Carl Ninck from Hamburg. He writes:—*"After leaving the smelly alleys (of Jaffa) we came to the fertile Plain of Saron, now at its springtime best and well known since antiquity. After half an hour we stopped at Sarona, a neat village with clean whitewashed houses, red tiled roofs and surrounded by small gardens. There are approximately 250 Germans from Wuerttemberg living here. [. . .] School children were playing in front of the school and called out a familiar Swabian "Gruess Gott". Oh how such a greeting in a foreign land reminds one of home! I jumped off our cart and the school children took me into their school. There I sang German songs with them and told them about their old homeland."*[75]

It is interesting to note that Ninck makes no reference to the initial hardships and deaths of the early years in Sarona. This suggests that at that time in 1884 the settlement had overcome the earlier difficulties, otherwise he would probably have mentioned them.

The need to help and support each other established both a strong bond between the settlers and a sense of community spirit. Morale was described as being good.

The community had developed a tradition of celebrating Thanksgiving (Dankfest) in October or November each year. It was always a day of religious service, as well as rejoicing, fellowship and festivities. It was an important event in the infant Sarona settlement each year and the whole community participated in the activities of that day.

Other community groups such as choirs and a brass band were formed. They were the core of social activities.[76]

By 1889, 269 persons lived in Sarona in 41 houses. There were also 30 other buildings which included community buildings, the winery, workshops, barns and sheds.[77]

The need to help and support each other established both a strong bond between the settlers and a sense of community spirit

23) Jaffa/Sarona Band—approx. 1890

Back Row (Left to Right): Gotthilf Hornung, Gotthilf Bulach, Reinhardt Lippmann, Christian Beck, David Eppinger

Front Row: Emil Joss, Karl Gollmer (Jnr), Herr Heinze, Theodor Fast

THE 1893-1897 SPLIT IN THE TEMPLE SOCIETY

The split that occurred in the Temple Society in 1893 directly affected many families in Sarona and caused divisions within the wider Templer Community.

During the late 1880s the Temple Society was overcoming its previous severe financial difficulties which stemmed in part from the costs and expenses it had incurred in establishing, developing and maintaining the settlements in Palestine. This work had been done without any financial assistance from the German Government although submissions had been made for assistance.[78] However, the Temple Society was still indebted at that time. It was also desirous of establishing a sound financial base for its future operations including the purchase of additional land.[79]

That tax was strongly opposed by many Templers who wanted it removed

In 1890 the Templer Council agreed to impose a tax, "Templer Tax", of 20 francs per family per year. That tax was strongly opposed by many Templers who wanted it removed. They contended that the Templer Council's decision was contrary to the spirit and intent of the Temple Society's spiritual objectives in that it pressured and compelled members to pay instead of appealing to their willingness to make contributions voluntarily and having trust in God's guidance.[80]

Finally, on 26 September 1893, after several years of disputing the Council's decision, 211 families and members from the Templer communities of Haifa (123—virtually the whole community), Sarona (70) and Jaffa (18) split from the main Temple Society and formed the "Freie Tempelgemeinde" (Free Templer Community)[81] In the above mentioned three settlements, only 11 families and members remained with the Temple Society in Haifa, 30 in Sarona and 70 in Jaffa.[82] This rift in the Temple Society lasted for four years.

Sarona families who remained with the Temple Society included—Venus, Wennagel, Laemmle, Lippmann, Edelmaier, Jung, Weeber[83]

24) Heading of official Temple Society publication

The Free Templer community agreed to and adopted a number of principles which in part stated:—". . . *that we (Author: The Free Templers) will continue to hold fast to the objectives of the Temple Society without wanting to quarrel with the "Warte" nor the Temple Society's Central Council*". The Free Templers also expressed their desire and hope that their differences with the Templer Council would be resolved and that they would become united again.[84]

Deep and bitter divisions continued between the two groups

Deep and bitter divisions continued between the two groups. Examples of this are: the Temple Society would not allow the Free Templers to express their views in or via the Templer Warte, so the Free Templers published their own newsletter *Mitteilungen aus der Freien Tempelgemeinde (Communications from the Free Templer Community)*.[85] The Temple Society would not report deaths in the "Warte" nor speak at funerals of even prominent and well respected persons who were Free Templers, such as Gottlieb Groll (1845-1895) and Johannes Dreher (1837-1896), teacher and mayor of Sarona for 19 years.[86] In Jaffa where the Free Templers were in the minority, they were denied access and use of the Jaffa Community Saal (hall) for religious gatherings. The Free Templers in Sarona, however, were in the majority and reached an understanding with the other Templers for joint use of the community's facilities.[87] The Free Templers claimed that they were at a financial disadvantage because the Temple Society would not allow any payments from the Templer financial assets. The Free Templers reported in their newsletter ". . . *it is unbelievable that progressive persons at the end of the 19th Century would impose such perverted measures . . .*"[88] Separate schools were started by the Free Templers and the small educational subsidies from the German government were divided within the communities between Templer and Free Templer schools.[89]

Sarona families who joined the "Free Templer Community" included—Steller, Weller, Groll, Dreher[90]

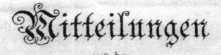

25) Heading of the Free Templers publication

All this occurred during Christoph Hoffmann's II (1847-1910) early years as President of the Temple Society. He became President following the two earlier Presidents, Christoph Hoffmann I and Christoph Paulus, who had both been founders of the Temple Society. The first two Presidents virtually enjoyed unquestioned authority within the Temple Society. Christoph Hoffmann II however, can be regarded as a new generation younger President. Similarly, there was a new generation of younger Templer settlers in the various settlements who were prepared to question the central control of the Templer Council and the authority of the President.[91]

The Templer Council regarded the move by the Free Templers as a vote of no confidence. The Council was also concerned that the Free Templers would seek self-enrichment by financial means and thereby compromise the attainment of the Kingdom of God, rather than seeking it through the teachings and beliefs of the Temple Society (Love of God and love of neighbour and of oneself).[92]

It was mainly due to Hoffmann's untiring efforts that eventually reconciliation was achieved between the Free Templers and the Temple Society

It was mainly due to Hoffmann's untiring efforts that eventually reconciliation was achieved between the Free Templers and the Temple Society. He was prepared to compromise some of his powers as President, as well as giving the individual communities a greater role and representation on the Templer Council. The Temple Society's constitution was amended to enlarge the Templer Council so as to include the Regional and Community leaders. He achieved this reconciliation without compromising any of the fundamental religious objectives of the Temple Society.[93]

He achieved this reconciliation without compromising any of the fundamental religious objectives of the Temple Society

Finally, after much negotiating and numerous conferences amongst the Templer communities in Palestine, Hoffmann was able to announce at the Tempelfest in 1897 that the Free Templers had agreed that they would in future be subject again to the constitution and direction of the Templer Council.[94]

Thus a difficult period ended for both the Sarona community as well as for the Temple Society as a whole. Both could now focus on expanding and developing the settlements again.

LAND OWNERSHIP

Since their arrival in the Holy Land in the late 1860s the Templers had been regarded with some suspicion by the Turkish authorities who at times frustrated the settlers' endeavours with bureaucratic difficulties. This occurred notwithstanding the work the Templers had done in improving and developing the land and their good relationships with the local inhabitants. The settlers did not have any protection

26) Official Turkish documents and Land Title Deeds

27) Second Sarona Winery built in 1890/91. The winery was a hive of activity in Sarona especially during the grape harvest

28) The first Sarona winery built in the 1870s

The Turkish Government announced that it intended to examine the entire real estate situation and convert previously privately owned land (Muelk) of the settlers into state owned land (Mire or Mirje) if no reliable documentation could be presented

A winery co-operative was formed to coordinate the making and sale of wine

by the German Government and were therefore powerless against nepotism and harassment by Turkish government officials.[95]

This was especially noticeable with landownership and the difficulties the settlers faced in having their properties entered in the land register in Jaffa. In 1891, the Turkish Government announced that it intended to examine the entire real estate situation and convert previously privately owned land (Muelk) of the settlers into state owned land (Mire or Mirje) if no reliable documentation could be presented. The settlers were dismayed by this decision and made representation and lodged a petition with the German Embassy in Constantinople. Their request for support was turned down by the Embassy. The settlers then turned to the King of Wuerttemberg, Wilhelm II, for assistance. He was sympathetic to the settlers and arranged for the Wuerttemberg legation in Berlin to take up the matter with the German Foreign Office. Some of the German press also reported on the plight of the German settlers in Palestine.[96]

The German Government finally took some action. In his report of Sarona in 1894 Mayor Johannes Dreher writes;—". . . *It is pleasing to report that the Imperial German Embassy in Constantinople has sent Count Muelinen as a delegate to oversee the property issues of Muelk and Mire. For several days Count Muelinen has been closely examining the property titles of the Germans. We thank the German Embassy for its involvement, because it is well known how easy it is in Turkey, even with His Majesty the Sultan's best intentions, to change Muelk into Mire.*"[97]

In 1898, to the relief of the settlers, the Sultan issued an irade (decree) to the Chief Land Registrar in Constantinople to issue title deeds for all German real estate, other than that land which had been identified as state land by a local commission.[98]

Thus ended 20 years of uncertainty in landownership.

A side effect of the landownership issue as well as the Turkish Government's prohibition on foreigners purchasing land[99] was that some Templer settlers started looking for new land outside Palestine. (see segment on "Impact of African Emigration" in chapter 4).

VITICULTURE

As the vineyards became established wine became an important product of the settlement. Sufficient quantities were produced to enable an export industry to develop. In 1874/75 a winery co-operative was formed to co-ordinate the making and sale of wine.

The co-operative required members to deliver their grapes to the Co-operative's winery. In addition, a monetary levy was imposed on the growers. The levy was based on the area each grower had under cultivation. In 1875 the co-operative had 23 members.[100] A communal winery with cellars (No 18) was built in 1874-75 and a cooper, Johann Bernhard Glenk and his son Georg, made wine barrels in Sarona in the late 1870s.[101]

The Temple Society Central Fund partnership was instrumental in opening a Division for Wine Export of the German Settlements of Jaffa-Sarona (Abteilung Weinexport der deutschen Kolonien Sarona-Jaffa) in 1891[102]. In 1894, the first shipment of 5000 litres of wine was sent to the Imberger Brothers and Co. in Stuttgart/Cannstatt, Germany. It was hoped that the wine would be accepted and sell readily.[103] In 1895 the division was replaced by an expanded co-operative—The German Winegrowers' Co-operative of Sarona-Jaffa (Deutsche Weinbaugenossenschaft Sarona-Jaffa) and a new larger winery (No 2a) was built in 1898.[104]

In 1894 the first shipment of 5000 litres of wine was sent to Germany

By the end of the 1890s there were 10 winegrowers cultivating 150 hectares of vineyards, three wine stores with their own winepresses, cellars, distilleries and cooper shops. The annual production of wine was 4000 hectolitres. There was also one producer of sparkling wines and liqueur.[105]

An interesting reference to the Sarona wine is made by Dr Danny Goldman in his publication:—*Sarona, Third Templer Colony.* He writes *"The Templer wine became so popular in Palestine, that the Rabbis legitimised the German wine for orthodox Jews and ruled out wine from Jewish colonies."*[106]

Haim Hissin one of the Jewish pioneers writes in his memoirs about the vineyards:—*"I saw the work of the Germans in the vineyards all day. They have a lot of Arab workers—but the owners, as well as their wives and children also work there. They give the Arabs a wonderful example how to work. During a work pause they gave me some wine—its taste was wonderful."*[107]

CATTLE PLAGUE OF 1895

On 11 August 1895 a type of cattle plague broke out simultaneously at three adjoining properties in Sarona—on the farms of Groll, Edelmaier and Haering—and 44 head of stock, mainly dairy cows, were immediately stricken. From these three properties the plague spread quickly to most other properties in the settlement. Only five farms in Sarona, with small numbers of stock, were not affected. The settlers were convinced that the cattle plague had been brought to Sarona by Arab workers.[108]

In the four month period from mid August to mid December 1895, over 190 cattle were affected by the plague

In the four month period from mid August to mid December 1895, over 190 cattle were affected by the plague, of these 137 mostly prime dairy cows died and 56 recovered. However, many of those that did recover were left in such poor condition that they took a long time to produce milk again, let alone be used for breeding.

The settlers were at a loss how to treat the infected stock as no known cure was available. A variety of innovative treatments were tried. A large shed was hastily constructed for sick stock outside the perimeter of the settlement. This proved impracticable because the distance from the settlement made it very difficult to treat individual sick animals. Even more so when several cows from one property were stricken at the same time and required several persons to look after them. The settlers massaged the sick beasts; steam was made to make the cows sweat; mild doses of boric, nitric and hydrochloric acid in luke warm water were administered by the settlers as they tried desperately to help their stricken stock to recover. Any beasts that were constipated were given laxatives and those suffering from diarrhoea were given opium or a mixture of nitrate of silver (Hoellenstein). The farmers also cooked special soups and other dishes to feed the sick stock.[109]

It was estimated that the cattle plague cost the Sarona community 10,000 francs not including the disruption to the milk deliveries

It was estimated that the cattle plague cost the Sarona community 10,000 francs not including the disruption to the milk deliveries.[110]

KAISER WILHELM II VISIT

On his journey to Jerusalem the Kaiser travelled through several German settlements including Sarona

In October 1898 the German Kaiser Wilhelm II and his wife, Kaiserin Augusta-Victoria, visited the Holy Land. The prime purpose of the visit was the consecration of the Protestant Church of the Redeemer in Jerusalem. On his journey to Jerusalem the Kaiser travelled through several German settlements including Sarona.[111] There he was warmly welcomed by the whole community. The Sarona settlement had been decorated with banners and flags and the young Pauline Glenk (later married Carl Kuebler) presented the Kaiser and his wife with a bouquet of flowers.[112]

There is an interesting description of the scene around Sarona as documented by Ludwig Schneller (1858-1953) the son of Johann Ludwig Schneller who built the Syrian Orphanage in Jerusalem, and author of *Die Kaiserfahrt durch's Heilige Land (The Kaiser's Journey through the Holy Land).*

29) Kaiser Wilhelm II on his journey from Sarona to Jaffa, 1898

He writes:—*"I took a walk through the orange groves, particularly the one of the community member Ellinger near Sarona, who in a few short years changed the sandy desert there into a flowering garden. After traversing the desert from Caesarea (Author: now known as Horbat Qesari), we were amazed by the wonderful contrast between the desert and the luxurious tropical vegetation. Everywhere there is greenery and blossom. The orange groves radiate their intoxicating scent across the plains, large oleander bushes in their red flowering glory make one forget that this is the drier part of the year in the Holy Land. This enticing district of dark green lemon and orange trees is really "the land where lemons flower and in the dark green foliage the golden oranges glow". I was able to pick and eat oranges to my heart's content and even take some as a greeting from the Holy Land to my family in Cologne. From the dark green leaves the ripening golden balls glow next to the white star flowers—such beauty which hits one in the eye as if it were golden fruit on a glittering silver platter[. . .].*

The extraordinary fertility of these gardens is possible because of a large subterranean river that flows the whole year from the far away mountains, even when the surface land dries out. Wherever bores are sunk, one finds water just a few metres down. The settlers near Jaffa are increasingly using this to their advantage. More recently, kerosene powered motors from Deutz are being installed to draw up water. By "little streams" the water is channelled into the gardens so that every tree has a small water channel around it. Without this water the country would be the same as the desert along the coast [. . .]."[113]

The Kaiser was very impressed by what the German settlers had achieved in the Holy Land. He praised the settlers and said their achievements and conduct was a credit to the German nation.[114]

The Kaiser's Birthday, 27 January, was always a day of festivities. Many houses displayed the black, white and red German flag. There was a flag raising ceremony, and sometimes speeches by the German Consul, and a get-together with drinks and food in the community hall. School children were given a holiday. A picture of the Kaiser was hung in many homes.[115] The settlers were very proud of their German nationality and heritage!

Sarona at the End of the 19th Century

By the end of the 19th century Sarona had overcome many of its initial hardships and had developed into a solid community of 243 comprising 54 families.[116] This also reflected that only a little growth in numbers had occurred over the previous ten years. Families had established themselves and children were attending school.

The Kaiser was very impressed by what the German settlers had achieved in the Holy Land

30) General view of Sarona at the end of the 19th century

31) Sarona school children and teachers approximately 1890

Back Row (left to right): Fritz Kuebler, Gottlieb Glenk, Wilhelm Kuebler, Immanuel Steller, August Venus, Georg Roller, Jakob Hoefer
Fifth Row: Luise Laemmle, (Richter), Dorle Doster, Martha Roller (Steller), Pauline (Laemmle) Wennagel, Paula Knoll (Glenk), Rosa Roller (Wennagel)
Fourth Row: Karl Weiss, Andreas Noz, Christian Kuebler, Friedrich Froeschle, Johannes Weiss, Paula Klotz
Third Row: Maria Weiberle, Bertha Venus (Knoll), Martha Venus (Loebert), Sophie Knoll (Wahl), Maria Graze (Kuebler), Frieda Blaich (Blaich), Pauline Dreher
Second Row: Samuel Weller, Mina Edelmaier (Hoefer), Selma Hasenpflug (Weiberle), Hulda Weiss, Martha Messerle (Frank), Klara Kuebler, Martha Kopp (Messerle), Theophil Messerle
Front Row: Otto Venus, Heinrich Hasenpflug, Margaret Blaich, Gotthilf Dreher, Hans Stueber
Teachers: Friedrich Dreher, (left) David Eppinger (right)
Girls married surname, if known, is shown in brackets

In 1895, 37 children were attending the school "Free Templer Community School" in Sarona and another 8 children were receiving regular higher education lessons on a part-time basis.[117] At the beginning of 1896, a second teacher was planned to be appointed. Due to the split in the Temple Society, problems had arisen in the education of children in the Templer settlements. Teachers from Sarona and Haifa continued to participate in the annual meetings of teachers. The community leaders wanted to ensure the children received an education equivalent to the standards of the German education system.[118] The Sarona community received a small subsidy (increased from 625 marks to 1000 marks in 1895) through the German Consulate from the German Government. In Sarona this amount divided—650 marks to the "Free Templer Community School" and 350 marks to the Temple Society School.[119]

Sarona was still primarily an agricultural settlement with 300 hectares being cultivated—150 ha of vineyards, 24 ha of orange groves and olives, with cereals and vegetables on the remainder.[120] One of the main agricultural activities in Sarona was the dairy industry and milk production. Professor Alex Carmel, Schumacher Institute, University of Haifa, describes the Sarona farmers as being the most successful farmers in the whole country at that time. Sarona is described as a well planned and beautiful settlement and looked upon with envy by the Jews.[121]

Professor Alex Carmel, Schumacher Institute, University of Haifa, describes the Sarona farmers as being the most successful farmers in the whole country at that time

Other trades, such as baker, butcher, builder, blacksmith, shoemaker and cobbler, cooper, miller, saddler, bricklayer and carpenter were also represented in the settlement.[122]

Children were born and four grades (each grade spanning two years) for various age groups established at the school in the community house. The community featured a brass band, mixed choir and a "Jugendverein" (Youth Club).

During the late 1890s and early 20th century there were significantly more young males than young females living in Sarona. In 1882 for example, nine boys and only one girl were born in the settlement. To overcome this gender imbalance the Mayor of Sarona, Friedrich Laemmle, went to Germany on several occasions to encourage young women to emigrate to Palestine. He was quite successful in his venture and a number of young ladies who were not Templers, did come and settle in Sarona. The names of some of these ladies were— Wilhelmine and Emilie Schillinger, Eugene Bauerle, Mina Schock, a Miss Hieber and Karoline Laemmle. All these young ladies lived with Fritz and Wilhelmine Laemmle until they found employment, accommodation or marriage.

Most of these ladies married young Templer settlers and became valued members of the Sarona Templer Community.[123]

CONSTRUCTION AND BUILDINGS IN SARONA

Building commenced shortly after the initial land lots had been allocated. Details of the early houses has been referred to previously. Despite the enormous hardships during 1872 and 1873, 14 private homes were built as well as the community house (Gemeindehaus).[124] An extraordinary achievement under the circumstances!

The builders at that time and right through to WW I were the Wennagels. Johann Martin Wennagel, a bricklayer (Maurer) by trade, arrived in the Holy Land in 1870. Wennagel was specifically requested to emigrate to the Holy Land to assist with the construction of houses and buildings in the new settlements of Jaffa and Sarona. He was a builder from Dornstetten-Aach, Black Forest, Germany.[125]

The community house was consecrated on 2 February 1873.[126] This was the first public building in Sarona. It was an important building for the community as it was used as the community centre for meetings, church services and also as a school.

The early buildings were built out of "kurkar" blocks—these blocks were cut out of sandstone layers on-site as Sarona was located on kurkar bed rock. The blocks were laid in rows and the walls were up to a meter thick. This thickness provided the house with sufficient insulation so that no cooling or heating was necessary inside the building. Other buildings were constructed out of "Debbish" stone. This sandstone was quarried at Hasan's Hill near the Arab village of Selemeh. The corner stones of buildings were often made out of concrete.[127] The window frames and other wooden fittings were built from timber imported from Europe by Breisch in Jaffa.[128]

32) Josef M. Wennagel 1878-1949 —master builder of Sarona

A community bakehouse was constructed near the community building. This was a small single storey building—one room only with a large, wood-fired brick oven in one corner. A small blackboard allowed Sarona residents to indicate when they wished to use the oven. A table and bench were also located in the room and so became a place for ladies to chat whilst waiting for their bread/ cakes to bake.[129]

A well was constructed and water was pumped, initially by wind power, to a large concrete tank at the highest part of Sarona, and from there it was piped to many homes in the settlement. Most early houses had their own well. Water had to be drawn manually with buckets. The residents and farmers dug their own wells to a depth

33) Community bakehouse (left) near the old community house

34) Sketch of windmill used to pump water for Sarona. This was the initial means to pump water to the settlement.

of 20-22 metres with the assistance of Arab labourers. Sarona was blessed with good artesian water once the bed rock was broken through. This water was clean and suitable for drinking and was used for both domestic and agricultural purposes.[130] The settlers also assisted the Jewish settlers at the newly established Jewish settlement of Rishon-le-Zion to find water. At its beginning this settlement was short of water and the settlers proposed building a water storage. In February 1883 some German settlers from Jaffa and Sarona helped the Jewish settlers to dig a well and good water was found at a depth of eight meters.[131]

The Wennagels not only built homes in Sarona but their reputation as master builders involved them in significant public works for the Government, including railway stations and, in the early 20th century, a major bridge over a wadi in Gaza.[132]

In the late 1890s, the Wagner Engineering works commenced the installation of motorised pumps in the wells.[133] This allowed better access to the water and significantly changed and improved agricultural production.

Another significant building constructed was the Winery in the 1890s for the German Wine Growers Co-operative.[134] Jakob Edelmaier and Christian Orth were the early Kellermeisters (winemakers).[135]

35) Original Deutz motor and pump installed by Wagner Bros. The pump and motor were recently discovered in Israel. The pump was in the Sarona Settlement well which was approx. 3 meters in diameter and about 40 meters deep. The motor is marked "Gebrueder Wagner, Jaffa, Palaestina".

36) *Construction of railway station on the Bagdad line built by Josef M. Wennagel. Mr Wennagel is seen in the middle of the photograph as indicated by an arrow*

37) *Twenty pillar bridge over Wadi Ghazze built by Josef M. Wennagel*

NEW DEVELOPMENTS

About this time a significant development was occurring outside the Templer settlements which would eventually have a major impact on the settlements, particularly Sarona. In 1896 Theodor Herzl (1860-1904), founder of modern political Zionism, proposed the establishment of a Jewish Homeland in the Holy Land. In 1898 (the same year the Kaiser visited Palestine) Herzl also went there to look at the possibilities of fulfilling his proposal and to meet with Kaiser Wilhelm II. The Kaiser was very polite during their meeting and then tried to determine what the Sultan in Constantinople thought of the idea. After getting a negative answer the Kaiser let the matter rest.[136]

The achievements of the few early Templer settlers made a significant initial contribution to the modernisation of the Holy Land

The achievements of the relatively few early Templer settlers before the first wave of significant Jewish immigration in 1882, are attributed largely to the settlers' faith and diligence. They made a significant initial contribution to the modernisation of the Holy Land without any assistance from Government. They demonstrated that European settlement was possible in the Holy Land.[137]

CHAPTER THREE

1900 TO WORLD WAR I

THERE IS NO BETTER WAY of starting this chapter than with a translated version of a report of the Thanksgiving Day in Sarona in November 1900. This article was printed in the *Warte des Tempels,* the monthly German publication of the TGD, in September 1980.

"At Thanksgiving in 1900 people started to already congregate at 9.00 am for the morning service at which several children were to be presented. The mixed choir of the community provided the musical backdrop.

In the afternoon around 2.00pm the whole community—young and old, nobody stayed at home—assembled not at the community hall but on the festival area. This area had been prepared by many willing hands. It was located between the Community House and various neighbouring homes. Ropes had been stretched between the buildings and large sheets (sails) were slung over the ropes to provide shade. The entrance was framed with palm fronds and the side facing the road was screened with greenery. Around the stage the products of the settlement were displayed—wine, honey, wheat and oat sheaves, marrows, oranges, sugar cane etc. Interspersed among the produce were the prettiest flowers that were still in blossom at that time of year. Above the stage in large letters for everyone to read was written "Opfere Gott Dank und bezahle dem Höchsten deine Gelübde" (Sacrifice Thanks to God and give the Highest your solemn vow)

The band played, the community sang hymns and the community leader Friedrich Laemmle reminded everyone as to the significance of this occasion. He cast his mind back on former years and said 'We have a reason to thank God to-day, because he has helped us through to now even though we may not have deserved it. For some time now the plague has been around us but we have been shielded from it. Also our expectations were blessed beyond our hopes, all fruits of our land thrived, the grape harvest was more abundant than anyone could have hoped for and for all that, in word and deed, we thank our Heavenly Father, from whom everything comes, fortune and misfortune.'

38) Arab worker with box of Jaffa oranges. The orange industry developed rapidly during the first decade of the 20th Century

41

Following this short service a number of musical items, songs, and poetry readings were performed. Wine, bread, hot sausages and potato salad were served and grapes were eaten for dessert. People stayed right into the night talking, singing, and listening to presentations from the various community groups. At 9.30 pm evening prayers were said and everyone made their way home and to bed . . . . so as to be able to get up early and start their daily work."[138]

A further report on Sarona, published in *Die Warte des Temples* in 1902 makes reference to several deaths due to malaria. It also reports that there were 40 children now in the school and two new teachers had been appointed—Immanuel Knoll, who had returned to Sarona after having completed his teacher training in Nagold, Germany, and Miss Anna Jung.[139]

As always Christmas in Sarona was celebrated both by families at home and by the community generally. The following is a description of the community Christmas celebration in December 1901.

"Again this year we decorated a Christmas tree in the community house for the school children. Each child received a small gift and a plate of Christmas cookies. The celebrations were held on Sunday evening the 22nd December and the school children participated in a small stage production. At this celebration, young and old, women and men all participated. The community house was filled to overflowing, as everyone wanted to see the happy faces of the children and one felt happy in oneself."[140]

An observation of Sarona in 1903 is provided by Elise Loebert (nee Hornung) when she recalls:—*"Sarona—the colony in the sun, wide clean streets without footpaths, clean, cared for gardens, homely houses [. . .]*

Father worked as head cooper in the winery. A cool wine aroma was always present there, and everything was spotlessly clean. Celebrations such as weddings were celebrated there.

Father belonged to the "Concordia" violin club. My mother loved music and sang in the mixed choir of Sarona. [. . .]

Sarona was very beautiful, but malaria was still present. We also had malaria. Father was ill and always had to carry his medicine bottle with him, even when working in the winery. We children also suffered from malaria, and probably our mother as well. Friedrich had a malaria attack in the first week of his life. The midwife, Mrs Baldenhofer, wrapped the child in a wet towel to reduce the fever."[141]

In 1902 the new German Templer agricultural settlement of Wilhelma was founded. 20 of the 69 original settlers of Wilhelma came from Sarona.[142]

IMPACT OF THE AFRICA EMIGRATION

Even though the settlement had begun to grow, the economic situation for many settlers, especially the young wishing to buy land or those wishing to expand their livelihoods, proved beyond their meagre financial means. In the 1890s, the ongoing uncertainty of landownership and titles also created unease amongst many settlers. The settlers considered German East Africa (a German colony, known as Tanzania today) as a possible place to acquire additional land. In 1896 the Chief Clerk of the German East Africa Administration visited the Holy Land and met with the Templer settlers.[143]

In 1896 the first families (two Reinhardt families from Jaffa) left for German East Africa.[144]

The Temple Society Central Council itself had been trying for years to raise money and attract finance, either through grants or loans and/or at least a line of credit with governments and banks in Germany.[145]

In the 1890s, the ongoing uncertainty of landownership and titles also created unease amongst many settlers

39) Mt Meru area in German East Africa where several Templer families from Palestine settled. The Templers cleared the land and started coffee plantations in this area.

40) Jakob Blaich in his coffee plantation in German East Africa.

The attractiveness of land settlement in German East Africa was probably raised again during the Kaiser's visit in 1898. Especially after seeing first hand what had been achieved by the German settlers in Palestine.[146] Due to the financial difficulties in acquiring land in Palestine, several families decided to emigrate to German East Africa where they believed it would be easier to secure their future. Young Germans (in this case Templers) were tempted by the allocation of large tracts of virtually "free" land near Arusha and the Mt Meru region by the German Government and a spirit of adventure to try their luck in German East Africa. They started to cultivate virgin land by planting coffee plantations and maize crops as well as having to cope with the wildlife of Africa as they commenced their new lives there.[147]

In 1907/08 there was debate within the Temple Society, and especially in Sarona, regarding the question of starting settlements in East Africa. There were strong opinions against going there as it was considered contrary to the original concept of the Holy Land settlements. Attempts were made to dissuade farmers and families from going. Karl Knoll from Sarona was in charge of examining the feasibility of new settlements in Africa. In 1908 the first families left Sarona and ventured to Africa. In 1909 other families followed—the names of some of the families who left were:—Jakob Blaich, Karl Knoll,

41) Lion hunt in German East Africa

42) Fritz Blaich (left) and Bernhard Blaich (right) buffalo hunting in German East Africa.

Gottlieb Glenk, P Egger, Bauer, Groezinger and Kappus. Some of these families returned after a few years, either because of health reasons or because the venture was not as successful as anticipated.[148] It appears that mainly families from the Sarona settlement emigrated, although several families from Jaffa, including the Oldorf, Lorch and Reinhardt families, also left for German East Africa.[149]

The repercussions of the families leaving caused concern in Sarona and with the Temple Society Central Council. A major concern was that the vacant land the settlers were leaving behind would fall into non Templer ownership. The land prices around Sarona had risen substantially due to the improved irrigation systems and the crops that could be grown. Good prices were being offered for the land. The Templer Central Council approached the German Government for a loan to purchase the land as it was being vacated but this was unsuccessful. Thus the Templers had to deal with the situation themselves.[150]

Most Templers abandoned their enterprises in Africa before World War I. A few families—notably the Blaichs and Reinhardts remained in Africa for many years.

ESTABLISHMENT OF THE SARONA DAIRY

The establishment of the Sarona Molkerei (Dairy) came about mainly because of the difficulties and costs experienced by the individual milk producers in distributing their milk. In October 1902, on the initiative of J. Edelmaier, S. Groll and Otto Jung a meeting was called for all milk producers and interested people to establish a Co-operative. F Laemmle, L Jung, J Edelmaier, H Weeber, C Scheerle, G Haag, S Groll and Otto Jung were elected to develop the constitution of the new co-operative.

At a meeting on 27 December 1902 a constitution for the new body was adopted and on 1 January 1903 the constitution came into effect and the Milk Delivery Co-operative was formed in Sarona.

Messrs F Glenk and G Haag initially administered the co-operative and the milk deliveries were at first received at the "Zehnt House" a small house owned by the community near the community house. Later a building for milk delivery was rented in Jaffa. Some initial difficulties were experienced with delivery times and competition in Jaffa from the Arabs. A separator was purchased as well as butter barrels and soon the business improved. In March 1903 the business was renamed "Agricultural Union Sarona". Agreement was reached with the Winegrowers Co-operative of Sarona to allow for the sale of milk and butter through its Jaffa outlet. The business continued to

43) Dairy cows near Laemmle's barn

Having a local dairy was a big saving for the dairy farmers and reduced their delivery and distribution costs substantially

grow. Mr Lippmann became involved with the administration of the business, K Richter was employed as a driver and a horse and cart was hired from G Graze.

During 1903, illness and other personal commitments required changes to the running of the co-operative: first F Graze then K Froeschle ran the business until, finally, Jakob Blaich took over.

In 1904, with the completion of a water main, the dairy was finally established in Sarona. Having a local dairy was a big saving for the dairy farmers and reduced their delivery and distribution costs substantially.

In 1905 an extraordinary general meeting was addressed by Heinrich Bulach, at which he presented the case for amalgamation of the milk delivery co-operative and the wine co-operative. It was resolved that:—"The German Wine Growers Co-operative will take over the business for the milk, butter, vegetable etc from the members of the Agricultural Union". This resolution came into effect on 1 December 1905. The Agricultural Union Sarona was liquidated and all members were paid out a modest return with a reasonable profit.

This was a major development for the young settlement and it took energy and patience, as well as co-operation to fulfil both the needs of the individual as well as those of the community.[151]

44) Georg Laemmle on horseback in the main street of Sarona in the early 1900s

A VIBRANT COMMUNITY

At the end of the first decade of the twentieth century (40 years after its founding) Sarona had developed into a vibrant community. A number of new homes were being built, and as the "new generation", that is those born in the Holy Land were contributing to the settlement, another generation was being born.

The Temple Society's constitution as previously amended allowed for representation on the Central Council of Community Chairmen and Regional Representatives. Sarona's members on the Central Council in 1911 were—Friedrich Laemmle, Heinrich Weiss and Jakob Prinz.[152]

Education for the children was provided in the community house which had a long room that could be sub-divided—Grades 1 and 2 were in one room and Grades 3 and 4 in the other. The teachers were Anna Hoffmann and Imanuel Knoll.[153]

A kindergarten with 24 pre-school children was operating—Maria Wennagel who had been the kindergarten teacher for many years retired and Christiane Weiss was appointed as the new teacher.[154]

The vineyards, winery, banana plantations (these were started by settlers returning from Africa[155]), vegetable gardens, plant nursery,

45) Rose garden in Orth's nursery

orange groves and animal husbandry were producing a good income. In some cases, due to the shortage of working capital by individuals, several agricultural producers would combine to buy land and establish orange groves. It took nearly five years to establish a good productive orange grove and therefore there was very little return on capital during that initial period. Thus several "company farms" were formed. It is estimated that orange production nearly doubled in five years.[156]

On the other hand, wine sales remained stable with only a 5% increase over a five year period. At one stage the winery was storing 1,000,000 litres of wine and there were real concerns whether there would be sufficient storage space for the next vintage. Serious consideration was given to not harvesting the grapes for one year. Fortunately for the settlers in Sarona, the grape crops failed in Spain and southern France and due to the demand for wine in Europe, much of the stored wine was able to be sold.[157]

46) The Wagner Bros. works in Walhalla

47) Advertisement for Sarona wine

48) Advertisement for Sarona wine

49) Advertisement for Gebr. Wagner (Wagner Bros.). It says the foundry and machine shop are the lagest business of this type in Palestine and Syria.

The dairy industry was well established and thriving. The Sarona dairy was operating successfully and milk and dairy products were sold in nearby Jaffa and to the local community. A problem facing the dairy farmers was the recurrence of the cattle plague which had been brought to Sarona by cows purchased in, and shipped from Beirut. These cows had been in contact on board ship with infected stock from other parts of Asia Minor. Much of the local herd was affected by this disease. The only way to overcome it, other than killing the cows, was by vaccination. The vaccine had to be bought in Constantinople, Turkey.[158]

Due to additional land purchases by the settlers, Sarona's agricultural enterprises stretched south to the old city of Jaffa, in the west to the sand dunes near the Mediterranean, in the north to the river flats of the Audsche River and in the east to the barren hills. The increase in acreage for agricultural enterprises was mainly due to the installation of motorised pumps for irrigation.[159] The first pumps for the Sarona fields were installed in 1898 and many others after 1900.[160]

Following the establishment of the new Wilhelma settlement in 1902, the winery had been expanded and renamed the Wilhelma-Jaffa-Sarona Wine Growers Co-operative (Weinbaugenossenschaft Wilhelma—Jaffa-Sarona) in 1904.[161] The communities of Sarona and Wilhelma also agreed to establish an Orange Export Company. Heinrich Bulach was appointed as its head.[162]

Other enterprises had been started near Sarona and these provided additional employment other than in farming and agriculture.

The Wagner brothers, Wilhelm (1853-1893), Georg (1857-1940) and Adolf (1873-1952), had started a foundry, engineering works, and a mechanical and repair workshop in the early 1890s at Walhalla near Jaffa. These works were known as "Gebrueder Wagner" (Wagner Bros). In 1895 Wagners started to import and install Deutz motors and pumps from Germany which modernised the irrigation system.[163] This was a very rapidly growing enterprise, with foundry, repair and engineering works in nearby Jaffa, providing additional employment opportunities for the Sarona community.[164]

In nearby Walhalla (another Templer community, established in 1888 on the outskirts of Jaffa) a cement product factory was developed at the beginning of the 20th century by Hugo Wieland (1853-1922) who had arrived in 1871 and lived in Jaffa. Cement was imported from Heidelberg in Germany and the factory produced floor tiles and building blocks, and patterned and coloured tiles for buildings throughout the Holy Land. This reduced the necessity to import many of these items from Italy. The factory was expanded and from 1903 roof tiles

50) The Wieland house with concrete
pipes they manufactured

and pipes were being produced from cement. From 1906 the factory started producing building materials in large quantities. This had a major impact on building in Sarona and most buildings built in the eight years before WWI were built with these cement blocks (known as Wieland stone), which were often patterned to give a better effect to the external walls. Wieland stones also started to replace the timber window frames in many homes built after 1904.[165]

Other enterprises were started in Sarona, an olive press and mill by the Pflugfelder family and olive and sesame oil was produced there until 1938; and a joinery workshop by Otto Venus.

In many cases Arabs were employed to help both domestically and on the farms. Arab guards were employed to protect the orange groves during the ripening period.

The development of a railway network early in the 20th century throughout Palestine also provided some employment opportunities, but it also meant some of the men having to move away from Sarona. The Jaffa to Jerusalem railway had been built and was operational by 1892. It passed to the south of Sarona.[166] When it was opened and the first steam train with its belching smoke and steam went by some of the very "old" settlers remarked that "it must be the work of the devil".[167]

Sunday was always a day of rest and religious significance.

51) In front of the Venus house and joinery workshop

A bowling alley (Kegelbahn) was built and provided an additional social venue at Kuebler's Bar/tavern. A brass band, male and mixed choirs as well as a ladies' auxiliary were active in the community. Young people organised excursions (on horseback, with donkeys and horse and cart) to nearby beaches north and south of Jaffa and to other places outside the settlement. The Mai Ausflug (May Picnic) was an important annual event for the whole community. The Mai Ausflug was generally held in conjunction with the Wilhelma Templer community and was a day of enjoyment and social interaction at a place away from their own settlement.[168]

52) An outing to the Audsche Mill

53) Young Men's Club Sarona approx. 1910

Back Row (left to right): Christian Orth, Christian Weiss, Johannes Wennagel, Hermann Graze, Samuel Weller

Front Row: Gotthold Steller, Johannes Weiss, Daniel Richter, Peter Franz, Fritz Weiberle, Heinrich Heimann.

54) Prince Eitel Friedrich and Princess Sophie depart from the Mount of Olives, Jerusalem in 1910

The visit was described as follows by Elise Loebert (nee Hornung):—"The streets of Sarona were wonderfully decorated. Garlands were strung from tree to tree across the street. These had been handmade by the girls from Sarona out of flowers and foliage. From every house a red-white-and black flag was fluttering. We all lined the street. A type of pavilion from the Kaiser's visit in 1898 was still standing and had been refitted for the princely couple. The Sarona Brass Band was assembled ready to play the welcoming march as soon as the carriages entered the street. 21 mortar rounds were fired to greet the couple in Jaffa. Soon a black carriage appeared with the princely couple (all the following carriages were also black) and the band played "Heil Dir im Siegerkranz", our national anthem at that time. We were all very excited and ready to celebrate. For us children it was very uplifting, when young girls curtsied as they presented bouquets to our guests."[171]

A Princely Visit

In April 1910, Prince Eitel Friedrich and his wife Princess Sophie Charlotte visited the Holy Land for the dedication of the Empress Auguste Victoria-Foundation Complex and the Church of the Ascension on the Mount of Olives in Jerusalem. During the visit, of the Princely Couple presented the main builders of the church—Ehmann and Blaich with State Service medals for their work. They also praised the German Templer craftsmen who had assisted with the construction and fitout of the whole complex.[169]

The Prince and Princess also visited Sarona.[170] They were received with great honours and Sarona's streets were festively decorated to welcome them.

Shortly after the Prince's visit the German Consul in Jaffa presented the Sarona community with 1000 francs to be put towards the construction of a new school and a new community hall which could be used on occasions such as Thanksgiving, weddings, Kaiser's birthday celebrations.[172]

New School and Community House (Hall)

On October 15, 1911 the traditional Thanksgiving was celebrated in Sarona but on that occasion there was an additional reason for celebration as the newly constructed school and community house (hall) (No 9a) was consecrated.

For many years the Sarona community had been grappling with the idea of building a new school and community facility. Due to the number of school children now in the settlement the old school

55) Opening of the new community hall and school in Sarona in 1911

56) Sebastian Blaich
—one of the builders
of the Church of the
Ascension

58

59

60) Sarona school children and teachers 1912

Back row (left to right): Rudolf Weller, Fritz Jung, Ernst Kuebler

Fourth row: Frieda Orth (Steller), Hulda Haering, Friedrich Haering, Wilhelm Groll, Maria Orth, ? Ottmar*

Third row: Wilhelma Weeber (Steller), Emilie Jung, Frieda Froeschle (Heselschwerdt), Thea Jung, ? Ottmar*, Elsa Jung (Groll), Maria Reinhardt, ? Ottmar*

Second row: Anna Hoffmann (teacher), Auguste Lippmann (Orth), Mathilde Baldenhofer (Lippmann), Else Froeschle (Hermann), Helene Groll (Orth), Lydia Scheerle (Froeschle), Adelheid Groll, Luise Jung, Imanuel Knoll, teacher

Front row: Hertha Lippmann (Weller), Erhard Baldenhofer, ? Sickinger, Willy Groezinger, ? Ottmar*, Tabea Glenk, Irene Haering (Blaich), Walter Kuebler, Heinrich Weeber, Walter Jung, Hermann Kuebler, Ottmar*

Girls married surname, if known, is shown in brackets

*There were five Ottmar boys—Gottfried, Phillip, Hans, Karl and Fritz. We were unable to identify them on the photograph

57) Top left—Church of the Ascension on top of Mt of Olives in Jerusalem

58) Far Left—The German service medal received by Sebastian Blaich from the German Government in recognition for his work in the construction of the Church of the Ascension.

59) Left—Interior view of the Church of the Ascension

could not accommodate all classes and additional rooms had to be rented. Furthermore, the community had grown and the old community house was inadequate for the community's needs. Due to lack of funds the community had postponed the building of a new school and community facility. A special fund had been established to which money could be donated or bequeathed. Over several years some funds had accrued but due to two large donations in 1910 the fund had grown substantially. At the annual general meeting of the Sarona community in February 1911, the community agreed to proceed without delay with the building of a new school and community house. Virtually everyone in the community made additional donations so that the final building cost of approximately 12,000 francs could be met.

At the consecration service speeches were made by Friedrich Laemmle, Mayor of Sarona, Herr Professor Prinz, Consul Dr Brode as the representative of the German government, and Christian Rohrer, Head of the Temple Society. The celebrations included the singing of hymns, playing of music by the Sarona brass band and singing by the male choir from Jaffa, the mixed choir from Sarona and the school choir.[173]

Other matters of interest in Sarona at that time were:—

In 1910 Halley's Comet could be clearly seen from Sarona and this astronomical phenomenon caused considerable interest amongst the settlers.

In the same year the settlement experienced the wettest year since establishment. The wadi flooded and at one stage was over a kilometre in width. Considerable damage was caused by the flood waters.[174]

An article by Davis Trietsch published in the *"Koloniale Rundschau"* (Colonial Review) in 1915 and entitled *"German and Jewish Settlements in Palestine"* made reference to the value of German settlements (properties)—Sarona was valued at four million francs.[175] One could assume that a number of the settlers were now relatively prosperous.

Appendix 3 lists the home owners in Sarona at the beginning of WWI. This listing was derived by comparing a detailed sketch of houses prepared by Carl Kuebler in 1920 (no new homes were built during WWI) with another sketch done in 1937. Details of when houses were built were also researched by interviewing persons.

THE FLOURISHING ORANGE EXPORT INDUSTRY

By the end of 1912 the export of oranges from the Jaffa district had become a major industry. As mentioned previously, this growth only

61) Arab workers picking oranges

62) Wrapper for the famous Jaffa
oranges

63) Right—Packing oranges

64) Camels transporting oranges from
Sarona to Jaffa for export

became possible by the installation of motorised pumps which
enabled large new areas to be irrigated. The improved ability to
irrigate also forced up land prices.

Orange groves had been established by grafting the orange trees onto
either a lime root-stock or onto a wild orange root-stock (Khush-
khash). Grafting onto lime root-stock produced a tree that bore fruit
faster whereas grafting onto a wild orange root-stock a stronger tree
that took longer to produce oranges resulted. The trees were planted
in rows approximately five metres apart. Manure was added to the
soil to help the growth of the trees.[176]

65) The old port of Jaffa. There were no wharves at Jaffa—ships had to lay at anchor off the coast and passengers and cargo was shipped by boats from the shore to the ships

The settlers experimented biological control methods to fight some of the insect pests

The settlers experimented with biological control methods to fight some of the insect pests, for example, lady bird beetles were imported from Italy to combat leaf lice (aphids) and similar beetles were imported from America to combat field bugs. To control lichen and moss, the settlers used gardening lime and copper, and iron vitriol was used against ants and beetles. The greatest danger for the orange trees was, however, the very hot easterly desert wind (Sirocco).[177]

Germans, Jews and Arabs all started to expand their orange groves. It was estimated that in 1912 in the area around Jaffa approximately 2000 hectares were under orange grove cultivation—150 hectares owned by the Germans, 600 hectares in Jewish hands and 1250 hectares under Arab control.

The *Jerusalemer Warte* of 17 February 1913 describes the scene:—*"At orange blossom time, which normally starts in March, the air of the whole area of many kilometres is filled with a sweet calming scent. Millions of white flowers cover the lush green trees. The harvest starts at the end of October and extends right through to spring time. The fruit itself has a better aroma than the Italian or Spanish oranges, it is larger and hardly has any pips, and it is sweet and can be stored for considerably longer because of its thicker skin."*[178]

Oranges were first wrapped in fine paper and then packed in cases—on average 150 oranges per case—each case weighed about 35 kilograms. An indication of the expansion of orange production exported through the Jaffa port is shown below:—

1905/06 ....531,000 cases exported
1907/8 .... 849,000 cases exported
1909/10... 903,000 cases exported
1912/13 .... 1 million cases (estimated)

As there was very little timber grown in the Holy Land nearly all wood for the packing cases had to be imported from Austria, Rumania and Russia, thus adding to the costs of production. It was hoped that in the future, a Jewish enterprise, the Pardess Company, in the Jewish settlement of Chedera, would make some of the boxes from locally grown eucalypt timber which was to be cut and sawn in the Holy Land.

It was estimated that one tenth of the orange crop was sold on the domestic market in the Holy Land. Approximately two thirds of the exported crop at that time was shipped to Liverpool in England by the Jaffa/Liverpool Line and a smaller quantity to other British ports. Other destinations to which the oranges were exported included Hamburg, Germany; Cairo, Egypt; Odessa, Russia and Constantinople, Turkey.[179]

66) Orange boxes for export loaded on boat to be taken to ships

67) Postcard from Sarona. The writing on the postcard states "Dear Luise, received your letter many thanks. The largest ship in the world is in Jaffa at the moment. It is 225m long. You'd be amazed to see such a giant. Regards to you all. Sarona 16/3/1902 signed F. Laemmle. Please give my regards to Sophie Schatteram. She learnt sewing with me at Ludwigsburg Ladies School in Backnang, signed Emilie Schillinger"[80]

CHAPTER FOUR

WORLD WAR I AND INTERNMENT IN EGYPT

68) Typical German World War I postcard. These postcards were sent by soldiers to their families and friends from Germany to Palestine.

EARLY WAR YEARS

The outbreak of war in August 1914 had an immediate impact on Sarona. A number of young men of military age were called-up for military service. These young men were joined by volunteers and left for Germany. Their sudden departure meant that the remaining persons had to take on additional work, as best they could, to maintain the agricultural and other commercial businesses.[181] The *Jerusalemer Warte* (the regular Templer publication of those years) published ongoing news from the war and updates on the battles being fought. This news was obtained by official news releases (telegrams) from the Consulate and also letters and postcards from serving soldiers. Sadness and grief came to the close-knit community of Sarona as casualties were reported from the European theatres of war.

The war itself was being fought mostly in Europe. There were skirmishes in the southern Sinai Peninsula near the Suez Canal where German and Turkish troops tried to capture the Canal. Sarona, as well as the other German settlements were, nevertheless, important for the German troops in the Middle East. The settlements provided valuable food supplies, as well as resources such as local tradesmen, horse-drawn vehicles and other goods. Water was pumped over long distances to some of the military bases. Horses and carts were used to bring supplies to the fighting troops.[182]

In August 1915, Jaffa was shelled by a French warship. The shells were aimed at the Wagner Bros. factory in Walhalla. Further shelling occurred in January 1916 and again in February 1917.[183] In 1916 the allies made an attempt to capture Palestine but although advancing as far as Gaza the attempt failed.[184]

69) Typical German World War I postcard

70) Jakob Weller in German Middle East soldier uniform

The First Car

The first car ever to come to Sarona occurred in the very early war years 1914 or 1915. It was green soft-top Stoewer with a pointed radiator and had its hand-brake and gear lever mounted on the outside. It was owned by Adolf Wagner from Wagner Bros. of Walhalla. He drove it to Sarona and parked it outside Christian Kuebler's Café. Everyone came to look at it. It was quite an occasion.[185]

The 1915 Locust Plague

All older residents remember the locust plague in 1915 which caused so much damage and which the community was powerless to halt. The locusts appeared without warning. The locust first appeared on Easter Monday 5 April 1915. It was a clear spring day when a black cloud "that darkened the day" suddenly appeared from the east (the desert). Millions of locusts descended onto the green orchards and fields around Sarona. Some of the other Templer settlements suffered a similar fate. The desert locusts were about 12 centimetres long, yellow in colour with reddish wings. They immediately started to devour everything in sight—all plants and leaves (only cypress and peppercorn trees were spared), many orchards and vineyards were annihilated, crops in productive fields just vanished—the devastation was enormous! Suddenly overnight, the locusts vanished.

Worse was to come as the locusts had laid their eggs in the sandy soil. The Turkish administration called on the whole population to dig up the eggs. A bounty was offered for each bag of eggs that was dug up. School children worked with hoes in the fields on this task.

However their efforts were futile.

About a month later, in May, these eggs hatched and millions and millions of small black locusts appeared and moved through the settlement like a flow of lava, devouring everything in sight, including the bark of trees. Residents, young and old, all worked feverishly to combat this disaster. Trenches were dug, up to a metre deep, and the crawling mass was swept into them. When the trenches were nearly full, they were quickly covered. Kerosene was poured onto the ground and set alight, but due to wartime only limited supplies of kerosene were available. Children were given time off from school and, "armed" with sticks and tins, were told to make as much noise as possible to frighten away the locusts. The locusts crawled under doors and through cracks into buildings. The hens ate that many locusts that the egg yolks were red and the eggs became unusable. It is uncertain how long the locusts were in Sarona but eventually they grew wings and could fly. A north easterly wind blew most of the swarm into the Mediterranean Sea. The agricultural settlement's

71) German children with members of the Bavarian Flying Corps. German service personnel often came to Sarona where they enjoyed the friendship and hospitality of the settlers

72) German soldiers with Sarona settlers at the Sarona bowling alley

crops were ruined and people despaired. Hunger became a widespread problem, but fortunately the Temple Society was able to purchase some wheat from Jordan from which flour was ground. It took years for many plants to recover from the locust plague and for the vineyards and orchards to become productive again.[186]

WAR YEARS 1917-1918

On 10 August 1916, the Swede Sven Hedin, a well-known researcher and author, visited Sarona and wrote "*I was shown through the colony where many plants were in blossom.[. . .] The land that the settlers had bought and made productive now sustains them. They mainly grow grapes, oranges and vegetables. Like in old times they also produce milk and honey.*

Of special enjoyment was my walk through the village streets, splendid avenues of eucalyptus, acacia, peppercorn and mulberry trees. Everywhere there was cleanliness, order and contentment.[. . .] With admiration I observed quiet men, their pious wives and their clean, alert children. The community members live in spartan simplicity and exemplary harmony. Class hatred and striving for power is unknown to them. Everyone works hard all day long for the benefit of all.[187]

63

73) German soldiers helping with the grape harvest during World War I

In his book *The Holy Land Called* Sauer writes:—*"This was no doubt a very flattering testimony; but the fact that it was given by a man who was in no way under any obligation to the Templers, lends more weight to his judgement."*[188]

In the early war years the war seemed a long way off and despite many young men being absent on war service and the manpower difficulties this caused, the daily life in the settlements continued. News reached the settlements of the battles around the Suez Canal and in the Sinai. During early 1917 the German and Turkish troops twice repelled the British forces near Gaza and Beersheba. In July 1917 the British under General Lord Allenby, who had taken over command from Murray, began planning a new offensive. After some preliminary and diversionary manoeuvres and the seizure of Beersheba at the end of October 1917, the main attack to capture Jaffa and Jerusalem was launched on 6 November 1917. By November 14 the port of Jaffa was captured by the British and by 9 December Jerusalem was also in allied hands.[189]

It was during orange harvest time when war came to Sarona in November 1917

It was during orange harvest time when war came to Sarona in November 1917. Only old men, women and children were in the settlement as all males from 18 to 48 years and of military capability had been conscripted for military service.[190] Furthermore, most of the horses and carts had been requisitioned for military purposes.

Prior to the arrival of allied troops, Sarona witnessed some war action first hand. A couple of German double-decker planes (the main German airbase was at Ramleh) landed in the vacant paddocks on the outskirts of Sarona. They took off again unhindered.[191] Then came the retreat of the Turkish forces. Some of the troops (officers) were on

*74) Sarona/Jaffa Confirmation group
1916*

*Back row (left to right): Luise Dreher,
Hilda Wennagel (Eppinger), Wilhelma
Weeber (Steller), Maria Orth, Maria
Reinhardt (Haar)*

*Front row: Meta Imberger (Hardegg),
Helene Aberle (Niemeyer), Wilhelm
Groll, Elsa Jung (Groll), Frieda Froeschle
(Heselschwerdt), Auguste Lippmann
(Orth), Albert Guenthner, Mariele
Schnerring (Koby), Johannes Frank, Elder*

*Girls' married surname, if known, is
shown in brackets.*

*The first allied troops to arrive in Sarona
were "Australian Cavalry" (soldiers from
the Australian Light Horse Brigade)*

motorised transports—these vehicles had no tyres only iron wheels
and were driven by a chain. However, most of the troops that passed
through Sarona were Turkish soldiers on foot. They were disorganised
and dispirited, just walking hungry and thirsty—begging for "ek mek,
ek mek" (bread, bread) or "Yemek yok" (no food). Only a little food
was provided as the settlement itself was short of supplies.[192]

The first allied troops to arrive in Sarona were "Australian Cavalry"
(soldiers from the Australian Light Horse Brigade). Their wide
brimmed hats and horses made an impression, especially on the
children. Heinrich Weeber (Snr), mayor at that time, had asked all
adults to remain indoors but children with flowers and oranges were
asked to line the street to demonstrate to the allies that the population
was not hostile.[193]

More allied troops arrived, including a contingent of Indian troops.
Trenches were dug in the fields of Sarona and the troops lived there.
After a few days shooting and shelling erupted across the River
Audsche. The Germans and Turks had put up some resistance there.

75) Aerial view of Sarona showing the extent of orange groves, vineyards and fields surrounding the settlement. The photograph was taken by the German Flying Corps in 1917

The hills on the other side of the Audsche provided a good vantage point over the river valley. The allied positions were being shelled and one shell landed and exploded in Sarona in the street where a short time before children had been playing. Luckily no one was hurt and only a little damage done. The "battle" went on for three days and everyone had to stay indoors during that period. As nearly all houses had cellars and thick walls most people stayed in that secure area of their homes. The allies took over the community house as a field hospital to tend to their wounded soldiers. The military also commandeered and occupied some other buildings.[194]

An incident occurred where the British saw a Templer resident watching the hostilities across the Audsche River from his house with binoculars. They accused him of spying and would most likely have shot him, but fortunately the community elder intervened and he was spared.[195]

After the hostilities ceased, people came out again. The children exchanged ripe oranges for biscuits. On other occasions the Indian troops gave the children tins of bully beef (from Argentina) and some very hard biscuits. A close watch was kept on livestock, hens and eggs to make sure they were not stolen.[196]

The Allied troops were generally well behaved and good to the families in Sarona

The Allied troops were generally well behaved and good to the families in Sarona. A number of the Australian troops were of German descent and could speak German. An incident did occur when some New Zealander troops broke into the Wine Cellar and became inebriated. The drunken soldiers entered the clubhouse and, in a rampage, smashed the furniture and many musical instruments, and went "marching" with a drum and some horns and trumpets up and down the main street during the night.[197]

The front moved on but where were the men? What had happened to them?

Many of the men were captured in Nazareth

Many of the men were captured in Nazareth. In a surprise early morning attack the allies overran the garrison of German troops stationed at Nazareth. Many men from Sarona were there. A few escaped and fled overland. The others were rounded up and taken as prisoners of war. They were forced to march from Nazareth to Lydda, a distance of approximately 90 kilometres. The weather was still relatively warm and the distance had to be covered in three days. During the march very little water was available and some of the men did not make it. Most, however, finally reached the spring of the Audsche River and were able to drink. From there they were taken to Lydda, near Ramleh, site of a vital railway junction with one line going south to Egypt and another east to Jerusalem. The POWs were put on a train and taken to Rafa near Gaza before being transferred to Sidi Bishr in Egypt. Some other men and soldiers were interned at Maadi and Tura in Egypt.[198]

Early in 1918, the allies claimed (no proof to substantiate this) that the remaining residents of Sarona had spied for the German and Turkish forces. So an order was given that Sarona had to be evacuated and everyone had to go to the Templer settlement in Jaffa—some three kilometres away. There the Sarona settlers were billeted to the families of the Jaffa community.[199]

All the elderly men had to report twice daily to the allied military command at the town hall (serail) in Jaffa.

Before leaving Sarona the boys in particular had a field day after the allies moved on. The vacated camp sites of the allies provided many "war souvenirs"—steel helmets, shells and live ammunition etc which had been left behind. The young boys collected these items and compared each others' collections, doing swaps. Some boys had 100s of rounds of live ammunition![200]

INTERNMENT IN HELOUAN IN EGYPT
1918-1920

In July 1918, an order was given that all women and children were to prepare themselves for deportation. The destination, Egypt, was not initially revealed to the settlers. This order applied to all the 850 German settlers from Jaffa, Sarona, Wilhelma and Jerusalem but not the Templer settlements (Haifa, Waldheim and Betlehem) in the north of the country. They were given two days to pack, each person was allowed approximately 40 kilograms of luggage. Before sunrise on 14 July 1918 they were picked up by trucks fitted with bunk type seats

76) Al Hayat Hotel at Helouan, Egypt where the women and children were accommodated during their internment 1918-1920

and taken to Lydda, where they boarded a train and were taken to Egypt. They arrived in Cairo on 15 July and from there their journey continued by truck to Helouan on the outskirts of Cairo.[201]

The sick and elderly were brought to Helouan a few weeks later by a special hospital train.

At Helouan they were quartered in the "Al Hayat Hotel" which had once been a grand hotel before being converted to a sanatorium for asthma and tuberculosis sufferers before the war. During the war the sanatorium had been used by the military as a garrison. The women and children were all accommodated in the main two storey building. The elderly men and all boys over nine years were taken from their families and put into a dormitory (a converted convalescing hall) near the main building. They were guarded by military personnel.[202]

The internment at Helouan lasted for two years. At the beginning, things were rather chaotic and disorganised. Local women cooked the meals and some meals were unhygienic and could not be eaten.

77) Sketch of Sidi Bishr POW camp, Eygpt, where the men were interned. Drawn by Carl Kuebler during his internment

78) German prisoners of war in the Sidi
Bishr prison camp

As the internees organised themselves, life settled down and a routine
was developed. The German women began to prepare and cook the
meals. Rosters for kitchen and other duties were drawn up by the
internees. All clothes that were needed were sewn in the complex
during the internment period. There were no shoes and people
walked barefoot. Entertainment was organised and on one occasion a
brass band comprising German soldiers at Sidi Bishr gave a concert.
Church services were held in a church opposite the Al Hayat. Some
girls and boys were confirmed during their internment. Some very
basic education (schooling) was given to the children. There were
only a few qualified teachers who were supported by some adults for
this purpose. There was a wash house outside the hotel where the
washing was done—it dried very quickly in the heat.[203]

Severe sandstorms were experienced and the male dormitory in
particular felt the brunt of these storms as it could not be sealed
properly and the fine desert sand blew in. During these storms the
men and boys would pull the sheets and blankets down the side of
their beds and then crawl under the bed to get away from the sand
and wait for the storm to abate. Afterwards came the big task of
cleaning everything up again. The country around Helouan was
often called "lentil country" by the internees because the ground was
littered with small stones the shape of lentils.[204]

79) Recreational activity in the desert
near Sidi Bishr

80) Women, old men and children, including the Kaiserswerth Sisters, during their internment in Helouan

81) Templer school boys during their internment at Helouan

Anyone wanting to leave the complex had to get permission and once out they were always under guard

Children at the time of the Helouan internment remember their days there as filled with carefree play and exciting desert adventures. Their parents, however, anxiously awaited news of a return to their homeland.[205]

After the war ended, excursions were sometimes arranged for the internees to such places as Cairo—the museum and zoological gardens and to the nearby pyramids and sphinx. Anyone wanting to leave the complex had to get permission and once out they were always under guard. These restrictions eased once the war finished. At the end of the war the married men from Sidi Bishr and the other camps were allowed to visit their wives and families on week-ends.[206]

*83) Headstones of German internees
buried in the Helouan cemetery*

During the time of internment several internees died. The deceased
from the internment camp were buried in the cemetery at Helouan.

IMPACT OF THE WAR

With the defeat of Germany and Turkey the empires of both these
nations came to an end. During the war the British, on 2 November
1917, issued a declaration, known as the Balfour Declaration (Arthur
Balfour was the British Foreign Secretary at that time), which in
general terms stated that the British Government would favourably
view the establishment of a national homeland for the Jewish people
in Palestine. The Arabs in Palestine had hoped that following the
defeat of Turkey they would be able to get self determination. In
Palestine, the British who were the military occupying power, had
to try and reconcile the differences between the Arabs and Jews and
their political aspirations.[207]

*The European nations were involved
in the protracted peace conferences
and post war discussions and were not
interested in the plight of the Germans
from Palestine who were interned in
Egypt*

On 1 July 1920, the British appointed Sir Herbert Samuel as the
High Commissioner of Palestine. From that date also the military
administration was replaced by a civilian one. English, Arabic and
Hebrew became the official languages of Palestine.[208]

In the meantime, the European nations were involved in the protracted
peace conferences and post war discussions and were not interested in
the plight of the Germans from Palestine who were interned in Egypt.
One could say they were forgotten. Initially some of the Templers
from Palestine, including some who had been soldiers and who had
retreated with the German army from Palestine, made representations
to the State Government in Wuerttemberg to be allowed to return
to Palestine. They also brought the plight of the internees in Egypt
to the attention of the authorities. An association of Germans

*82) Left—Ladies excursion form Helouan
to the Sphinx and pyramids during their
internment at Helouan*

Foreign Office,
November 2nd, 1917.

Dear Lord Rothschild,

I have much pleasure in conveying to you, on behalf of His Majesty's Government, the following declaration of sympathy with Jewish Zionist aspirations which has been submitted to, and approved by, the Cabinet

"His Majesty's Government view with favour the establishment in Palestine of a national home for the Jewish people, and will use their best endeavours to facilitate the achievement of this object, it being clearly understood that nothing shall be done which may prejudice the civil and religious rights of existing non-Jewish communities in Palestine, or the rights and political status enjoyed by Jews in any other country"

I should be grateful if you would bring this declaration to the knowledge of the Zionist Federation.

84) The Balfour Declaration 1917

from Palestine was formed in Germany to take up the cause for a return to Palestine.[209]

The internees were concerned that their properties in Palestine might be confiscated by the British military administration and they might not be allowed to return home. There were real fears that this would occur.[210]

Lobbying for the return of the Templers continued throughout 1919 and 1920. The Red Cross, the Quakers (who had been very supportive of the Templers) and Unitarians, as well as other community groups all lent their support. German newspapers as well as those in England and Holland took up the cause of the internees. The Foreign Office in Britain was petitioned and Questions were asked in the British Parliament.[211]

Eventually, on 29 July 1920, it was announced in the House of Lords, that the remaining internees in Egypt could return to Palestine.[212]

RETURN TO SARONA

The expectations of the Templer internees in Egypt at the end of the war was one of being able to return quickly to their settlements and continue their lives which had been so severely disrupted by war. No one had contemplated that their internment would continue. However times had changed—Germany had been defeated, the Ottoman Empire had collapsed and Palestine had become a British Mandate Territory.

In April 1920, the British authorities decided to deport/repatriate 270 internees to Germany. The reasons why only some were chosen has not been established. The men of the families selected for repatriation were released from their camp at Sidi Bishr to help with the packing. This decision came as a complete surprise to the internees.[213]

A delightful poem by an unknown author in Helouan, was recited by the interned children. It gives a glimpse of what leaving the internment camp and going to Germany meant:—

Sind der deutschen Kinder viel
Wir moechten gern aus hier heraus
Und wieder mal in unser Haus

There are many German children
Who would love to get out of here
To return once more to our home

In unserm Heim da war es schoen
Da konnt man frei spazieren gehn
Hier aber duerfen aus dem Haus
Wir alle 14 Tage nur raus

At home it was so beautiful
Where one could freely walk about
But here we're allowed out
All of us only once a fortnight

Es sieht zwar heute grad so aus
Als duerfen wir hier bald heraus
Doch nicht zurueck ins Heilige
Nach Deutschland werden wir versandt

To-day it seems likely
That we will soon be out of here
Land Not to return to the Holy Land
But to Germany we'll be sent

In Deutschland aber ist es kalt In
Da werden wir schon frieren bald
Nur fehlen Kleider, Strumpf und Schuh
Und Lebensmittel noch dazu

Germany it's very cold
And soon we'll all be freezing
We have no clothes, socks nor shoes
Let alone foodstuffs too

Doch, wohin auch wir werden versandt
Ins Deutsche oder Mohrenland
Wir wollen immer Deutsche sein
Gott fuerchten und den boesen Schein

However, no matter where we are sent
To Germany or any other land
We always will remain German
Respect God and shun evil.[214]

85) Sketch of Sarona drawn by Carl Kuebler in 1920 during his internment at Sidi Bishr

86) Copy of envelope addressed to Mina Laemmle whilst at Bad Mergentheim in Germany

In July 1920 the British began planning for the return of the Templers to Palestine

On 13 April 1920, the internees to be deported left Alexandria on a converted freighter, *Kypros,* for Germany. They arrived in Hamburg on 7 May 1920 and from there 230 internees were taken by train to a castle at Bad Mergentheim. This was their home for the next seven months. The men and some women tried to get employment wherever possible to support their families.[215]

Meanwhile, the internees who had remained in Helouan waited anxiously as to what was to happen to them. In July 1920 the British began planning for the return of the Templers to Palestine. Many of the Templer houses were still occupied by military personnel.

In July 1920 the internees elected 29 representatives to travel to Palestine with the British Public Custodian, Keith Roach, to assist and plan for the return of the internees. This group became known as the Wiederaufbaukommission (Reconstruction Commission) abbreviated WAKO. WAKO's role was initially to prepare some accommodation for the returning internees from Egypt. Heinrich Weeber, Sarona's mayor during the latter war years, was appointed to the executive committee of WAKO together with Georg Wagner and Philipp Wurst. A later role undertaken by WAKO was to gain the release from the Public Custodian of some of the frozen funds of the settlers when they returned to Sarona. The distribution of some of these funds was important in the rebuilding of the settlements and the settlers' enterprises.[216]

In June 1920, 388 internees left Helouan and were moved to the Shubrah camp, in a northern suburb of Cairo. Shubrah was a former Austro-Hungarian hospital.[217] On 8 September 1920 they left there and arrived in Palestine on 9 September 1920.[218] The settlers from Sarona left the train, which had stopped as close as possible to Sarona on the Jaffa/Jerusalem railway—there was no railway station there. Their luggage was unloaded and they then had to walk the rest of the distance to Sarona.[219]

Although presents were few there was, nevertheless, hope and joy that the homeward journey had commenced

In September 1920 there were 93 former Saronians in Germany.[220] The Quakers again were very supportive and helpful during that period. In December 1920 the Palestine Templers were advised that they would be allowed to return "home" again. On 23 December 1920, 264 Germans from Palestine (including 114 children) left Bad Mergentheim[221]. Christmas 1920 was spent on the special train which took them from Bad Mergentheim via Austria to Trieste. Although presents were few, there was, nevertheless, hope and joy that the homeward journey had commenced. In Trieste they boarded a freighter for the trip across the Mediterranean Sea to Jaffa. It was a slow trip as the ship called at many ports on the way.[222]

87) The castle in Bad Mergentheim where many Templers were placed during their stay in Germany after World War I

Finally, on 13 January 1921, the Templers from Sarona, Jaffa, Jerusalem and Wilhelma settlements disembarked at Jaffa. The others were taken to Haifa. What joy it must have been for the people on board

to see the Palestinian coastline and the buildings of Jaffa again! They were greeted by the Jaffa Templer brass band playing in an open boat and were warmly welcomed as they finally stepped ashore.[223]

The late Otto Laemmle writes of a moving personal experience on his return:—*"As I arrived in Jaffa on the small ship in January 1921, together with the other "Palestine Germans" from Bad Mergentheim in Germany and then rowed ashore in the familiar row boats, we were given a small snack at Stefanus Frank's restaurant in Jaffa. As a young 10 year old I was game enough to leave the other travellers and by myself went through the familiar gate which led to the eastern side of the settlement and onto the road no more than a sandy track which ran along the settlements eastern perimeter. By chance, I saw on close examination of some passing Arabs an elderly man who caught my eye. I recognised him as our former gardener, Abdul Asis, whom I had not seen for over three years. I ran towards him and shook hands and introduced myself. He also was pleasantly surprised, put his hand into the pockets of his baggy pants and gave me two beautiful big golden oranges, which he told me were from our garden. I took his hand and went with him through the familiar gate and introduced Adbul Asis to my mother and my brother and sister. We all had tears in our eyes from the joy of return and reunion, it was a piece of our homeland!"*[224]

CHAPTER FIVE

THE EARLY 1920'S

Many homes were in such a state that they were uninhabitable

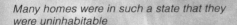

88) Restored water pump after World War I. Family group rejoicing as the water for irrigation flows once again

R EBUILDING
The residents of Sarona returned to a plundered and dilapidated settlement. Some of the homes were gone, others were in urgent need of repair and maintenance—windows smashed, shutters flapping in the wind, little or no furniture left. All crockery, cooking and kitchen utensils were missing, as well as any loose items which had been left behind. Many homes were in such a state that they were uninhabitable. Anything made or constructed of wood, such as doors and windows, had been used for firewood whilst the settlers were away. Most barns and sheds had only the walls left standing.[225]

The British military were still occupying some homes and buildings. The British Public Custodian of Enemy Property maintained control over several community buildings. These homes and buildings were gradually relinquished and handed back to the owners. The British vacated the last building they had been occupying at Easter in 1921.[226]

The citrus orchards had been neglected. No irrigation had been undertaken for several years and the trees had either died or were suffering badly from lack of water. Vineyards and vegetable fields were totally overgrown and damaged by heavy vehicles and armoured cars having been driven through them. The cows and other livestock had disappeared; many had been slaughtered and killed during the war years.[227]

89) Left Top—Sarona/Jaffa Confirmation group 1922. This was the first group of youth confirmed in Jaffa/Sarona following the return of the settlers after their internment during World War I

Back Row (left to right): Hugo Hahn, Arnolf Eppinger, Erhard Baldenhofer, Ida Hahn, Olga Wennagel (Hoersch), Else Froeschle (Hermann), Irene Haering (Blaich)

Middle Row: Walter Kuebler, Fritz Ottmar, Eugen Sickinger, Heinrich Weeber, Roland Frank, Erna Tietz, Elly Wennagel (Grant), Luise Kazenwadel (Katz), Helene Guenthner (Koeper)

Front row: Rudolf Imberger, Herbert Uhlherr, Bruno John, Johannes Frank, Elder, Anni Gollmer (Kruegler), Luise Bulach (Imberger), Ernstine Messerle

The girls' married surname, if known, is shown in brackets.

Elder Frank is renowned for telling each of the confirmands that during life "always trust your conscience"

91) Sarona/Jaffa Confirmation group 1925

Back row: Elsa Eppinger (Beck), Lotte Frank, Walter Wagner, Erich Steller, Ilse Wieland (Weller)

Middle row: Martha Hoffmann (Janzec), Rifka Tannenbaum, Erika Steller (Guenthner), Maria Messerle (Wagner), Elly Lippmann (Steller), Rosa Baldenhofer (Schmidt)

Front row: Willy Guenthner, Edmund Steller, Ewald Glenk, Johannes Frank, Elder, Karl Weller, Helmut Sickinger, Ludwig Buchhalter

The premises of pre-war commercial and trade businesses had been ransacked and, of course, the business clientele was gone.[228]

This was the situation facing the Sarona settlers on their return. A new start had to be made.

90) Left Bottom—Sarona/Jaffa Grade 3 School Class 1922. This class was part of the combined Sarona/Jaffa school at that time

Back row (left to right): Erika Steller, Rosa Baldenhofer, Elly Lippmann, Walter Wagner, Karl Weller, Ewald Glenk

Middle row: Lotte Frank, Rosa Weinmann, Elsa Eppinger, Maria Messerle, Erich Steller, Walter Guenthner, Edmund Steller

Front row: Ludwig Buchhalter, Mr Kuckhi (teacher), Johannes Frank (teacher), David Eppinger (teacher), Anna Bulach (teacher), Rifka Tannenbaum

The people (families) moved in together into the houses that were habitable and gathered whatever furniture could be found or repaired. Wooden boxes were used for chairs and tables. All the cutlery and crockery was gone. People shared with one another whatever meagre things they still had. Steps were taken immediately to clear the fields and plant vegetables. Orange groves were cleared. Dead trees removed and other trees pruned and the pumps repaired so that water could be pumped for irrigation. To help with the food shortages some foodstuffs and live chickens were sent to Sarona from the Templer settlements of Haifa and Betlehem. "Backle" leaves from a green plant growing wild in the orchards were picked and eaten as salads. Gradually, livestock was bought again. Dairy cows were purchased from as far away as Beirut and Damascus. The new livestock was, in some instances, driven overland from Damascus to Sarona. The tradesmen were busy repairing damaged homes and buildings. Others were making furniture.

The settlers also quickly re-established their religious and social activities. There was a high level of community spirit and co-operation to get things organised and to get Sarona up and running again.[229]

The British authorities visited Sarona a number of times to see how the settlers were progressing. Requests were made to the British administration for assistance with reconstruction and for compensation due to war damage. In some cases compensation was paid. It is estimated that approximately half the value of the claims for the settlers' war losses in livestock and equipment was received.[230]

After two to three years of very hard work the situation in Sarona had improved and the worst was behind the settlers. There were no longer

92) Male choir from Sarona on excursion

any food shortages—the gardens, vineyards and orange groves were becoming productive again, cows were bought and milk production restarted, homes and buildings had been repaired and restored, the school had been re-established and community life had settled down again. All buildings had been returned to their owners.[231] Children were born after a period of two to three years in which no children were born. The community spirit had not diminished—it had in fact been enhanced during the post-war years. There was an air of optimism.

The community spirit had not diminished— it had in fact been enhanced during the post-war years. There was an air of optimism

During the early 1920s the economic conditions in Palestine were beneficial to the inhabitants of Sarona—there was a ready market for much of their produce. Some settlers entered into a "share farming" arrangement whereby they would lease land from Arab or even other settlers, cultivate it and then share the income. Most primary producers opted for a mixed farming production during these early post war years. Vegetables in particular were in demand. Sale of vegetables gave the landowners of Sarona a good disposable income and the capital for restoring their homes and businesses.[232] Tel Aviv was expanding rapidly with the increasing number of Jewish immigrants.

Approximately 80,000 Jewish immigrants arrived in Palestine between 1920 and 1926[233].

By 1925 Sarona was still a very small German settlement on the outskirts of Tel Aviv. Its size was:—

Population 225
Buildings 46
Outbuildings 41
Farmers 25
Tradesmen 28
Civil servants.. 1
Teachers 4
Area of properties .... 492ha.[234]

Sarona which had started as, and was still primarily an agricultural settlement, now had more tradesmen in its midst than farmers

Sarona which had started as, and still was primarily an agricultural settlement, now had more tradesmen in its midst than farmers. The overall population had in fact decreased by 18 since the turn of the century. This was largely due to the lack of availability of land, the casualties of the war, and the few births that occurred in the period 1917-1921 due to war and internment.

During the rebuilding period the settlers established a sound relationship with the Public Custodian of Enemy Property, Keith Roach. On termination of his Office in 1925, Keith Roach stated:—

They were the first to offer new directions to agriculture in Palestine

"I am particularly pleased to say that, throughout the duration of my often very difficult task, there has always been a good relationship with the representatives of the Temple Society. I may tell you, and here I am in full agreement with the first High Commissioner for Palestine, Sir Herbert Samuel, that the German settlers are a valuable part of the population of Palestine and are appreciated as such. They were the first to offer new directions to agriculture in Palestine."[235]

INFLUENCE OF BRITISH RULE

As outlined previously, a civilian administration replaced the military one in Palestine in 1920. During 1920/21 both the Arabs and Jews tried to influence the wording of the mandate instrument. On 24 July 1923, the Council of the League of Nations passed the mandate resolution, which was to be administered by Great Britain. It came into effect in September 1923. Initially the British wanted to establish a constitution and create a Legislative Council with Muslim, Jewish and Christian representatives and chaired by the High Commissioner. This, however, did not eventuate, largely due to Arab opposition.[236]

*93) British forces controlling Arab riots in
Jaffa*

*The British had a most difficult role as
mandate administrator in having to act as
adjudicator and peace keeper between
Arab and Jewish aspirations for Palestine*

94) Palestinian currency coin

The old Ottoman laws were abolished and the British introduced
English type laws and administrative procedures which were better
suited to the changing conditions in Palestine.[237] Law and order was
upgraded and infra-structure works such as rail, road, harbour and
bridge works commenced. Building of power stations for electricity
was supported, the education system improved, health standards
implemented, certain businesses licensed and agricultural and
commercial/trade enterprises were promoted and encouraged.[238]

The British, throughout the 1920s and until 1948, when the State of
Israel was founded, had a most difficult role as mandate administrator
in having to act as adjudicator and peace keeper between Arab and
Jewish aspirations for Palestine. In 1929 there was an Arab uprising.
A further revolt in April 1936 by the Arabs forced the British to call
on its military to help restore law and order. Military courts were
established and curfews imposed. In August 1936, a Royal Commission

*95) British forces controlling Arab riots in
Jaffa*

was appointed by the British authorities to inter alia ". . . ascertain the underlying causes of the disturbances which broke out in Palestine in the middle of April . . ."[239] The hostile relations between the Arabs and Jews worsened even further during the late 1930s and continued to escalate during the war years.[240]

THE ISSUE OF NATIONALITY

Most of the Templers who had migrated to Palestine in the late 1800s and early 1900s had come from Germany. They and their children had remained German Nationals whilst living in the Holy Land. Up to 1918, Palestine was part of the Turkish Ottoman Empire and the Turks and Muslims were suspicious of Europeans and their religions. The question of becoming a Turkish citizen was not contemplated by the German Templers.[241]

Sir Herbert advised the delegation that the Templers should retain their German nationality

However, when Palestine became a mandated territory in 1923 Palestinian citizenship came into being. In order to clarify the question of citizenship a delegation from the Templers met with Sir Herbert Samuel, British High Commissioner in Palestine to discuss this issue. Sir Herbert advised the delegation, that due to both the unsettled political structure and the unclear situation prevailing in Palestine, as well as the doubtful value of the mandated territory's citizenship, the Templers should retain their German nationality. Thus they remained patriotic German nationals but Palestine was their home.[242]

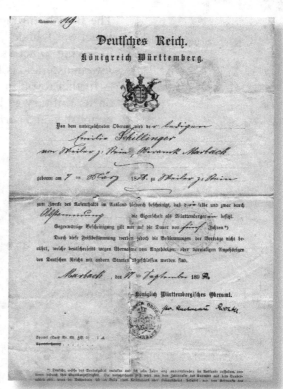

96) Pre World War I German identification certificate

CHAPTER SIX

AMALGAMATION WITH THE
JAFFA COMMUNITY

FOR SOME TIME IT HAD BEEN APPARENT to the leaders of the Temple Society Central Council that there was a need to start new settlements as the opportunities for young Templers in Palestine were very limited. This became even more evident in the 1920s when young persons could not afford to buy land to start agricultural production, and other employment opportunities were few. Many of the young men went to Germany to further their education or technical training. Some found employment there and did not return.[243]

97) General view of Sarona in late 1920s

Sarona had increased in area by only 18 ha. since early in the century. In the early twenties the settlers who had returned to Sarona concentrated on rebuilding their existing enterprises and were not looking at expanding their holdings. Land prices had risen sharply within the settlement due to the agricultural development of the land. The small amount of additional land that had been purchased was used to expand existing farms and orchards and not by "new" farmers wanting to start an agricultural enterprise. Land prices around Sarona were rapidly escalating as the new Jewish city of Tel Aviv was expanding and new Jewish settlements were being established near Sarona.[244]

Land prices around Sarona were rapidly escalating as the new Jewish city of Tel Aviv was expanding

The Temple Society Central Council although desirous of buying a large tract of land in Palestine to start a new settlement did not have the financial means to do so. Although some costings were done for a new settlement, the project did not proceed.[245]

The Jaffa settlement in the meantime had also reached a stage where it could not expand. Its community members were living in a confined area around the Hotel Jerusalem, whilst another group was located in another part of the city known as Walhalla. Jaffa, with its predominantely Arab population, was also expanding. Land prices were soaring, and again the members of the community did not have the means to purchase land for increasing the size of the settlement. In 1925, the Jaffa community sought assistance from Sarona for the purchase of land and proposed an amalgamation with Sarona. The two communities had been closely associated with each other since the founding of Sarona in 1871. In the mid 1920s there were 35 to 40 building blocks available for homes in Sarona. The amalgamation proposal was supported by the Templer Central Council. It made sense to share facilities between these two communities.[246]

The amalgamation of a primarily agricultural settlement with an urban settlement was not an easy task

The amalgamation of a primarily agricultural settlement with an urban settlement was not an easy task. A commission was established to deal with and resolve the problems associated with the proposed merger. One of the outcomes was that the Jaffa settlers were given the opportunity to purchase building lots at a "cheaper" price but in return had to pay a higher levy/rate to the community council.[247]

After lengthy negotiations, the two communities of Sarona and Jaffa/Walhalla were finally merged on 2 September 1929. The new community now numbered approximately 500 persons.[248] It was not until 17 May 1936 that the Constitution for the new combined community was finally endorsed by the Sarona/Jaffa Templer Community. The introduction in the constitution stated:—

"The Temple Community of Sarona and the Temple Community of Jaffa have joined together to form a new Community which has taken over all the rights and obligations of both the members and the former communities without holding each other to account.

The joint Community is a Community of the Temple Society and will be known as the "German Templer Community Sarona/Jaffa".

The Community's mission is to foster and increase the Christian community spirit in the sense of the Temple Society.

The Community has adopted this constitution to achieve its mission with harmony and orderliness.

For the Community, as well as its individual members, respect for law and order is self-evident".[249]

Satzung

der

**Deutschen Tempelgemeinde
Sarona/Jaffa.**

1936.

Buchdruckerei des Syr. Waisenhauses, Jerusalem.

Einleitung.

Die Tempelgemeinde Sarona und die Tempelgemeinde Jaffa haben sich zu einer Gemeinde zusammengeschlossen, welche die Mitglieder sowie die gesamten Rechte und Pflichten (Aktiva und Passiva) der beiden Tempelgemeinden ohne Verrechnung übernommen hat.

Die vereinigte Gemeinde ist eine Gemeinde der Tempelgesellschaft und führt den Namen „Deutsche Tempelgemeinde Sarona/Jaffa".

Ihre Aufgabe ist die Schaffung und Ausbreitung christlicher Gemeinschaft im Sinn der Tempelgesellschaft.

Um diese Aufgabe in Eintracht und Ordnung durchführen zu können, hat sich die Gemeinde diese Satzung gegeben.

Für die Gemeinde, wie für ihre einzelnen Mitglieder ist die Achtung vor Gesetz und Obrigkeit selbstverständlich.

98) Cover of the Sarona/Jaffa Templer community constitution document

99) Aerial view of Jaffa. Jaffa Templer settlement with church spire in foreground

LIFE IN SARONA IN THE LATE 1920's AND 1930's

(The details of the following chapter are mainly based on personal interviews conducted with persons who lived and grew up in Sarona. In other instances individuals sent letters or other written material of their recollections and experiences in Sarona. Care was taken so that the information provided by one individual was wherever possible corroborated by someone else. A copy of the notes of the interviews, other printed material and in some cases tape recordings was given to the Temple Society of Australia Archives by M Haering and H Glenk.)[250]

(For material from other sources a separate reference endnote is shown)

100) Official stamp of the Sarona Templer community

During the 1920s and early 1930s as Sarona recovered from WW I, it experienced a considerable period of growth and prosperity. Europe was recovering from the ravages of war and offered good markets for primary products. In Palestine the influx of Jewish immigrants created a demand not only for primary produce but also for services and tradesmen. The Arabs also traded and worked with the Sarona community which provided employment for many Arabs. The changing political scene in Europe and Palestine affected all residents of Sarona during the latter 1930s.[251]

By 1926/27 Sarona had grown into a settlement with a population of 225 persons (212 Templers and 13 Non-Templers) living in 47 houses. There were 45 buildings (dairy, winery, sheds, barns, workshops etc) associated with businesses as well as notable public buildings such as a school and community hall. The Sarona settlement and surrounding agricultural areas covered an area of approximately 458 hectares.[252]

101) Street scene in Sarona

ADMINISTRATION

The central organisation of the Temple Society was in Jerusalem with its own constitution and conventions. In 1935 the extended Central Council of the Temple Society included the permanent members of the Central Council, the Board of the Temple Society Central Fund, the Community Chairmen, Mayors and Chairmen of the Economic Councils of the Templer communities in Palestine, as well as the Regional Heads. The Sarona community's representatives were: Johannes Frank, Wilhelm Aberle, Samuel Weller, Walter Hoffmann, Alfred Weller and Richard Hoffmann.[253]

102) Membership card of the Temple Society

The Sarona community had its own agreed constitution which was binding on all the community members. The responsibility to administer and comply with the constitution was vested in the elected mayor and his fellow councillors and the community elders.[254]

The Sarona community organisation had a dual role—firstly a religious and spiritual one and secondly the economic and administrative affairs and well being of the community members. To fulfil these roles it was structured as a Council of Elders, with a chairman (Gemeindevorsteher) appointed by the President of the Temple Society (Tempelvorsteher) for the spiritual role; as well as a community council under the chairmanship of a Mayor (Buergermeister). The

103) Palestinian Postage Stamp post-marked in Sarona

Mayor and four Community Council members were elected for a four year term and a two year term respectively (half the council members retiring each year). A Community Chief Executive Officer (Gemeinderechner) was also elected every four years. The community council was responsible for administrative matters of the settlement.[255]

Mr. Timotheus Lange was the "manager" in charge of the office in Sarona. He lived on the top floor of the community house. (No.09a)

Disputes between settlers within the community were settled by the Mayor and Gemeindevorsteher and the community council in an amicable manner, wherever possible. A settler who felt aggrieved by the mayor's (Sarona Council's) decision could appeal to the central Temple Society Council in Jerusalem. There is no record of a community member taking action through a higher or external court of law.

Luftpostverbindungen von Deutschland nach Palästina:			
(nach Angabe des Hauptpostamtes, Stuttgart).			
letzte Auslieferungszeit beim Postamt 1 in Stuttgart:		Linie:	Ankunft in Lydda:
Dienstag	22 Uhr	niederl.	Donnerstag 12,30
Donnerstag	22 "	polnische	Samstag 17,05
Freitag	22 "	niederl.	Sonntag 12,30
Sonntag	18,20 "	polnische	Dienstag 17,05

104) Airmail time table from Stuttgart in Germany to Palestine.

105) The old pre World War I German Post Office in Jerusalem

Internal matters affecting the whole community were discussed at annual general meetings of the community and voted on. The majority decision then prevailed and was binding on community members.[256]

The community office was located in a special room in the community house. This also served as a post office from where letters could be collected, or dispatched by posting them in a mail box. In the 1930s an Arab boy delivered the mail to the various homes in Sarona. There were no letter boxes and the mail would be left under the door or on the top step. The mail was brought to the community house on

a daily basis by someone from Jaffa—it had to be collected from Stephanus Frank in Jaffa. For many years Friedrich Haering fulfilled this task as he was employed as a patternmaker by Streker in Jaffa and picked up the mail on his way home. In the late 1930s an airmail service operated between Germany and Palestine.

There was a (public) **telephone** at the office which could be used. Initially the other telephone in Sarona was at Albrecht Aberle's house (No.43) (He was the Honorary Swedish Consul).[257] Later there were telephones at the winery, Wilhelm Aberle (No 29) and Christian Kuebler's Bar.

The settlement of Sarona was given an independent local government authority status with one vote on the city council

As Tel Aviv grew into a substantial city, the British established a city council for the twin towns of Jaffa/Tel Aviv. Within this city council the settlement of Sarona was given an independent local government authority status with one vote on the city council. Mr Gotthilf Wagner fulfilled this representative role.

Since the very early days of Sarona the community bell would be tolled at noon and again at 1.00pm. This was done to mark the midday break and was used by the whole community for the lunch break and especially for the many Arab workers that were employed.

Honesty was a priority amongst the Sarona community—there were no thefts

Honesty was a priority amongst the Sarona community—there were no thefts. However, in order to protect property from outsiders, an Arab policeman named Hassan, was placed in Sarona by the British authorities. In addition, the Sarona community employed a night watchman—an Arab named Abdullah. He was very dark but spoke fluent "schwaebisch" (the German Swabian dialect spoken by the Templers in Palestine). Initially he lived in a little house, known as the "Zehnthaeusle" (the one tenth cottage), which was owned by the community. The cottage was located between Kueblers and the main community house. Later he was moved to rooms in the winery and the Jewish Rabbi who blessed the local produce so that it was kosher, then lived in the cottage.

There was no **garbage collection** in Sarona. Food waste was either composted or fed to the chickens or pigs. Some settlers used their unsoaped dishwater for livestock purposes. The settlers were not wasteful and anything that could be recycled was. Occasionally, some waste was buried or burnt. As Tel Aviv grew a municipal tip was organised. Sarona farmers sometimes loaded their carts with organic matter from the tip and later ploughed it into their fields. There was a garbage collection arrangement in the city of Jaffa.

The British authorities imposed speed limits on roads (60kph). A number of registration and licensing requirements were introduced

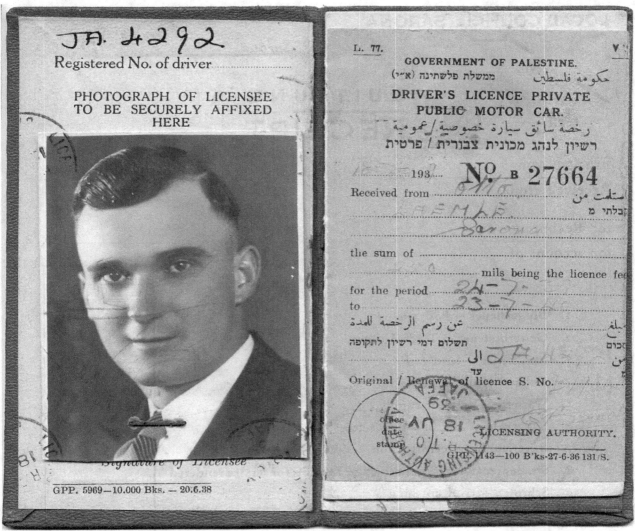

106) Driver's licence. Licence issued to Otto Laemmle in 1930s

107) Certificate of Registration (title) issued by the Land Registry Office, Palestine Government

for the whole population of Palestine. These included the registration of businesses, land titles, motor car and motor cycle driving licences, motor cars, motor cycles, bicycles and firearms.

RATES AND TAXES

A series of rates and taxes were payable by the Sarona settlers. Payments for these rates and taxes were paid to the "Local Council Sarona".

The Sarona community paid a **"Buergersteuer" (Poll (Citizen) Tax)** —initially a 10% levy on their income to the community council. This levy had been in force since the very beginning of the founding of Sarona. After WW I the community adopted a different method of assessing tax and a "Steuerkommission" (taxation commission) was established to deal with taxation matters.[258]

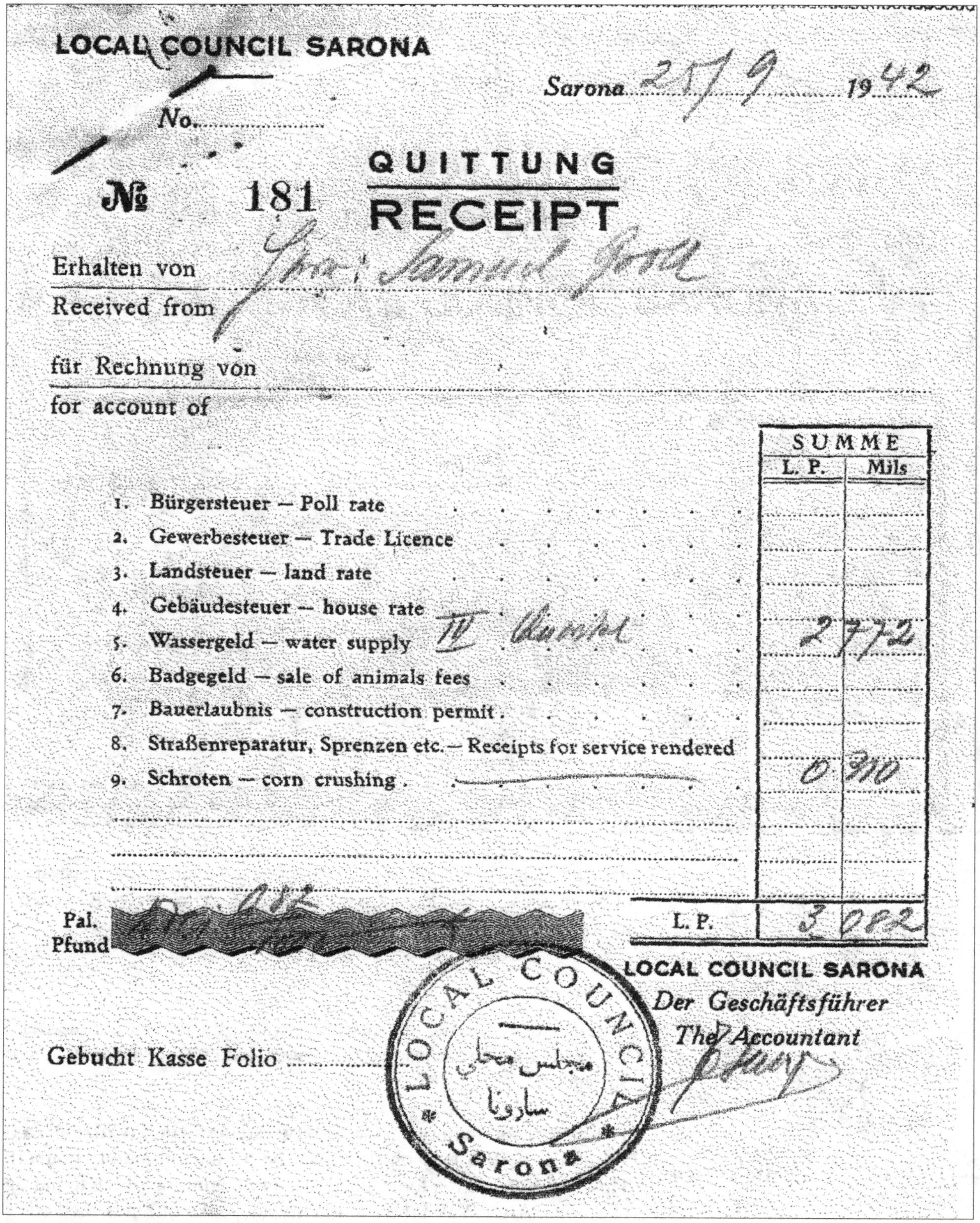

LOCAL COUNCIL SARONA

Sarona 25/9 1942

No.

№ 181

QUITTUNG
RECEIPT

Erhalten von *Herr Samuel ....*

Received from

für Rechnung von

for account of

	SUMME	
	L. P.	Mils
1. Bürgersteuer — Poll rate		
2. Gewerbesteuer — Trade Licence		
3. Landsteuer — land rate		
4. Gebäudesteuer — house rate		
5. Wassergeld — water supply *IV Quartal*	2	772
6. Badgegeld — sale of animals fees		
7. Bauerlaubnis — construction permit		
8. Straßenreparatur, Sprenzen etc. — Receipts for service rendered		
9. Schroten — corn crushing	0	910

Pal.
Pfund

L. P. 3 082

LOCAL COUNCIL SARONA
Der Geschäftsführer
The Accountant

Gebucht Kasse Folio

LOCAL COUNCIL مجلس محلي سارونا Sarona

108) Receipt issued by the Sarona Local Council. Note the various rates and charges that were levied

In 1933, for example, the following matters were included in the assessment of the Citizen Tax (Poll Rate).

1. Assets:—
- personal (non real estate) a rate of 1½% of the value—cash money, gold, loans to other persons, deposits with banks, shares etc
- property (real estate)—building blocks £P150 per dunum (1000sqm)
- buildings—various rates depending on type of building
  i. modern houses without cellar
  ii. modern houses with a cellar
  iii. houses built before or during WW I without cellar
  iv. houses built before WW I with a cellar
  v. houses with wooden floors and special type of wall
  vi. barns built in modern style
  vii. old style barns
  viii. other buildings
- orange groves—rate based on size (area) and age of grove
  i. new groves—less than 2 years, 2-4 years, 4-6 years
  ii. old groves—first class groves, lesser quality groves
- banana plantations with irrigation systems—rate based on value of the system and water consumption
- vineyards—rate based on size (area)
- other agricultural land—rate based on size (area) and soil quality
- businesses—rate based on value of machinery, plant, equipment etc
- other possessions—rate based on value
- other real estate outside Jaffa/Sarona settlement—not assessed but net income derived from these properties had to be declared.

2. Income
- a rate of 3½% was levied on net income from:—
  i. wages, salary and honorariums
  ii. business enterprises, agricultural enterprises and commercial undertakings
  iii. dividends, interest, leases, rents, share of a business etc

3. Deductions from the above amount of tax payable could be made for the membership fee for the community—a scale of rates applied for single persons, married couples with children and married couples without children.

4. School fees—an annual rate was payable which was based on the number of children from a family attending school.

5. Kindergarten fees—a flat annual rate for each child attending.[259]

In addition to this, the British introduced a property rating system on property **"Landsteuer (Property Rating Tax).** This rate was determined by an Assessment Committee in accordance with the "Urban Property Tax Ordinance". An aggrieved land owner could appeal against the committee's assessment to an Appeal Commission.

Other rates and fees were **"Gebaeudesteuer" (Building Rate), "Badgegeld" (Sale of Animals Fees), "Bauerlaubnis" (Construction Permit)** and **"Schroten" (Corn Crushing).**

"Wassergeld" (Water Supply Charge) was paid for water used and supplied from the community water supply.

109) *Urban rate assessment notice issued for rating purposes*

102

110) Peaceful street scene in Sarona

Every Saturday afternoon people swept and raked the roadway outside their places . . . by Saturday evening Sarona always looked very neat and tidy

"Strassenreparatur, Sprenzen etc"(Road Repairs and Sprinkling) costs were paid for services rendered. The **roads** in Sarona had been built by the community. They were all unmade—very dusty in summer and wet and soggy in winter. In summer, the roads were initially watered by the residents, using watering cans to settle the dust. Later, they were sprinkled by a horse or mule drawn water cart which was owned by the community. The roads were maintained by the local community who employed an Arab worker for that purpose. Every Saturday afternoon people swept and raked the roadway outside their places. This was a thankless chore, especially if a camel train had recently passed through, or during the jacaranda blossom season. However, by Saturday evening Sarona always looked very neat and tidy.

AGED CARE

There was an old people's home (Altersheim) in Sarona. It was located in the Jenner house (No.53) which had been left to the Sarona community when the Jenners died—they had no children. Ms Paula Kloz was in charge of the home. She cooked and cared for the two or three residents who lived there.

111) A Sunday afternoon stroll in beautiful Sarona.

LIBRARY SERVICES

At the community house (No. 09a), English *(The Palestine Post,* printed in Jaffa) and German newspapers, as well as a range of other reading material, was available for the whole community's use and access. Reading the newspapers was popular to catch up with overseas news.

In the 1930s news from the "Deutsches Nachrichtenbuero" (German News Bureau) was received in Jerusalem and sent to Sarona. There it was typed, duplicated and delivered to the settlers' homes by several boys.

A range of library books was able to be borrowed and read.

EDUCATION

The education of the young had always been a priority for the Templers

The education of the young had always been a priority for the Templers. Ever since the first school was established and a teacher appointed in 1873, the Sarona community had cared for the education of its children. Before WW I the school was located initially in the old community house (Saeulensaal) (No. 25) and from 1911 in the new community house (09a). Even during internment in Helouan, basic classes in reading and writing were provided by dedicated adults.

In summary, education up to WW I had comprised four years (grades 1 and 2) primary school education; four years (grades 3 and 4) junior school education; and, for those students wishing to continue a further two years at the Lyzeum Tempelstift in Jerusalem. Secondary education was provided there up to the Untersekunda level of the German education system.[260]

112) Entrance to the Lyzeum Tempelstift in Jerusalem

On return from internment in 1920, schooling was recommenced. Many children had missed out on proper education whilst interned and in Germany. A concerted effort was made to catch up on the lack of education for these children. The school in Sarona could not be used because it was occupied by the British, so the children from Sarona went each day by horse drawn wagon to the Templer school of the Jaffa community which was located in the Walhalla settlement some three kilometres away. There were some days when the children and their teacher, Johannes Frank, had to walk. Later a bus was organised to take the children to school. The cabin of the bus was

113) The new Sarona/Jaffa school opened in September 1931. Teachers and pupils of the school in 1935—
see over page for names

Names for Saron/Jaffa School Photo 1935 (for previous page)

1. Oskar Hoffmann
2. Kurt Ehnis
3. Heinrich Hasenpflug
4. Hans Hoefer
5. Paul Sickinger
6. Bruno Steller
7. Herbert Kuebler
8. Theo Weller
9. Ernst Aberle
10. Udo Strasser
11. Ulrich Reinhardt
12. Hans-Joachim Wieland
13. Gerd Aberle
14. Berthold Tannenbaum
15. Hilde Kuebler
16. Gerda Kuebler
17. Charlotte Hoffmann
18. Elisabeth Frank
19. Charlotte Asenstorfer
20. Gisela Wurst
21. Emma Baumert
22. Helene Strecker
23. Paula Hahn (teacher)
24. Eugen Neun (teacher)
25. Olga Frank (teacher)
26. Eugen Koch (teacher)

27. Eugen Faber (teacher)
28. Siegfried Hahn
29. Rolf Weller
30. Horst Kolb
31. Margrit Wagner
32. Elsa Hasenpflug
33. Annemarie Trefz
34. Rosemarie Hasenpflug
35. Aline Zollinger
36. Emma Noz
37. Inge Weller
38. Dieter Baldenhofer
39. Erich Baldenhofer
40. Alfred Lorenz
41. Adnan Esaue
42. Elham Hallag
43. Eleonore Ehnis
44. Edelgard Rohwer
45. Anni Kuebler
46. Rosemarie Lange
47. Maria Strecker
48. Gertrud Strecker
49. Egon Kuebler
50. Gertrud Strasser
51. Klaus Reinhardt
52. Werner Baldenhofer

53. Siegfried Hasenpflug
54. Brunhilde Noz
55. Lieselotte Steller
56. Ilse Blaich
57. Eva Wieland
58. Gertrud Weiss
59. Emma Hoffmann
60. Elfriede Hardegg
61. Gisela Hennig
62. Gisela Rubitschung
63. Irene Wagner
64. Heinz (or Erich) Aberle
65. Helmut Baumert
66. (Erich or) Heinz Aberle
67. Erich Hahn
68. Hugo Weller
69. Ulrich Asenstorfer
70. Heinz Kuebler
71. Bruno Venus
72. Gerhard Wagner
73. Kurt Lorenz
74. Paul Rubitschung
75. Otto Hoffmann
76. Klaus Hoffmann
77. Hugo Hoffmann
78. Reinhold Orth

114) School concert program, 1936

separated from the back where the children sat on long bench type seats. On the sides of the bus were canvas sheets which would be rolled up in the warm weather. As the Monday to Friday bus driver was an orthodox Jew a non orthodox Jewish driver had to be employed on Saturdays, the Jewish Sabbath, to drive the children to school. The teachers at this combined school were Johannes Frank, Anna Bulach, David Eppinger, Julie Aberle and Dr Alfred Schwab (from Germany).

As Sarona recovered and buildings became available again school classes were held in the old community house (No 25) (grades 1 and 2) and Geschwister Haering's house (No. 26) for grade 3 and the Saal (hall) (No. 09a) for grade 4. The teachers in Sarona during that period were Johannes Frank, Olga Frank and Kurt Lange. Girls were taught needlework (Handarbeit) for two hours on Saturday afternoons initially by Christine Weiss and later by Adelheid Groll.

With the amalgamation of Sarona and Jaffa communities in 1929 a joint new school was planned for Sarona. The school was designed by Theo Wieland and built by the Wennagels. Construction of the new school (No. 84) started in 1930 (the foundation stone was laid by the Templer President Christian Rohrer on 28 July (1930),[261] and was completed and opened in September 1931. Some financial assistance was provided by the German government to build the school. The teachers in Sarona during this time included Ms Olga Frank (grade 1, writing and arithmetic), Dr Horn (German and history), Mr E Neun (music and general subjects), Dr E Koch (English and mathematics), Mr Malem Costanti (Arabic), Dr H Rohrer (general subjects), Kurt Lange, Ms Paula Hahn (general subjects and sport), Dr Schwab, Rektor Ehmann (senior grades), Ms Thea Frank (sport).

When the new school was opened, all classes were held at the new school. The school hours were 8.30am to 12 noon and 2.00pm to 4.00pm, Monday to Friday, and half a day on Saturdays.

115) View of new school and community complex

The importance of good morals and community spirit was emphasised

Qualified teachers were appointed. Some teachers had grown up in Palestine and gone to Germany for formal teacher training and returned, whilst others were recruited as qualified teachers from Germany. There were four grades and the curriculum covered German, writing (in gothic script), reading, mathematics, physics, history (German, Greek and Roman), geography, nature study, singing, drawing, Latin, French, Arabic and English in the latter years. Sporting activities took place twice per week. Girls were taught knitting and needlework (sewing) whilst the boys were taught woodwork. For nature study there was a small garden where pupils could grow plants and a small shallow pond where aquatic plants and papyrus were grown. David Eppinger conducted Bible studies. The importance of good morals and community spirit was emphasised. Homework was given regularly to the students. Unruly student behaviour was punished in the Grades 1 and 2 by making the offender stand in a corner. In Grades 3 and 4 boys would be given the cane either on the flat of the hand or on occasion across the backside. At times boys would receive a cuff behind the ears from male teachers.

116) School class in 1935
Front desk on left: Siegfried Hasenpflug (left), Reinhold Orth (right), 2nd desk: Frieder Krafft, Ulrich Asenstorfer, 3rd desk: Klaus Reinhardt, Hugo Hoffmann, 4th desk: Arberle twins, Olga Frank (teacher), Werner Baldenhofer

Front desk on right: Gisela Hennig (left), Gertrud Weiss (right), 2nd desk: Emma Hoffmann, Irene Wagner, 3rd desk: Brunhilde Noz, Ilse Blaich, 4th desk: Gisela Rubitschung, Elfriede Hardegg, 5th desk: Trudi Strasser, Gertrud Strecker

A few Arab children attended the school. They spoke Swabian and
learnt to read and write proper German. They caught the school bus
to and from Jaffa the same as the Templer children from Jaffa and
Walhalla.

The school year was split by short breaks at Christmas, Easter and
Whitsuntide and an eight week break in the summer months of
July and August. Due to small class sizes, there were sometimes
problems with children of different ages and learning abilities. The
school intake always occurred every two years after the Dankfest
(Thanksgiving). On the first day of school every child received a
"Zuckertuete" which was filled with a variety of goodies—chocolates,
lollies and biscuits—to sweeten the school days from day one!

After completing their eight years of schooling, many students either
started a trade or found work. Others (boys and girls) went on to
secondary schooling at the Lyzeum Tempelstift in Jerusalem, under the
auspices of Dr Rohrer. The boys and girls from Sarona who attended

117) Boys' football (soccer) team,
Back row (left to right): Kurt Ehnis (kneeling), Bruno Steller, Theo Weller, Paul Sickinger, Rolf Weller (kneeling)
Front row: Heinrich Hasenpflug, Ernst Aberle, Oskar Hoffmann

118) Girls' sewing class

*Back row (left to right): Thekla Groll,
Ella Weller, Rosel Sickinger, Witta
Baldenhofer, Hedwig Weller, Christine
Weiss (teacher), Erna Graze, Ruth Groll,
Hanna Baldenhofer, Lina Laemmle, Nelly
Glenk, Gunda Steller
Front row: Annelies Lippmann, Helene
Knoll, Waldtraut Asenstorfer, Kaete
Kuebler, Agnes Groll, Elfriede Noz*

JERUSALEM GIRLS' COLLEGE.

HUMILITY

LOVE

JERUSALEM
GIRLS'
COLLEGE

TRUTH

I SERVE

PROSPECTUS.

*119) Cover of Jerusalem Girls' College
Prospectus*

that school had to board in Jerusalem with Nikolai Schmidt. The Schmidts had no children of their own but owned a very large house.

During the 1920s the issue of secondary education in Palestine was considered by the Templer Council and discussions were held with the German Protestant Community in Palestine. In the 1920s the curriculum at the Lyzeum Tempelstift had been expanded to a level where it reached the Obertertia level of the German education system. However, continuing problems were experienced in providing and maintaining the academic standards required at this level. In 1927, it was announced that no new higher secondary education institution would be provided, but that a limited secondary education level (middle school) would continue. In 1928, under the auspices of Dr Herbert Rohrer, the Lyzeum Tempelstift introduced a course which provided a higher education curriculum which equated to the Untersekunda and Obersekunda levels of the German education system. The Lyzeum Tempelstift received a small subsidy from the German government for the education it provided.[262]

The alternative for boys was to go to the "Frèreschule" (L'Ecole des Frères) a Catholic school run by French Brothers/Monks in Jaffa. Here the classes were conducted in French and English. A condition of attending was that all students had to attend a religious service and prayers at the beginning of each day. Arabic was taught as well as Literature (French classics). Some children were sent to Germany (either billeted or to a boarding school) to further their education or technical training.

120) Kindergarten class playing "ring-a-ring-a-rosie" under the watchful eye of "Tante" Cornelia Graze (kindergarten teacher)

Further options for girls were the Soeurs de St Joseph School, run by French nuns and a private girls' college, the Jerusalem Girls' College.

A kindergarten for pre schoolers had been established. It was located next to the community house. Its teacher was "Tante" (auntie) Cornelia Graze. The kindergarten had a large sandpit and, if new sand was needed, it was brought by camel from the beach. An Arab driver on a donkey would lead the camels, each camel had a bag of sand tied

121) Kindergarten class with Cornelia Graze (teacher) ca 1939

122) Kindergarten class with Cornelia Graze

to each side of the saddle. It stepped into the sand box and the sand was emptied from the bags into the sandpit.

Whenever "Tante Cornelia" took the children for a walk she would tie a long rope around her midriff and each child had to hold onto the rope during the walk.

"Tante Lula" Julie Aberle was the kindergarten teacher in the former Walhalla school building.

CITRUS INDUSTRY AND THE FAMOUS JAFFA ORANGES

Citrus production was one of the main industries of Sarona—oranges are synonymous with Jaffa/Sarona. After WW I the orange groves had been replanted and revived, and irrigation systems repaired, improved and extended. Citrus fruits provided a good income and many of the orange groves adjoined the settlement.

Oranges are synonymous with Jaffa/ Sarona

All owners of larger orange groves employed an Arab overseer (Waechter) who lived at the orange grove. His job was to guard the grove and he was also responsible for the irrigation of the trees during the hot dry summer months. The trees were irrigated by digging a trench around the tree and running water into it.

The main orange harvest in late October and November was always a very busy time in Sarona. The owner/growers picked many oranges themselves but they also employed many Arab workers during harvest and packing time. Great care was taken to ensure the orange rinds were not damaged during harvesting—the pickers had to have short finger nails and the picked oranges were placed in lined baskets by the pickers. In actual fact the oranges were not picked they were

123) Overlooking orange groves from Lippmann's irrigation storage (swimming pool) with the Tel Aviv skyline in the background.

124) Packing wrapper for the famous Jaffa oranges from Sarona

cut from the trees before they were fully ripe (many still green but juicy and sweet) so that they would keep better for export. Guards had to be employed to prevent the oranges from being stolen before and during harvesting.

After picking, the oranges were sorted according to quality and size. The oranges had to be completely dry before being wrapped in tissue paper and packed in boxes, which had a divider in the middle. These boxes were made on site. The packing process was carried out in a packing shed at the orange grove. From there the oranges were taken by camel to Jaffa—later, trucks were used to take the packed orange cases to Jaffa. The Arab boatmen of Jaffa would load the oranges on to ships (in the 1920s and 1930s there was no wharf at Jaffa). The ships lay at anchor at sea and Arab boatmen would take passengers and freight to the ships in longboats. With great skill in reading the wave movements, they lifted the goods in and out of the boats on to the ships.[263] As before WW I, the oranges were exported to Europe (Germany and England) and marketed as "Jaffa Oranges". Some grapefruit were grown and also exported.

In the 1920s the growers experimented with growing and exporting mandarins but this was not successful because mandarins had soft peels and did not keep. After the trial, mandarins were only grown for domestic (local) consumption.

115

125) A newly established orange grove showing the extent of the orchards

126) Orange packing shed scene with Arab workers

As well as the Sarona Citrus Growers Co-operative (which was made up of actual growers) a company was formed with the shareholders, in most cases, not being orange growers from Sarona. This company was known as Siedlungsgenossenschaft (SG) (Settlement Cooperative of the Templer Community Sarona/Jaffa) Ltd. SG owned an orange grove outside of Sarona and sold the oranges. The profits were

127) Carefully handpicking the golden oranges

128) Sealing the boxes before export

distributed amongst the shareholders. Friedrich Froeschle was manager of the company. Another partnership, Knoll and Co was also involved in growing oranges.

The German Templer Bank in Jaffa organised the selling of the citrus crops to brokers/merchants in England and Germany. When the monies were received for the orange crop, months after the harvest, payment was then made to the growers.

Some growers sold their crop directly to English or Arab merchants. The merchants would come whilst the oranges were still green to inspect the crop, a count was done of the trees to calculate a value and a price was then negotiated. The merchants then took responsibility

129) Orange cases stacked ready for transport

130) Orange wrapper

for harvesting and packing the crop. This method of selling, which was based on tree numbers, encouraged some farmers to plant more trees. Growers who opted for this type of sale usually got their money more quickly than those who sold via the bank. However, in the more densely planted orange groves the trees tended to grow into each other and in the long term the quality and quantity of the crop suffered.

131) Convoy of trucks taking the packed oranges to Jaffa for export

„**Orangen-Geschenkkisten nach Deutschland.**

Wir geben hierdurch bekannt, daß wir auch in dieser Saison Geschenkkisten nach Deutschland liefern können. Der Preis dürfte ungefähr derselbe wie im Vorjahre sein. Lieferungszeit von Ende Dezember 1937 bis Ende Januar 1938 nach Maßgabe der Verschiffungsmöglichkeit.

Wegen der zu erledigenden, behördlicherseits vorgeschriebenen Formalitäten sind die Bestellungen bei unieren Filialen persönlich aufzugeben und zwar

bis spätestens 31. Januar 1938.

Später einlaufende Bestellungen werden nicht mehr angenommen.

Bank der Tempelgesellschaft
(Bank of the Temple Society) Limited."

132) Advertisement for sending oranges as gifts to Germany

Translation of "Orange Gift Boxes to Germany"

"Notice is hereby given that we are able during this season to arrange gift boxes to Germany. The price will be approximately the same as last year Delivery will be between the end of December 1937 and the end of January 1938 depending on shipping arrangements.

Due to the official formalities it is necessary to personally place an order through one of our agencies by no later than 31 January 1938.

Late orders will not be accepted.

(Bank of the Temple Society) Ltd"

The main orange growers of Sarona were Sam Weller, Karl and Friedrich Froeschle, Gottlieb Glenk, Reinhardt Lippmann, Fritz Kuebler, Karl Kuebler, Karl Steller, Immanuel Steller, Samuel and Philipp Groll, Fritz and Otto Laemmle, Johannes Weiss and Johannes Orth. Other people owned smaller orange groves. The SG Company owned one orange grove on the outskirts of Sarona and the partners of Knoll and Co. owned several orange groves. All the orange groves were outside of the actual "township" of Sarona.

The settlers could if they wished send individual cases of oranges to family and friends overseas. This practice became quite popular during the 1930s as many of the settlers had immediate family members in Germany or relations through marriage outside Palestine. These "orange" gifts were received with joy by the recipients overseas.

Jaffa oranges were well known, even before World War I, and sought after in Europe for their sweetness and quality. It is interesting that some famous orange covered chocolate sweets in Australia are known as a "Jaffas". Their reputation has indeed spread far and wide!

DAIRY INDUSTRY

The good cow herd, that had been in Sarona before the war, was lost in the war years

Dairy production, especially milk, was still a significant industry in Sarona although it had declined in importance when compared to pre World War 1.

The quality of Sarona's cow herd was lost during the war years. The new dairy cows acquired after the war did not have the same milk producing qualities as the pre-war cows. Arrangements were therefore made to import bulls from Friesland (Netherlands), East Prussia, Poland and England and so improve the herd quality again.

The Jakob Blaich family ran the dairy (No.56). In Sarona the main

133) Scene with dairy cows outside Laemmle's barn

dairy farmers were Otto and Fritz Laemmle, Sam, Jonathan and Jakob Weller, Karl Steller, Karl Froeschle, Katharine Jung, Ernst Kuebler, Samuel Groll, Johannes Weiss (1920s) and Erwin Haering. The cows were kept mainly indoors in sheds and only let out once or twice a day. The cows were hand milked, mostly by Arab workers, at least twice a day. Some milk was blessed by a Rabbi so that the milk was kosher and could be sold and consumed by the Jews. The milk was not pasteurised, it was put into milk cans for transport to the Sarona dairy. Germans, Jews and Arabs all bought milk direct from the dairy. Some milk was transported to Jaffa and Tel Aviv and sold.

Butter and cheese were made at the dairy by Arab women turning a churn. "Lebben" (yoghurt) was produced and sold in bottles. A Rabbi also visited the dairy to ensure these products were kosher.

In 1937/38 agreement was reached in principle for the milk processing and distribution from Sarona to be done by the Wilhelma dairy. The dairy co-operative of Wilhelma had modernised their dairy thus

134) Herd of dairy cows

135) The tunnel between the old and new wine cellar

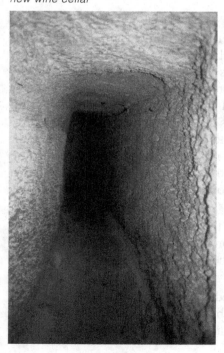

enabling that dairy to undertake additional work under a contractual arrangement which was finalised during the war years.[264]

WINE INDUSTRY

Another important industry since the beginning of Sarona was the wine industry. The winery (No.2a) and the large cellars were the largest buildings in Sarona. The old and new cellars were joined by a tunnel. After the war, the neglected vineyards were quickly restored and wine production re-commenced. Both red and white wine grapes were grown. These wines were marketed overseas including an exhibit at the 1924 International British Empire Exhibition at Wembley, England.

As can be imagined the wine cellar had been "visited" during the war and all the wine that was there in 1917 was gone. Already before the war Wilhelma had joined with the Sarona-Jaffa Wine-growers Co-operative to form an enlarged co-operative known as "Deutscher Weinbau Verein G.m.b.H.—Wilhelma-Sarona Jaffa".

After WW I, that co-operative was reconstituted under British Mandate laws. It became known as the Deutsche Weinbau-Genossenschaft Wilhelma-Sarona (The German Co-operative Vine-culture Society Wilhelma-Sarona Ltd). The British version of the Society's rules was the one that applied in the case of disputes. The Society's objective was *"to workup and sell in common, grapes of*

136) Sarona wine exhibit at the British Empire Exhibition at Wembley in 1924

the vineyards of the members". The Society's rules also provided a wide range of capabilities to carry out its objectives. Included in these capabilities were:—

"a. To carry on the business of food and fruit-preservers, flower and fruit-extractors, brewers, distillers, sugar manufacturers and merchants, manufacturers of and dealers in oils, wine, liquors and spirits of any description.

b. To carry on the business of planters, vine-growers, farmers, land exploitators and buyers of every kind of vegetable, produce of the soil, to prepare, manufacture and to render marketable any such produce and to sell, dispose of and deal in every such produce, either in its prepared, manufactured, or raw state and whether by wholesale or retail.

c. To carry on the business of coopers, bottle-makers, bottle-stop makers and potters . . . ."[265]

The Society appears to have concentrated on the production of wine and spirits. Some methylated spirit and vinegar was also produced. All bottles and corks were imported.

The area under vineyard cultivation in Sarona decreased steadily after WW I. Many vineyards were replaced by orange and citrus orchards as these provided a better financial return in the longer term. By the 1930s most of the wine grapes delivered to the winery in Sarona came from the growers in Wilhelma. This is reflected in the membership of the Society where the majority of members came from Wilhelma.

137) Delivery of grapes to the winery in Sarona

138) Scene outside the winery with wine barrels ready for shipment

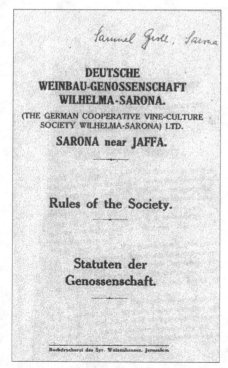

139) Cover of the constitution of the Wilhelma-Sarona Wine Co-operative

The Co-operative had a rule whereby a person could be a member of the Society only if he/she had an area under vineyard cultivation. Members were required to deliver all their grapes (except those for their own personal use) to the Society's winery.

Sarona always had its own cooper and wine maker. Georg Roller was the winemaker throughout the period between WW I and WW II. In the early and mid 1920s a Mr Grosshans was the cooper. In 1929, the Society recruited, through advertisement in Germany, Hermann Hoersch from Germany to come to Sarona to be its main cooper, initially for a period of three years. Mr Hoersch remained cooper until 1939. He lived with his family in a dwelling above the wine cellar. A number of settlers worked at the winery, an apprentice was employed in the cooper trade and another in winemaking. Mr Hennig was office manager of the winery.

The grape harvest in the summer months was, of course, the busy time, when grapes from Sarona and Wilhelma were delivered and processed.

In 1936, the winery was closed as it underwent a major upgrade during which the winemaking facilities were modernised. The wine was stored inside the winery and in the tunnel which ran between the old winery (No.18) and the wine cellar (No. 2). From there it was sold mostly around the Cannstatt/Stuttgart area in southern Germany where Doh and Imberger both had retail outlets. Some wine of course was sold within the Templer settlements and to other local buyers. The local Saronians could buy wine from Abdullah, an Arab who hand-delivered the wine to their homes.

140) Wine label for Wermuthwein

The wines were known as—"Wermuthwein" a vermouth wine; "Hoffnung der Kreuzfahrer" (Hope of the Crusaders) a red table wine; "Perle von Jericho" (Pearl of Jericho) a sweet wine; "Wilhelma Auslese"; "Sarona White"; "Jaffa Gold"; and "Silvaner" (Sylvaner) all white wines.

Arak, brandy and liqueurs were produced at the winery. A large chimney was built about 1927 when distilling was started. As the arak and brandy were distilled, they gave off a very distinct odour.

The wonderful description below from Herbert Steller, of how the grapes were brought from Wilhelma to Sarona in the 1930s provides a good written picture of this aspect of activity.

"At 7 to 9 years of age I helped to harvest and transport the grapes by horse drawn wagons (Leiterwagen) over a sandy stretch of road to Petah Tiqvah and the good bitumen road to Sarona.

On harvest days, after the milk was delivered to the Dairy (Molkerei) in Wilhelma at 3.00am, we proceeded in the dark with the wagon in the direction of our vineyard. You could hear, but not see the other people going in the same direction.

We picked up the large baskets from our orange orchard where they had been washed in the water reservoir. It was still dark when we arrived at the assembly spot where all the Arab pickers, men and women, were waiting. You could hardly see them, but hear them talking, huddled together.

141) Label for arac

As soon as it was light enough they started picking. I was fascinated by the noise (yelling) and singing) and the speed with which the large baskets filled. Everyone wanted to be first off and to get to the Weinkeller (wine cellar).

It was heavy going through the sand until we hit the good road in Petah Tiqvah (Em Lebbes). Some wagons needed extra help. From there it was a straight run to Sarona past eucalyptus plantations where the Templers from Sarona, Jaffa and Wilhelma came together for the Mai Ausflug (May Picnic). Arriving at the Weinkeller there was, most of the time, a lengthy waiting time until your wagon could be unloaded, sorted out, red—white. First in, first out.

We young folks were sent to get something to eat and drink—pretzels and buns at Guenthners, wurst (sausages) etc at Groezingers—and were rewarded for our trouble. The horses then had to be fed and watered.

On the way back after we dropped off the baskets at the orchard, from there the horses found their own way home, and I was allowed to be Kutscher (coachman). Then rest and sleep."

ORTH'S NURSERY

A plant nursery was started by Johannes Orth in 1911. After WW1 he developed it into a large nursery (No. 35) from which plants and flowers were grown and sold. It was a well known enterprise throughout Palestine. Orths had five glass houses—one of which was used solely by a Swiss scientist who studied cactus plants. Orth's nursery had some large shade houses to protect plants and seedlings from the hot summer sun. The shade houses were open structures with wooden slats over the top to provide the shade. Plants were propagated at the nursery. The packing and sorting of plants and flowers was done in the packing sheds at the nursery. The nursery had its own water supply from a well and a pressure pump was installed from which a large gun-type sprinkler could be used or alternatively it would provide enough pressure for up to 200 small sprinklers.

142) Scene in Orth's nursery

Orths exhibited their products at several exhibitions—in 1924 at the British Empire Exhibition at Wembley, England and at the Jerusalem (International) Horticultural Society show in 1938. At the latter exhibition Orths won several prizes for their flower and ornamental plant exhibits.[266]

Flowers were an important income—Orths were growers, wholesalers and retailers. They owned three florist shops themselves—in

143) View of Orth's nursery with propogation beds and glass house. These were some of the first glass houses built in Palestine for flower and vegetable cultivation.

144) Erich Hermann attending young plants in Orth's nursery

Jerusalem, Jaffa and Tel Aviv. Demand for flowers was good, especially amongst the British living in Palestine. They bought many flowers for their wives and girlfriends. Many flowers were also used for wreaths, which were made by Orths. They had to import all the rings and wire for wreath making.

Orths were the "Fleurop" representatives in Palestine, and through them floral arrangements could be sent overseas.[267]

Orths employed a Jewish foreman and up to twenty Arabs for weeding. Couch grass especially was a problem and had to be physically dug out. Also cultivation work associated with their business required intense labour. Erich Hermann, from Germany, was employed by Orths as he was an expert with roses and fruit trees. Some fruit trees were imported from Italy.

Orths imported spruce trees each year from Germany. These were sold to families who wanted a spruce tree rather than a cypress tree at Christmas time. They also imported and sold a range of ceramic ornaments such as wedding decorations and Easter ornaments.

As well as the nursery business Orths grew oranges and vegetables for commercial purposes

OTHER PRIMARY INDUSTRIES

There were a number of other primary industries on a smaller scale in Sarona.

145) Exhibition stand of Orth's nursery promoting orange trees and other plants

146) View of Orth's flower growing fields

Only a small amount of **meat** for local consumption was produced in Sarona. The animals for slaughter, mainly pigs and calves, were purchased from the Wilhelma farmers. Some calves were bought from Arab and later Jewish farmers. Shortly after his family returned to Sarona after WW I, Willi Groezinger went to Germany to learn his trade as butcher and smallgoods maker. Groezingers, who owned the butcher shop (No.38a) and the nearby slaughter house (No.38b), raised some pigs themselves. W Groezinger also slaughtered pigs for Sarona residents—a tradition known as "Schlachtfest" (see below). The British employed "meat inspectors" to check the quality of the meat, smoked hams and small goods. Groezingers had a cooling system with ice to keep the meat. In 1937, this was upgraded to a refrigerated cool room. At times Groezingers bought in some meat from a larger butcher outside the Sarona settlement to sell in their shop or to make smallgoods.

In 1931, Groezingers bought the business of Sarona's other butcher Hermann Wurst. The contract of sale provided that Mr Wurst was not allowed to establish another butcher/smallgoods business for five years within 10 kilometres of Sarona. Mr Wurst started another business in Haifa. The British authorities required butcher shops to be licensed under the "Regulation of Trades and Industries Ordinance".

Some of Groezinger's products were kosher and sold to the Jews.

A tradition with many families was a **"Schlachtfest".** This was when one or two pigs that had been reared during the year were slaughtered. The whole family would assemble and they would divide the meat as well as the sausages and smoked ham (Schinken) amongst themselves. Sometimes some meat would be sold as well. Schlachtfests always took place in the winter months because of the cooler weather.

From August 1941 Wilhelm Groll continued to run Groezinger's butcher shop.

Many settlers raised their own chickens for both meat and eggs. Pigeons (squabs) were raised for meat and often made tasty Sunday roasts. Some families had many chickens and sold the **eggs.** To overcome the shortage of eggs in winter, when the hens virtually stop laying, excess eggs from autumn were stored (preserved) in lime mixed with water in drums (in Kalk gelegt) for later use. Although the eggs were not quite like fresh eggs, they were suitable for cooking and baking.

Many families grew their own **vegetables.** There were several commercial vegetable growers in Sarona, Gottlieb Glenk, Johannes

Weiss, Samuel and Wilhelm Groll, Jakob and Jonathan Weller, Fritz and Otto Laemmle and Georg Weinmann. They sold vegetables within Sarona but the bulk of their crop was sold in Jaffa and Tel Aviv. They grew summer and winter crops. In summer, tomatoes, capsicums, cucumbers, zucchinis, pumpkins, lettuce, egg plants, water melons and cantaloupes were harvested and the winter crop included cabbages, cauliflowers, potatoes, carrots and spinach.

147) Water melon harvest

Arab workers tended to the fields and assisted with the harvest. The melon crop was often sold as one lot to a buyer. Other settlers had smaller gardens which produced fresh vegetables in smaller quantities.

148) Cauliflower harvest ready to transport to market

Fruits such as apricots, plums, stone fruits, olives, apples and pears were grown often by each individual family.

Fritz and Otto Laemmle started the first **apple** orchard in Sarona. Unfortunately at the beginning of World War II, this small new enterprise was just beginning—the trees were only two to three years old. The last residents of Sarona in 1945/46 remember the apples as specifically large, juicy and sweet—an unusual sight in Palestine at that time.

Georg Weller was one of the first to grow **bananas** for commercial purposes. This was a somewhat risky business due to the cold nights with minus degree temperatures in winter. He was successful and other settlers followed suit. For export the whole banana bunch was cut and put in a bag and sold. The bananas were exported to Rumania.

Field and Grain crops—wheat, oats, barley, maize, turnips (Futterrueben), clover and lucerne were cultivated in fields around Sarona. Much of the crop was threshed either by hand or in Sarona itself where a threshing machine was located near the Dairy. The grains that were used for human consumption were taken to the other mills in Jaffa and Walhalla, owned by Buchhalter, Heselschwerdt and Gollmer, for grinding.

The other grain and field crops were used for stock feed as well as pumpkins which were specifically grown for that purpose. Clover, lucerene and lupins were cut for hay.

149) Pumpkins for cattle feed

150) Banana crop

151) Corn crop

133

152) Chaff cutting

153) Threshing barley and making hay

Sugar Cane—small quantities of sugar cane were grown by the Laemmles and Carl Kuebler. The cane needed to be irrigated regularly. Pieces of cane were cut and given to children as a sweet to suck and chew. No sugar was refined but the crop was cut and taken to the winery where it was processed and distilled into spirits.

Unsuccessful attempts were made to grow **tobacco.**

154) Cutting sugar cane, 1923

*155) Bee hives in field next to orange
grove*

Honey—some bee hives were kept in Sarona. Before WW I, the
Laemmles, Orths and Ottmers supplied honey in Sarona. F. Laemmle
bred and exported Queen Bees to Europe. Later some bee hives were
kept by Friedrich Orth, Eugen Sickinger and Luise Jung. Some honey
was also brought to Sarona from the Wilhelma settlement. After the
orange trees had finished blossoming, the honey suppliers sold sweet
orange-blossom honey.

Peanut Butter—The Glenks bought peanuts which were then roasted
and processed into peanut butter. No peanuts were grown in Sarona.

BUILDING INDUSTRY

Up to World War I the Wennagel master builders had been virtually
the only builders in Sarona. They had built the wine cellar, most
homes, sheds, bowling alley and other significant community
buildings. They also built many homes in Wilhelma. They continued
this role after the war. There were no new homes built for several
years after the war, however, there was much work to be done in
restoring the damaged homes and other buildings.

Hugo Wennagel (3rd generation builder in Sarona) and Fritz Steller
both studied architecture in Germany after they had completed their
building apprenticeship with Josef Wennagel

In 1930/31 Fritz Steller started his own building business. He went on
and built several houses in Sarona.

156) The Sarona water tower—a real landmark
Walter Kuebler, Friedrich Haering and Edmund Steller

Theo Wieland studied architecture and designed a number of homes and buildings.

In 1925, the Sarona community arranged for the construction of a water tower. This was a major undertaking and the tower was owned by the community. During construction, the tower required a continuous concrete pour. First all the form work was prepared with reinforcement, then over 100 Arab labourers worked in relays—the concrete was mixed by using shovels, and then carried manually in 4 gallon (20 litre) tin buckets to the formwork and emptied. To complete the upper level (storage area) the heavy buckets full of concrete were manually carried up ladders. In some instances at the higher levels the concrete was hoisted up.

Before WW I, no building permits or approvals were needed. However, after the war the British authorities required that building approvals be obtained. Buildings, and homes had to comply with sanitary requirements. For building approvals in Sarona plans were lodged with the community office. Paul Frank checked the plans and submitted them to the authorities for approval.

The construction of the new Sarona school and community complex (No 84) was the largest construction project undertaken by the Wennagels.

In the late 1920s and into the 1930s, the building industry was very active. New homes were built not only in Sarona but in the other Templer settlements as well. Outside the settlements, much building occurred, and building works were undertaken by the Sarona builders for Arabs, Jews and for the Jaffa City Council. During the 1930s, when more than 30 building blocks were made available in Sarona there was a "housing building boom" as many Jaffa settlers relocated to Sarona.

The builders Wennagel and Steller often had several houses on the go at the same time. The houses were built of sandstone or cement bricks. Some German trades people were employed, however, most labouring work was done by Arab workmen—some were very good and employed as "permanents", others were employed on "a needs basis". The laying of cement bricks was mostly done by Arab workers. The walls were then concrete rendered. All concrete was hand mixed. Wood was used sparingly as it was very expensive and had to be imported from Sweden by a Jewish importer. Many homes had concrete floors and the concrete was covered by tiles. All the cement was imported from Heidelberg, Germany. Wall and floor tiles were made at the Wielands concrete factory in Walhalla/Jaffa. Some homes had flat roofs and others were gabled and tiled. Some of the roof tiles came from Schnellers in Jerusalem and some from

This was a major undertaking and the tower was owned by the community

157) Fritz Steller and Hugo Wennagel as architect students in Germany

During the 1930s when 30 additional building blocks were made available in Sarona there was a "housing building boom"

Wielands. Most building materials were brought to the building site by horse and cart and in later times by truck.

The carpentry and joinery workshops of Otto Venus (established before WW I) (No. 89) and Hermann Wied (started in 1930/31) (No.50) were also busy with making furniture and fittings for the new homes. A number of tradesmen from the Sarona/Jaffa settlements worked at these joinery workshops.

Wennagels employed a very good Jewish plumber named Stern who lived in Tel Aviv. This man was also an expert in reinforcing work. He supplied the steel reinforcing for the concrete water storage tanks.

158) Copy of invoice issued by Josef Wennagel—Masterbuilder

140

The painting work was done by a Jewish painter named Lehmann.
He was affectionately known as the "Schmierer" (smearer). He
always called any off-white colour "dinkelweiss" instead of dunkel
weiss (dark white).

HOUSES AND HOMES

As described above, all houses were built of stone and concrete. This
segment does not describe one house or home but is a generic outline
of what was in a typical house and how the homes functioned.

All homes had a formal living room, often with a piano or pianola
where family members would play music. The floors of the entry and
most living areas were usually tiled with decorative colourful tiles
mostly supplied by the Wieland factory.

*159) Interior view of Steller's enclosed
verandah with floor tiles supplied by
Wielands*

160) Beautiful Wieland tiles in the Weiss house in Sarona

161) Helene Groll at the piano

All the early homes as well as those built in the 1930s had a built-in wood-fired stove/oven which was used for everyday cooking and some baking. Some kerosene stoves as well as primus cookers were used later. The main community bakehouse was used for baking bread, round flat loaves (Fladen), pretzels and cakes. When the oven was fired, numerous families would use it.

Hot water was heated on the stoves for normal household needs or in the laundry coppers for baths. A hot bath was usually taken once a week, mainly on Saturdays. The farmers who had orchards had plenty of wood but the others had to buy wood—often olive tree timber was burnt and this was quite expensive. No forms of heating were installed. Many homes had small kerosene heaters. People just dressed warmly in the cooler winter months. The windows were glazed but also fitted with wooden slatted shutters—in summer these were used when the windows were left open so that air could circulate in the rooms.

The ladies did all the cooking and baking. The cuisine was a mixture of Swabian (German) dishes and of traditional Middle Eastern food. The best of both worlds!

Initially, there were no refrigerators but some people had ice-boxes. The ice was made at Gollmer's mill in Walhalla and cost one piastre, delivered. Later, some households had electric refrigerators.

162) Above—Entrance to Orth's nursery with their house in background 163) Below—Beautiful front garden and entrance to home in Sarona.

164) Beautiful garden around a home in Sarona (Reinhardt and Fritz Lippmann and son. Neef family house on left)

165) Edith Lippmann (Neef) watering the home garden

Originally all homes used kerosene lamps for lighting. Each day the glass cylinders of the lamps had to be cleaned. Electricity came to Sarona in approximately 1929/30. This changed many things in the homes as lighting and electrical appliances started to be used.

Most houses were double storey and usually had a cellar.

Up to the 1920s, all houses had pan toilets and the waste was buried. With the building of the water tower in 1925, and a good pressure water supply, septic tanks were installed for sanitary waste. All other waste water was also discharged into the septic tanks (soak pits). The newer homes installed showers but with cold water only.

There were mesh wire fences between most houses. These fences marked the boundary of the properties. Surrounding the houses were gardens where flowers, decorative plants and trees were planted. Along the street front nearly all owners had a picket fence.

Many families had small backyard vegetable gardens and a few fruit trees—apricot trees were popular.

Young Jewish ladies or girls were often employed for domestic work in the homes. Many of them lived in Montefiore and walked to and from work each day. Arab women were employed to do the washing.

166) Erna Graze (left) and friend in reflective mood in their front garden

Charlotte Laemmle has provided a very precise description of the Laemmle family home (No. 07) based on the recollections of her auntie Lina Laemmle. This is an indicative description of an early Sarona home and its fittings. The following is an excerpt of this description.

"The Laemmle House
The Laemmle house was built of local sandstone and rendered with a cement-like surface. It was painted a cream colour. Windows were painted green. The roof was tiled with terracotta tiling. Floors were of painted wood, apart from the kitchen and entry, which were tiled. All interior walls were whitewashed—not wallpapered. Sometimes colour, cream or a light lilac, was added to the whitewash. Cornices were simple and sometimes painted a different colour.

167) The old Laemmle's family house

A Tour Through the House

Front Garden

The front garden was approximately 5-7 metres deep. Plants which grew there included—oleander bushes, a jacaranda tree, a trumpet bush, geraniums, rose (Koenigin der Nacht), white cactus and pots of begonias and impatiens.

Indoor potted plants lined the entrance and verandah area. On the left hand side of the garden was a "garden house". This was an open structure with climbers growing up its posts. It housed a table and benches and was a pleasant place for social get-togethers—or simply having lunch.

Three steps led to the front door and entry hallway.

***Entry**—An entry hall of 2-3 meters width welcomed one into the house. From this, the hallway doors opened into four main downstairs rooms.*

***Dining Room**—This room housed a large cabinet of books originally owned by Christian Friedrich Laemmle (Fritz)—an unusual possession in this rural village! Table and chairs from his third wife were added later. Later the furniture was updated with a new dining table and chairs brought from a nursing sister who returned to Germany.*

***Sewing Room**—Sewing was an integral part of life for the women of Sarona. Mina Laemmle was, however, fully occupied with running her home and land and hence employed a Jewish sewing lady who came every few weeks and sewed clothes and mended garments. The room contained a sewing machine on a table facing the front window, a couch and chairs and a tall cupboard with curtain front.*

***Kitchen**—One entered the kitchen through the hallway. A large wood fired stove, bought from Mergentheim in Germany, served the cooking needs of the family. A sink sitting in a wooden bench was located under a window facing the garden.*

Washing up was done with hot water only, soap was rarely used as the washing up water was collected in a bucket underneath the sink and added to the feed given to the pigs.

***Crockery-cupboards**— lined the wall abutting the grain area. A rectangular table was located along the inside wall of the kitchen with bench and chairs.*

***Pantry**—A large room close to the kitchen, this housed shelves of preserves, jams and home produce. Flour, sugar, etc. was bought in bulk and kept there. Products could be bought from the Templer Konsum (store) run by Jakob Jung. Later many Templers bought cheaper goods from the Jewish settlers in Montefiore and Tel Aviv and the Arab merchants in Jaffa, causing the Konsum some financial difficulties.*

***Laundry**—Here there were large troughs for soaking and washing clothes and linen. A wood fired boiler provided hot water for the*

Laemmle family. Three or four metal tubs were placed on trestles in the yard and the washing was done outside. In the early days, Mina L. would make up a lye solution from ashes to do the washing. The washing was hung up to dry on a clothes line in the yard. Bed linen was washed only once every four weeks. An Arab woman often helped with the laundry.

"Kraftfutter" room, grain room or "Suttroy" (sous terrain)—This housed some of the feed for the animals. One stepped down 2-3 steps from the laundry. There one found barley and oats for the horses, wheat for the chickens, Kleie (bran), and Oelkuchen (lees of olives) for the dairy cows.

Bienenzimmer (bee keeping room)—Here old Fritz L. kept his bee keeping equipment and produced his honey. After his death it became a storage area where tools were kept. Later it became a hen house for brooding hens and later again a pantry.

Toilet—There was an outside toilet located to the left of the back entrance in the garden area. In later years many families had an inside toilet.

Stairway—A narrow stairway led to the first floor landing/open area.

168) House plan of Laemmle's family house, ground floor

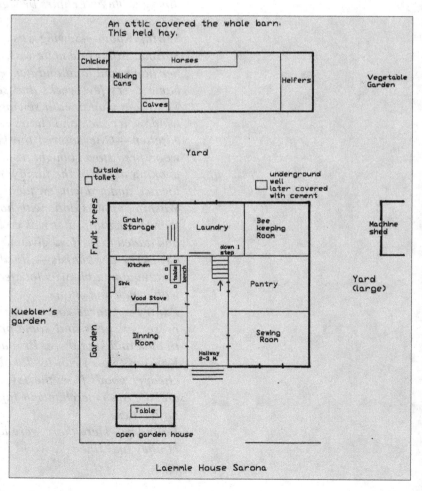

Laemmle House Sarona

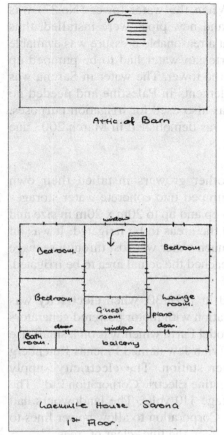

169) House plan of Laemmle's family house, upstairs

170) Barn next to Laemmle's house

Guest room—this was a pleasant room with a window onto the balcony

Bedrooms—the bedrooms were located on the first floor. Two had doors leading to the balcony. Various family members used the bedrooms over the years according to the events of the family.

Bathroom—This was a small room on the balcony with just a bath in it. No hot water. Most of the family washed themselves in the laundry. A bath required that water had to be boiled in the laundry and carried upstairs in metal buckets. A hard earned bath!

Formal Room—this was the "special room" of the house. Good quality furniture with fine furnishings, including antique vases and ornaments, decorated the room. A large portrait of the Kaiser and his wife hung on the wall. The room was always kept tidy and a piano was kept there too.

Attic—Another staircase headed up to the attic from the landing on the first floor. This was a large open room used only for storage (old beds, toys, children's items and old kitchen equipment).

Cellar—Two underground storages occupied the entire area under the house. In the very early days, all food stuffs were kept there, especially milk and butter, as it was cool. Later it was used for storage of harvests and crops, such as water melons. [. . .]

Throughout the history of this house, with its joys and tragic events, there was always a sharing and caring feeling amongst all the family members.

They lived the Templer spirit in every way."[268]

UTILITY SERVICES—WATER AND ELECTRICITY

The early **water supply** came from the community storage tank. The water pressure from this system was poor and many homes drew

water from their own wells. When the water tower (No.37) was built—it was 25 metres high, and new pipes were installed, thus ensuring that good clean water at a reasonable pressure was available to all houses in Sarona. The artesian water had to be pumped up into the storage tank on top of the tower. The water in Sarona was the best of all the Templer settlements in Palestine and needed no additives. Some of the water was also used for irrigation purposes. Sarona's landmark water-tower was demolished in March 2003 due to it becoming unsafe.

Most of the orchardists and other growers installed their own bores and pumps. Water was pumped into concrete water storages (Bassins) approx. 120-150cms deep and up to 20m x 20m in size and from there it was channelled to the areas to be irrigated. It was an inefficient irrigation system as much water was lost through seepage in the sandy soil before it even reached the actual area to be irrigated.

A major improvement occurred in 1929/30, when **electricity** was connected to Sarona. A power station with motor powered generators was built at the site of the old Model Farm which was on a small rise between Sarona and Jaffa. A Latvian Jew named Pinchas Rutenberg owned and operated the power station. The electricity supply company was known as the "Palestine Electric Corporation Ltd". The current produced was high voltage 110 volts. The landowners had contractual agreements with the Corporation to allow power lines to be run across private land and to keep the lines clear of trees.[269]

When electricity was brought to Sarona, Paul Frank was asked by the electricity company to do the survey work and peg out the pole positions for the power lines. Mr Frank managed to place all the pole positions in backyards and gardens and not along the streets.

OTHER BUSINESSES, ENTERPRISES AND OCCUPATIONS

Although no new land was available for agricultural purposes in the 1930s, Sarona still grew due to the influx of families from the Jaffa settlement. This increase within the settlement, as well as the enormous and rapid development of Tel Aviv presented new business opportunities. A range of businesses and occupations could be found in Sarona or nearby. Many non-Saronians from outside the settlement were customers and users of these businesses. Below is a listing of businesses and services, some of which have already been referred to above, they were either in or near Sarona—they all had an impact on Sarona's economic well being.[270]

The water tower was built and new pipes were installed. This ensured that good clean water at a reasonable pressure was available to all houses in Sarona

A major improvement occurred in 1929/30 when electricity was connected to Sarona

The enormous and rapid development of Tel Aviv presented new business opportunities

Engineering and Mechanical Works—Gebrueder Wagner (Wagner
Bros). The factory and workshop which had been established in
1900 at Walhalla/Jaffa was the largest engineering and mechanical

171) Cover of the German Businesses in
Palestine Index

172) Far right—Extract of the German
Businesses in Palestine index

Nachweis
deutscher Geschäfte
in Palästina

Herausgegeben vom
Syrischen Waisenhaus in Jerusalem

1937

- Architekt, Bauingenieur.
Bauausführungen. Entwürfe.
Otto Venus
- Bank der Tempelgesellschaft
Ltd., Jaffa.
- Mechanische Bau- und
Möbelschreinerei.
J. Wennagel
- Bank der Tempelgesellschaft
Ltd., Jaffa.
- Bauunternehmer.
Hermann Wied
- Bank der Tempelgesellschaft
Ltd., Jaffa.
- Mechanische Bau- und
Möbelschreinerei.

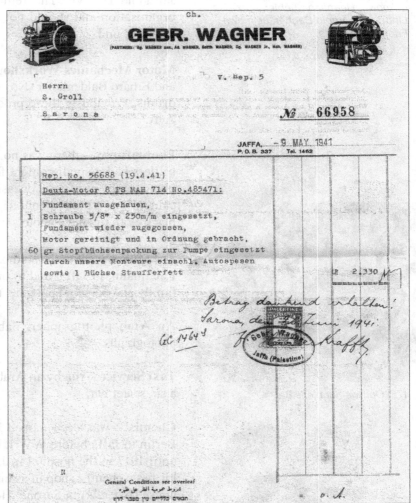

173) Invoice issued by Wagner Bros.

174) Scene of Sarona Brass Band members Wagner's Tavern in Haifa

Standing (left to right) Otto Venus, Waiter, Carl Kuebler, Reinhardt Lippmann, Georg Roller, unknown, Christian Kuebler

Seated: Unknown, Gottlieb Glenk, Carl Baldenhofer, Johannes Weiss, Immanuel Steller, unknown, Karl Steller, unknown, Rudolf Weller, Samuel Weller, unknown, Hermann Kuebler, Fritz Lippmann, Arnold Bacher, unknown, Friedrich Haering

works in Palestine. Over 40 residents (both male and female) from Jaffa/Sarona were employed there in a range of occupations and trades. The total workforce at Wagners was approximately 100 workers comprising Germans, Jews and Arabs. They worked together in harmony and the business experienced no difficulties in regard to this mixture of workers from different ethnic backgrounds.

The company was structured into five divisions—foundry, turning workshop, fitting workshop, patternmaking workshop and auto and motor repair workshop. The company also owned an automotive spare parts shop where replacement parts for motors and cars could be bought.

Banking—in 1924 the Bank der Templegesellschaft (Bank of the Temple Society Ltd.) was established.[271] The Head Office of the Bank was located in Jaffa. A number of Sarona residents worked there. There were other banks—the Barclay Bank and Ottoman Bank in Jaffa and Tel Aviv. The Templer Bank was an entirely independent organisation and should not be confused with the Temple Society Central Fund.

Motor Mechanics Workshop—started in 1934 by Herbert Uhlherr and Erhard Baldenhofer (No. 90). They sold petrol and kerosene from drums. Previously these products had to be bought in Jaffa or Tel Aviv.[272]

Photography—there was no official photographer in Sarona. Many settlers had a small camera for personal use. Otto Venus did some photography at official occasions and as a favour at weddings. The camera was mounted on a tripod and he had to put his head under a black cloth to take a photo.

The settlers went to the studios of professional photographers, such as Rachmann, in Jaffa, and to other photographers in Tel Aviv to have family and personal portraits taken.

An Arab photographer, Sabine, visited Sarona to take official photographs.

Taxi Service—run by an Arab named Said. He lived in Jaffa and had a six seater car.

Chemist—was a Jew named Isidor Mamlok who had migrated from Berlin to Jaffa before WW I. He worked as an assistant to Dr Lorch until 1917 in the hospital in Jaffa as the hospital chemist.[273] He had his basic chemist shop in a small rented building near Georg Weller's house (No. 22a) in Sarona. He rode his bicycle to Sarona every day to work there.

175) Outside Kuebler's Bar

176) Entrance to Kuebler's Bar

Before WW1 Luise Groll had operated a small chemist shop from which she sold and distributed medicines.

Veterinary Services—were provided by a Jew named Faerber who lived in Montefiore, a Jewish settlement established in 1855 not far from Sarona.[274]

Bar/Café—This was built by Christian Kuebler before WW I and was a focal point in Sarona (No. 69b). The bowling alley (Kegelbahn) (No. 87) was part of Kuebler's establishment. Beer, wine and spirits were sold and light meals were served. It was a favourite place for farmers, tradesmen and Wagner employees to meet and socialise. Women usually only went there for wedding receptions or birthday parties. If main course meals were required, they had to be ordered in advance. Several Arabs were employed as waiters.

Blacksmith—Grazes owned and operated the smithy (No. 24). They had established this business before WW I. Here horses were shod, carts and implements repaired.

177) Entrance to Groezinger's butcher and smallgoods shop

Butcher and Smallgoods—Willi Groezinger owned the butcher/ smallgoods shop (No.38a) in Sarona. Some residents bought their meat and smallgoods from Jakob Messerle who owned a butcher shop near the Lorenz Café on the Sarona/Jaffa Road.

Bakery and Pastry Cook—Willy and Erika Guenthner owned and operated the bakery. Bread, rolls and cakes could be bought there.

Cafés—Guenthner's Cafe—a patisserie and coffee restaurant was established in 1934 and was part of Guenthner's bakery. It became very popular with the younger married couples and singles. It had an outside area with tables and chairs set up under trees. Pot plants provided privacy between the tables. There was a small dance floor and music was played through a loud speaker connected to a gramophone. Some evenings the café remained open until midnight for dancing. British, Jewish and German visitors would patronise the Café. On Sundays, yeast rolls (Salzstangen) and apricot cakes (Krapfen) were sold. Guenthners employed a Somalian waiter named Osam.

Guenthners also sold ice cream. Parents would take their children there for a treat—vanilla and chocolate flavoured ice-cream was sold in small waxed cardboard containers and eaten with a small flat wooden spoon.

Lorenz Café—was located on the main road between Walhalla and Jaffa near the new German Consulate. It was a popular place for a cup of coffee when coming home from Jaffa or the beach. Alcoholic beverages were served there as well. The café was renowned for its "Mohrenkoepfe" (black round chocolate covered sponge cakes filled with cream).

It was also the first cinema for the Germans in Jaffa/Sarona.[275]

General Store/Shops—these were owned by Jakob Jung (that shop was known as the "Konsum" and provided mainly grocery lines) (No. 32) whilst Christian Weiss operated a general store (No.01) that sold mainly toys, novelties and sweets. He also sold petrol from a hand operated petrol bowser. These stores were open six days per week and only closed on Sundays.

Joinery/Cabinet Maker—Otto Venus owned the first joinery workshop (No.59) which he started before WWI. Later Hermann Wied started a similar workshop (No. 50). They made doors, windows, shutters, cabinets, furniture and coffins.

178) Lorenz Cafe/Bar on the road to Jaffa.

179) Scene in Venus' joinery workshop.
(l to r) Arnold Bacher, Otto Venus, Fritz
Weiberle

180) Otto Venus invoice heading

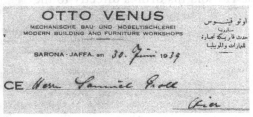

Plumbing—a Jew named Ignaz provided a plumbing service from
Tel Aviv. In the 1930s, Friedrich Haering changed his trade from
patternmaking to plumbing and started a successful plumbing
business in Sarona. (No. 52)

Watchmaker and Jeweller—Edgar Knoll established a watchmaking
and jewellery business on completion of his apprenticeship after he
returned from Germany. It was located in a front room of his parents'
house (No.71b).

Doctors—there were no medical doctors in Sarona. Miss Maria
Weiberle, a nurse, provided some first aid treatment in Sarona. Many
settlers consulted old Dr Lorch and his son-in-law Dr Rubitschung
in Jaffa. Here the doctors ran a small hospital where many children
were born. A German doctor, Dr E. Gmelin, Chief Doctor at the
Diakonissen Hospital in Jerusalem, treated a number of Sarona settlers.

Over the years, the settlers consulted Jewish doctors as well:
Doctors Stein, Bayer and Goldman in Tel Aviv, and Doctor Perter
in Montefiore. A young Jewish doctor, Doctor Kutting, also came to
live in Sarona. He rented, and practised from, a home owned by the
Wine-growers Co-operative.

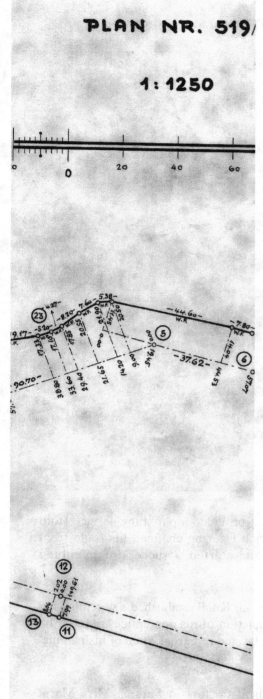

PLAN NR. 519/

1:1250

HE SURVEY EXECUTED BY ME ON DECEM
E POSITION AND BOUNDARIES OF IMMOVA
MED ON THE GROUND.

PAUL FRANK
GEOMETER
LICENSED SURVEYOR
SARONA bei JAFFA

LICENSED SURVEY

In later years a Templer doctor, Dr Alfred Weller practised from Annelies Lippmann's house.

In case of serious illness or surgery the patients were usually taken to Jerusalem. Another option was to go to the Haifa Hospital.

Dentists—There were several Jewish dentists in Tel Aviv: Doctors Stein, Wisowski and Warschavski who were usually visited for any dental problems. In the early 1930s a female Jewish dentist had her practice in Immanuel Knoll's house and later an Arab dentist practiced there. During the war a Jewish dentist, Dr Stein, came to Sarona. He treated the interned settlers next to Mamlok's Chemist shop.

Ophthalmologists—there was a well known Jewish eye doctor, Dr Ticho, as well as Dr Feigenbaum in Jerusalem and Doctors Friedman and Gruen in Tel Aviv.

Footwear—shoes were made and repaired by Andreas Noz. As Tel Aviv grew, a Jew named Schoenberg established a footwear business and sold German Salamander shoes in Tel Aviv. His shop was on the corner of Herzl and Jaffa Streets.

Hairdresser—The hairdresser's name was Tannenbaum. He married into the Templer Community and lived in Jaffa. Erika Kahlow worked as a hairdresser in her home (No 76). During WW II Mrs Elenore Wenz did hairdressing in Sarona.

Messenger Service—Machmud, an Arab boy, was a messenger boy in Sarona. Many businesses had their own Arab messenger boy to run errands and messages. Some of the boys were very adept and carried trays on their heads.

Printing Works—the "Rekord" Printing works were started by Hermann Kuebler and Horst Koeper in the early 1930s. The printing works were located in the old wine cellar (No.18), and printed and produced most printed material for Sarona and the surrounding industries—from wine labels to books. The works provided both employment and apprenticeship training opportunities.

Lemonade Factory—this was owned by Friedrich Orth who made "Gassos" (lemonade—both plain and flavoured) in small glass bottles and soda water in larger bottles. He sold his drinks directly to the public. (No. 42b)

181) Left—Example of a Paul Frank's survey plan

182) Part of the winery was converted to the Rekord printing works

183) Example of label printed by Rekord

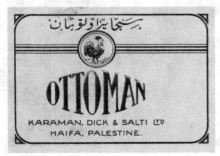

184) Example of label printed by Rekord

Gunsmith—Urban Beck leased a room of his house (No. 79) to a gunsmith from Germany. The gunsmith lived in Tel Aviv and made and repaired shotguns and rifles.

Surveyor—Paul Frank ran his surveying business from his house.

Well Drilling—this was done by Hahns who also did some smaller blacksmithing jobs.

Import and Export—Wilhelm Aberle had an import/export business in Jaffa and Paul Aberle had a similar business in Jerusalem. Through their businesses, many of the imported goods were procured and also exports arranged.

OVERSEAS WORKERS

In some cases workers were recruited from Germany/Austria or employed if they were in Palestine to fill specialist positions in businesses in Jaffa/Sarona. For example, Hermann Hoersch was recruited as cooper for the winery, Franz Messner worked as an electrician at Wagners, Erich Hermann was a specialist gardener at Orth's nursery and Johann Eckstein was a plumber. Wennagels employed Hans

157

185) Printing machine room at Rekord printing works

186) Printing machine room at Rekord printing works

187) Printer examining sheet for quality

188) Printing sample—printing was done in various languages

189) Females were also employed at the printing works

Pisch as a bricklayer and concrete renderer, as well as two top grade German/Hungarian carpenters—Wohmer and Doemler. Horst Koeper from Saxony, Germany, assisted in establishing the printing works. Other Germans and Austrians who had come to Palestine were also employed at times.

ARAB WORKERS

Arab workers provided an estimated 90% of the unskilled labour force for Sarona. Arab women were employed in some homes to provide domestic assistance with house work, laundry or sewing. Some others worked in the fields weeding, hoeing and carrying out other light work, such as harvesting and packing. Many male Arabs were employed in the various agricultural industries as guards and labouring duties, at the printing works, in the building and construction industry, as waiters and general assistants and labourers in most businesses. Seasonal activities had a bearing on the number employed. The Arabs were better paid by the Sarona employers than if they worked for other Arab employers—sometimes they were paid at piece rates, for example at Orth's nursery they were paid, when weeding, by so much per square metre. Often the workers would sleep over at the employers in a shed or outbuilding, or if employed

190) Arab families camped near Sarona

159

191) The Arab workers employed at the Rekord printing works

192) Arab workers often carried goods on their heads

193) Making tiles in the Wieland tile factory

194) An example of beautiful needlework embroidery by Lina Laemmle, 1924

on a building site, at the site. The Arab women would bring them their meals at these locations. Many workers formed life long relationships with the Templers and were loyal and trustworthy.

SHOPPING

There were virtually no shops, as we know them to-day, in Sarona. Most of the food requirements were either home grown or available in Sarona from the producers. Other items could be bought either in shops or at the markets (Suks) in Jaffa and later in the shops of Tel Aviv.

Rolf Breisch had a large shop in Jaffa with an extensive range of goods, including some clothing and giftware.

Original all **clothing,** dresses, trousers, jackets, shirts and underwear was made by the women in Sarona. Nearly every home had a sewing machine and the women were very proficient in sewing and needle work. Clothing patterns could be bought at Breischs in Jaffa. The early sewing machines had to be hand turned, later treadle machines became more popular. Hand knitting was done for a range of garments including socks. Only men's suits were tailor made.

In the 1930s finished dresses became available and could be bought from Jewish shops in Tel Aviv. There was a large department store, named Eckmanns, which sold virtually "everything".

CARS AND MOTOR CYCLES

As in other parts of the world transport and personal mobility changed dramatically after WW I. Initially during the late 1920s

195) Motor car outing during 1930s. Driver Heiner Hasenpflug, middle Marta and Otto Venus, rear?

196) Excursion on motor bikes were very popular with the younger generation—

From left to right: Nelly Glenk (Wied), Karl Wied, Jon Weller, Helene Knoll (Kuebler), Ewald Glenk, Ruth Groll.

197) Left—Car advertisement printed in "Die Warte des Tempels" in 1937

the young men bought motor cycles which remained popular right up to World War II. Many motor cycles had side carriages.

In the 1920s as the economic situation in Sarona improved, cars were purchased. Philipp Groll owned the first car in Sarona. Tragically in 1934, he became the first road fatality when his car overturned on the Jerusalem road and he was badly injured. He died a few weeks later of the injuries he sustained in the accident.

His daughter, Adelheid, was the first female licensed motor car driver in Sarona.

Drivers were licensed for both cars and motor cycles. To obtain a licence, one had to go to the Serail (town hall/city offices) in Jaffa and see a British Police sergeant. Usually there was a considerable wait to see the sergeant. He would then ask to be taken for a short drive after which a licence would be issued. Most youngsters drove motor cycles before they could get their licence and had no problems getting a licence.

Motor cars and motor cycles were given a five yearly "roadworthy check" especially for brake efficiency.

198) Otto Kuebler, proud owner of a new motor bike

199) "Wanderer", a German made motorbike with side car. Seated: Lina Asenstorfer (nee Messerle), son Tony and daughter Charlotte near the Audsche river on the North Beach

Cars and motor cycles had to be imported. Import agents for motor cars included the Faig Brothers—Wanderer, Horch and Audi, Wagner Brothers—Opel, Wieland Bros.—Mercedes Benz.

SPORTING ACTIVITIES

Sporting activities really developed after WW I.

200) Hugo Steller competing at the sportsfest

Sport was part of the school curriculum and children participated in sporting activities. During the 1920s, a **football (soccer)** club was formed in Sarona. The club's colours were a red top with the emblem in the form of a shield on the front and black shorts. This club was extended to include other sports such as **athletics, field sports—discus, shot put and javelin throwing, weight lifting, gymnastics**—both floor and bars and rings. Later **tennis** became popular with both men and ladies and a tennis court (No. 88) was built. The surface was concreted by Wennagels in 1929. The sports club became an important community organisation for younger persons and was named "Deutscher Sportverein Sarona" (DSS)—German Sports Club Sarona.

The teams for the various sports competed against teams from the other Templer settlements and against British military, Police and Jewish teams. Support and barracking for the Sarona team during football games was quite vocal at times. The sporting field was located

201) Athletes from the various competing teams parading at the opening of the sportsfest

163

203) The perpetual Hindenburg trophy was awarded to the winning team

202) The sporting arena in Wilhelma marked out for the annual Sportsfest

adjacent to the new school building where rooms for the DSS had been included in the building.

During the 1930s annual **Sportfests** would be organised among the German Templer settlements. They were held in a different settlement each year. Sportfests were mainly athletic competitions but taken very seriously. Sporting competition between the settlements was strong. In 1935 the British Police participated at the Sportfest. The teams competed for the Hindenburg trophy which was awarded to the most successful team. The build up to, as well as the 1936

204) Assembled athletes at the annual Sportsfest—note the British Union Jack—British teams also competed at these events

LIFE IN SARONA IN THE LATE 1920'S AND 1930'S - CHAPTER SEVEN

Olympic Games in Berlin, Germany may well have given a stimulus to this type of competition. The competing athletes would train many weeks beforehand to ensure peak fitness on competition day. The sports ground was clearly marked out for the various events. The athletes would march onto the sporting arena for an opening ceremony with the settlement emblems. Winners were rewarded with medals and certificates. The winners' certificates were proudly displayed on a wall in the clubrooms of the Sarona Sports Club.

In addition to sporting competition, these sportfests provided a good means of bringing people from the various Templer settlements together for social interaction. Contact on a day to day basis especially between the southern and northern settlements was generally limited by distance.

Swimming, although not done on a competitive basis, was very popular. Most primary producers had above ground concrete water storage tanks. These were usually about 1.2-1.5metres deep and several metres long and wide. Lippmann's had the biggest water storage tank—approximately 20m x 20m. It was shallow at one end and deeper at the other where the outlet was. There was an underwater ledge around the pool (No. 47).

At the start of summer, the tank was cleaned and scrubbed and prepared for swimming. Goldfish were kept in the tank—these had to be caught and put into another smaller tank whenever the big water storage tank was emptied. Lippmanns was a popular meeting place

205) Badge of the German Sports Club of Sarona (Deutscher Sportsverein Sarona)

206) Membership card for the German Sports Club of Sarona

![DSS] DEUTSCHER SPORTVEREIN SARONA

MITGLIEDSKARTE № 49.

für Frl. Luise Irmg.

aktiv / passiv

DEUTSCHER SPORTVEREIN SARONA

207) Swimming in Lippmann's water storage was a great summer pastime for old and young.

Back row (left to right): Ewald Glenk, Heinrich Wurst, Rudi Kuebler

Front row: Unknown in water, unknown, Hugo Steller, unknown, Otto Laemmle, Oskar Groll

165

in summer to go swimming and nearly all children learnt to swim there. There was no "dressing room" only some adjacent trees and an orange grove where one would change—boys one side and girls the other! Later a shed (a large wooden shipping crate) was placed near the pool and used by the girls to change.

There was one tragedy at Lippmann's tank when Fritz Werner Kuebler, an 18 month old toddler, drowned in June 1932.

Before WWI some **hunting** was done around Sarona by a few of the settlers. The hunting tradition continued after the war. One street in Sarona was locally known as the Jaeger Strasse (Hunter Street) because most of the hunters lived there! The British introduced hunting licences and declared hunting seasons. All firearms had to be registered. The game hunted included foxes, hares, ducks, quail, woodcock, chukka partridge and pigeon. The game birds were hunted in autumn and winter as they migrated through Palestine from Europe to the Middle East and Asia. There were times when gazelles were hunted and even wild pigs, but not in the Sarona area. Goats were not hunted. In the early years, people rode to their hunting grounds on horseback, or walked. Later, they had to go up to 20 or 30 kilometres further away from Sarona, using motor cycles or cars (Hasenpflug had a car and often drove hunters to the hunting areas). On occasion, a taxi was hired. Hunting guns and ammunition were imported from Germany.

Most of the sporting activities were male oriented. The ladies, however, did have regular gymnastic activities—mainly floor type exercises using hoops and balls. Thea Frank conducted these gymnastic exercises for the ladies. Some ladies played tennis socially. At one stage a small number of young ladies started an athletics group.

Social and Other Activities

Any entertainment or social activities had to be organised amongst the settlers themselves. There was a range of activities some on a regular basis whilst others were ad hoc. The following activities provide some insight into the extent of social and other entertainment activities available in Sarona.

The **Dankfest** (Thanksgiving) was held in October/November each year. It was both an important religious event as well as a social festival for the Sarona community.

A religious service was usually held in the morning, followed by a community get-to-gether in the afternoon in the Sarona "Waeldle" (treed area). On Thanksgiving Day, the brass band would play on a raised platform at the foot of the water tower. Many items of local

208) Youngsters at Lippmann's water storage

209) Hugo Wennagel out hunting

*210) The Sarona Band and friends at a
May picnic*

211) Relaxing at a May picnic

212) Happy get-together at an outing

213) Male choir performing in the M'Lebbes "Waeldle" at a May picnic

Left to right: Gottlieb Glenk, Ludwig Ehnis, Otto Venus, Paul Frank, Karl Steller, Carl Kuebler, unknown, Georg Roller, unknown, Oskar Groll, Imanuel Steller, Helmut Bacher, Hermann Kuebler, Friedrich Orth, Heinrich Steller, unknown, Georg Weller, Friedrich Haering, unknown, Walter Jung, Walter Kuebler, Eugen Steller, Arnold Bacher

agricultural produce would be displayed. Large cooking vessels were used to cook sausages (Saitenwuerstle) which were served with potato salad. In the earlier years roasts were sometimes cooked and served as the evening meal. This ceased as the community expanded. Local wine was served and consumed. Trestle tables were set up for people to sit at, eat their meal and enjoy each others company. Music was provided by the band, the choirs sang, poems or verses were recited and sometimes a play was performed. It was a tradition which had been carried forward since the very early years of Sarona.[276]

The **Mai Ausflug** (May picnic) was another traditional annual event that commenced in Sarona in 1875. The picnics were held at various locations near Sarona. In 1883 the picnic was held in Rishon-le-Zion, a Jewish settlement.[277]

The tradition of Mai Ausflug continued into the thirties, when it ceased. It was always held early in May. The Templers of Sarona, Jaffa and Wilhelma would all meet at Latrun, approximately 20-25 kilometres from Sarona off the Jaffa/Jerusalem road or in the "M'Lebbeser Waeldle", a wooded area towards Wilhelma. The families went there by horse and cart, some went by motor car, and an open air picnic was held. Families took their own food and drink to the picnic. It was a fun day—with bands playing, choirs, singing, tug-o-war, bag races, egg and spoon races etc.

There were two **ladies' auxiliaries** (Frauenverein) in Sarona—one for older ladies and another for younger women. The auxiliaries provided a social facility for the ladies to get together and socialise. They would meet at the community house and usually do needlework, knitting, crocheting etc.

214) An example of some beautiful fine
lace work made by the Ladies auxiliary

The Ladies Auxiliary would organise an "Unterhaltungs Abend" (entertainment night) at least once a year. A play would be performed, songs sung and jokes told—good entertainment!

In the evenings or on weekends the men would meet for a **Medschles** (Arabic, meaning a convivial get-together) at Kuebler's Bar. There they would enjoy a beer, a wine or an arak (aniseed based spirit—ouzo) with some olives and roasted peanuts or pumpkin seeds (bisser) whilst talking about the day's experiences and problems.[278]

The **beaches** were a favourite place for the settlers of Sarona. There were two beaches the **Nordstrand** (North Beach), that is north of Jaffa near the mouth of the Audsche River, and the **Suedstrand** (South Beach) just south of the old city of Jaffa.

The Nordstrand was readily accessible as it was only a few kilometres from Sarona. It was very popular for outings and bathing. After swimming in the sea, one could go to the Audsche River and wash off the seawater salt with fresh water. People went there by horse and cart, in the early days on horse back (ladies rode side saddle), bicycle, motor bike and motor car. Often people would take a picnic lunch with them. Some snacks and drinks could be bought from the Arabs there. Even persons from the Wilhelma settlement came by horse and cart to visit. Some Sarona settlers rented a small house or built shades (arische) on the beach. In later years as Tel Aviv grew, there were some large multi-story buildings on the beach front. There

215) Sewing class for young women
From left to right: Rosa Graze, Ida Lange,
Maria Weiss, Irma Graze

216) Relaxing at a picnic outing about 1930

Left to right: Bernhard Blaich, Hildegard Jung, Friedricke Blaich (nee Jung), Wilhelm Groll, Hulda Haering, Hulda Wurster (nee Sickinger), Irene Blaich (nee Haering), Elsa Groll (nee Jung), Luise Jung and Friedrich Haering

217) The Sarona brass band

Back row (left to right): Friedrich Haering, Otto Venus, Fritz Lippmann, Hermann Kuebler, Carl Kuebler, Arnold Bacher

Middle row: Christian Kuebler, Georg Roller, Samuel Weller, Reinhardt Lippmann, Imanuel Steller, Gottlieb Glenk, Karl Steller

Front row: Wilhelm Groll, Friedrich Orth, Rudolf Weller

218) Reinhardt Lippmann (mayor) with his family enjoying a Sunday afternoon at home

Left to right: Hertha, Edith, Father Reinhardt, Auguste, Fritz, Johanna, Mother Caroline with baby Elly and Paula

219) A pleasant afternoon at Kuebler's Cake/Bar outdoor courtyard

220) Typical shade shelter built on the beach

221) Sarona bathing beauties!

were shops and cafes on the ground floor for refreshments and deck chairs could be hired on the beach. Arabs would come to the beach and sell drinks, icy poles and water melons.

The Suedstrand was the first beach cove south of Jaffa—it was a beautiful beach. It was twenty minutes by bus from Sarona. One had to catch the regular bus to Tel Aviv and then another one to the beach. It was another popular place to go. People also went there by horse and cart, motor cycle and by car. Sarona families would sometimes rent a house there over the summer holidays.

There were no shops at the Suedstrand and one couldn't even buy water.

Children loved the Suedstrand—there was a wadeable rocky area with rock pools, or one could swim to a very small rocky "island" at low tide. Some children had small paddle boats.

During the summer months some shades were erected on the beach. An Arab "life guard" named Sliman would spend days on the beach to watch for swimmers caught in the undertow and rescue them with his paddle boat.

222) Young ladies beach picnic

223) The "Adamsfelsen" (Adam's Rock) on the Suedstrand—a popular destination to swim to. Other natural features on the beach were the "Insele" (little island) and the "Ei des Kolombus" (Egg of Colombus)

Gisela Hoffmann in her paper *South Beach Idyll* recalls a typical day during the school holidays in the late 1930s when her family stayed at the Suedstrand. She writes:—"*Early in the morning, already in our bathing costumes and with a beach towel across our shoulders, we and the neighbours' children trudged across the still cool sand along the path to the beach, on our left between small sand dunes past rows of Arab boats, called Maonen, and on our right the "Villa South Beach", and down the hill. We always went barefoot because the sand was deep and sandals or sand-shoes were an impediment to walking.*

Having reached the beach, we deposited our belongings under a canvas awning with Sliman. [. . .]Sliman was the Arab lookout and life-guard who knew and tolerated all of us. He was a trustworthy person who, whenever someone was in difficulties would set out on a rescue mission in his paddleboat.[. . .]

The wonderful, mild, blue sea was usually as smooth as glass, and on days like that we would cross the first shallow, a safe stretch of water more or less surrounded by coral reefs on two sides and protected from the open sea. From the coral reefs we then went to the next rock—which we called the "Egg of Columbus". That was the first stretch where we had to swim through deep water and then we scrambled up the rock to catch our breaths. After that, the challenge was to dive to the bottom and to prove that one had reached the bottom you had to come up with a handful of sand.[. . .]

The next goal was a larger rock, the "Insele" (island) as it was christened. Only the strongest swimmers would attempt it. It took a lot of stamina to swim to the "Insele". From the "Insele" we swam back to the shore because by that time it was nearly midday. The sun was high and hot and the waves started to get choppy from rising wind [. . .] Then it was back home by the shortest route, more hopping than walking across the hot burning sand.

We protected ourselves against sunburn with Nivea cream, but had no notion of putting on hats. [. . .]

In the afternoons we met other children[. . .] and played ball games and whatever other games were popular at the time.[. . .]

In late summer we sometimes had the chance to pick the fabulously scented white beach lilies, which flowered on the dunes near the steep cliffs. However, the scent was so strong and cloyingly sweet, that most grown-ups complained of headaches and did not like the flowers in their vicinity."[279]

The **hills** towards Jerusalem were not very popular for outings. People went there to hunt or to pick wildflowers in springtime. Bunches of poppies, cyclamen, corn-flowers and anemones were picked. When it snowed in the winter of 1937, the school children went on a hastily arranged excursion. It was the first time that many children from Sarona had seen snow.

The **Audsche River** provided several places of interest for the settlers. Its mouth near the Nordstrand (see above), the Audsche Mill or "Ras-el-Ain", the spring at its source near the hills.

The mill was a popular place for picnic outings and swimming. It was located approximately five kilometres north of Sarona near the only bridge across the Audsche. The mill comprised several buildings and some of the water was diverted to turn the millstones. The farmers were able to have their grain crops ground there. It was safe for fresh water swimming, without the danger of catching Bilharzia, a disease transmitted by tiny snails.

Donkey rides (Eselritt) were popular with the younger persons. A number of settlers owned donkeys or mules, and outings were organised by riding the donkeys to and from Sarona. Sometimes the outing would go to the old ruins of Antipatris near Wilhelma.

Bicycle Outings—during the 1920s it was popular to have bicycle outings. Everyone with a bicycle would join in and ride to a destination such as the North Beach. Later similar trips were organised by

224) The Audsche Mill—a popular place for an outing

225) Donkey ride on the beach. From left to right: Hildegard Jung, Erna Graze, Ella Groezinger

226) The Sarona Bicycle Club—men, women and children all participated

*227) Immanuel Knoll family
outing on bicycles
From left to right: Meta, Werner, Edgar,
Immanuel and Bertha Knoll*

the younger people with **motor cycles.** Pillion passengers were taken on the motor cycle trips.

Children continued to own bikes and bicycle outings were organised for the youngsters.

Excursions and trips were organised to a variety of locations— including the Dead Sea, Jerusalem and Beirut. In the early 1930s, a tour by train was organised to Helouan and Cairo in Egypt. Buses were hired on these occasions and many people from Sarona participated in these excursions.

A number of Sarona residents attended irregular **horse race meetings.** They were held in the cooler part of the year. The races were

228) Family outing with horse and cart

229) Horse racing at Sarafand

run by the Arabs and British at Sarafand on the sandy plains near Ramleh and Lydda. There was no proper race course and the horses would race over a straight stretch. On several occasions, horses from the German settlements won races there. Horses were mainly entered for racing by the British military and police force, or by prominent Arab and Jewish owners. There were Arab bookmakers at the "course" and one could have a bet.

As conditions improved in post WW I Sarona, **travel to Europe,** mainly Germany, became quite popular. Many Sarona families had relatives and friends in Germany whom they visited, others went there on their honeymoons. In 1936, a number of people travelled to the Olympic Games in Berlin. Other families visited relatives who were still in the former German colony of German East Africa. The tours were usually organised by and booked through Reiseagentur W. Fast, Jerusalem (travel agent), who had established a travel agency in Jerusalem after World War I. Travel to Europe was by ship, usually with the Lloyd Triestino Line, from Jaffa to Trieste or Genoa in Italy, and then by train to Germany. The German Levant Line had ships which went to Hamburg in Germany.

Kegeln (skittles)—playing skittles was more a social aspect of life than a sporting activity. The bowling alley was owned by Christian Kuebler and located at his bar. Built before WW I, it was in the open, with only the pin area being covered. After the war it was fully enclosed. Men would meet there and enjoy a game of skittles and social get-togethers. One had to pay to bowl and the pins were set up by boys—either youngsters from the settlement or Arab boys (Kegelbuben).

230) The old open air Kegel (skittle) alley at Kuebler's bar. It was enclosed during the 1930s

231) Program cover for a concert by the mixed choir of Sarona

232) Program of concert. Note last line "Rauchen verboten" (smoking prohibited)

The ladies would bowl on Sunday afternoons and on social occasions.

The traditional **brass band** was an institution in Sarona. It played at community occasions, at the Dankfest and sometimes at funerals and weddings.

A **mixed choir and a male choir** were other aspects of community life. They practised regularly and sang at church services, weddings, the Dankfest, and other community celebrations. The male choir was invited by Pater Mueller, to sing at the Emmaus monastery in the hills near Jerusalem on several occasions. The choir was usually accompanied by family and friends from Sarona whenever they went there.

A **concert** held in Sarona on 23 June 1935 is described as: *"In the evening[. . .]the second concert of the mixed choir of Sarona/Jaffa was held in the community hall. Mr Eugen Neun was the conductor. As well as the numbers sung by the choir, the program included performances by Mrs Irmgard Neun-Eyth (soprano), Mr Alfred Hoenig, the Wilhelma brass band, the Eppinger Music Quartet and the male choir from Sarona. Misses Linda Eppinger and Liselotte Wagner accompanied the choir on the piano or harmonium. The program included excerpts from operas and items by Schubert, Lortzing and Offenbach."* The description mentions the high quality of the performances.[280]

Once or twice a year **plays or dramas** would be performed at the community hall. The sets were very basic and simple. Humorous "Schwaebische Auffuehrungen" (Swabian plays) were very popular at weddings.

As the economic well-being of the Sarona settlers improved, they would sometimes **eat out** in cafés or restaurants in Jaffa or Tel Aviv.

During the 1930s, they could go to Tel Aviv to **watch films** at the movie theatre. German films were also shown at times in an outdoor setting at the Lorenz Café. People would sit at tables in the courtyard of the café and films would be projected on to a screen.

Dancing first came to the attention of the Sarona community in World War I when German Army officers were astounded that there were no women in Sarona who could dance. Reinhardt Lippmann arranged for some dancing lessons and his daughters had to play the piano to provide the music.

233) Left—Actors in a typical Swabian stage play

234) Cover of dancing school graduation dance program

I. Teil. (3⁰⁰h — 6³⁰h)	II. Teil. (7¹⁵h — 10⁵⁰h)
Polonaise mit Walzer	One-step
Rheinländer (Damenwahl)	Pas de quatre (Damenwahl)
Française mit Walzer	
	Klopfwalzer
Kettenwalzer	Française mit Boston
Boston	(Damenwahl)
Berliner Rheinländer	Walzer (Elterntour)
Klopfwalzer	Neckwalzer
Lanciers mit One step	Kreuzpolka
Boston (Damenwahl)	One-step (Damenwahl)
Walzer (Elterntour)	Blumenwalzer
	One-step-Galopp!
³/₄stündige Pause.	„Schlusswalzer"

235) Inside of dancing school program

LIFE IN SARONA IN THE LATE 1920'S AND 1930'S -
CHAPTER SEVEN

Dancing came into vogue during the 1920s. At first it was "frowned" upon by the older settlers. The dances were held initially in the community hall with gramophones providing the music. Sometimes, problems arose when young persons wanted to organise a dance and had to pick up the key for the hall from the mayor who would refuse permission. This problem was overcome when the new school and community complex was built in which the young people had their own rooms.

Dancing was taught at no cost by Fritz and Hertha Lippmann, Rudolf Weller, Erhard and Ilse Baldenhofer and later by Friedrich Haering. In Jaffa Mrs Wieland, as well as the nephew of the Spanish Consul and a Jew taught dancing. Curiosity got the better of some of the older settlers who could be observed peering through the windows to see who was dancing with whom. Similarly, some of the Arab workers were seen to watch what was happening at the dances—it was something the Muslim religion did not allow.

Some traditional German folk dancing was done. The girls would dress up in appropriate Trachten (costumes) and were taught by Paula Hahn.

During the 1930s, dancing became a regular social activity within the Sarona community, especially in conjunction with other social activities or get-togethers. It was now encouraged as it provided a form of entertainment for the younger generation.

Visits to Jaffa **by German ships** provided an opportunity for the captain and crew to be invited to the settlement and enjoy some local hospitality, usually at Kuebler's Bar. The crews were amazed to see so much German culture in a foreign land. In the evenings, the ship's band would often put on a concert or play some dance music, much to the enjoyment of the settlers. The school children were often invited to visit the German ships.

Children's activities and games included marbles, hop-scotch, a stick game, poison ball (Voelkerball), a form of baseball (Schlagball) and hide-and-seek. Older children played tennis and soccer. Kite flying was undertaken at times.

Toys were often handmade. Some toys could be bought at Breisch's store in Jaffa—Japanese tin cars, yo-yos, teddy bears, dolls, metal meccano sets etc. These toys were treasured and looked after by the children.

236) Folk dancing—Erna Graze and Ella Groezinger

In the 1920s, a **Circus** would sometimes come to Jaffa. This was always a welcome form of entertainment and many settlers and their children would go to the circus.

In the 1930s, an **Arab with a bear** visited Sarona on an irregular basis. He would set up in an area and play music whilst his bear would dance. A small contribution had to be paid to watch the performance. It was a popular show for children.

In 1929 and 1931, the **"Graf Zeppelin"** airship flew over Sarona. Both times this was a big event for the German settlers. Many gathered at the water tower awaiting its arrival. When it was sighted, there was great excitement and the call quickly went out "Der Zeppelin kommt" (The Zeppelin is coming). People were amazed how quietly the airship passed overhead and described it as "a beautiful sight".

237) The Zeppelin over Sarona

CHAPTER EIGHT

RELIGIOUS AND FAMILY SERVICES

(The details of the following chapter are mainly based on personal interviews conducted with persons who lived and grew up in Sarona. In other instances individuals sent letters or other written material of their recollections and experiences in Sarona. Care was taken so that the information provided by one individual was wherever possible corroborated by someone else. A copy of the notes of the interviews, other printed material and in some cases tape recordings was given to the Temple Society of Australia Archives by M Haering and H Glenk.)

RELIGIOUS SERVICES (SAAL) were held on Sunday mornings. People would dress in their "Sunday best" and go to "Saal". The community bell would be rung at 9.45 am for several minutes summoning the settlers to the service which started at 10.00 am. The services were conducted by a community Elder, who was appointed by the Templer Central Council. At the annual Dankfest service new born infants were presented to the community. Children in their early teens were confirmed. There was a confirmation service every two years. At these occasions, the religious services were shortened and confirmation lessons were held for the confirmands after the service. If they wished, the members of the congregation could stay on for the lessons. Occasionally, the Tempelvorsteher (President of the Temple Society) Christian Rohrer (1860-1934) from Jerusalem would visit and conduct a service. In later years, Johannes Weiss from Sarona conducted the services.

Kinderlehre (Sunday school) was held for children each Sunday before the main church service. Mr Johannes Frank usually conducted Sunday school, as well as the Saal.

238) Christian Rohrer and his wife Anna (nee Eppinger). Mr Rohrer was President of the Temple Society from 1911 to 1934 and conducted religious services in Sarona from time to time

World War I memorial in the Sarona cemetery (background)

239) Sarona/Jaffa Confirmation group 1929

Back row (left to right): Kurt Kuebler, Heinrich Wurst, Otto Kuebler, Fritz Sickinger, John Weller, Walter Weller, Hans Roller

Middle row: Hedwig Aberle (Wennagel), Elfriede Noz (Bechert), Helene Knoll (Kuebler), Martha Messerle, Annelies Baldenhofer (Trefz), Johanna Baldenhofer, Nelly Glenk (Wied)

Front row: Ilse Gollmer, Erika Kahlow, Ruth Groll, Johannes Frank, Elder, Lina Laemmle, Hugo Steller, Frieder Bulach

Weddings were always an important and big occasion in Sarona. The couple's engagement was always announced at the Sunday service.

In the old days the whole Sarona community was invited to the wedding. Later, as Sarona grew into a larger community, only family and friends were invited. The invitations were done on a personal basis when the engaged couple visited their guests and invited them to their wedding.

The bride and groom had to go to the German Consulate in Jaffa and later to the new Consulate in Walhalla for a civil marriage. There the marriage was registered and a certificate issued. If either of the couple was from overseas, they had to prove their bona fides before the marriage was approved.

The religious wedding service was usually held in the old community house (Saeulensaal), followed by the wedding celebration in the new community house where the large hall was appropriately decorated and tables and chairs set up.

The traditional food served at weddings was "Saitenwuerstle" (frankfurter type sausages) with potato salad, followed by coffee and cakes. The food was served by the girls from the community and the drinks by the boys. For entertainment during the wedding celebration choirs

240) Above—View inside the community hall during a religious service

241) Below—Wedding of Johannes Weiss and Pauline Weller

242) Hermann and Olga Hoersch leaving the community hall after their wedding ceremony

243) 1907 Wedding invitation to the Sarona community. In the early days the whole community would be invited to the wedding

sang, some guests, especially children, would recite rhymes or poems; and often a witty Swabian play would be performed.

During the 1930s, some wedding receptions were held at Christian Kuebler's tavern or at Guenthner's café. Sometimes a wedding reception was held in the home of the bride's parents.

Before WW I, practically all marriages were between Templer settlers not only from Sarona but from other settlements as well. During the 1920s and 1930s, as more and more of the young males went to Germany to study or for technical training, or alternatively some young Germans came to Palestine, marriages occurred with one partner being a non-Templer. These non-Templers, colloquially known as "Deutschlaender" (German lady or gentleman) or "Reingeschmeckte" (interlopers), were often regarded with a degree of suspicion within the local community before they were fully accepted.

244) Right—Engagement notice

245) Wedding of Eugen Steller and Elly Lippmann, 19 March 1931, Sarona

246) Large wedding procession in 1920s. Often the whole community was invited

247) Marriage certificate issued by the German Consulate

Ausfertigung.

Nachstehende Verhandlung, welche Blatt 23 Band III des bei dem Kaiserlich Deutschen Konsulate zu Jaffa in Gemäßheit des Gesetzes vom 4. Mai 1870 geführten Registers über Geburten eingetragen ist und welche wörtlich, wie folgt, lautet:

№ 4.

Verhandelt zu Jaffa, den achtzehnten Mai neunzehnhundertsechzehn.

Vor mir, dem unterzeichneten Beamten, erschienen heute im Amtslokale, bekannt und verfügungsfähig:

Der württembergische Staatsangehörige, Landwirt Samuel Groll,

wohnhaft in Sarona bei Jaffa,

welcher mir

erklärte,

daß ihm am neunzehnten April neunzehnhundertsechzehn, um zehn einhalb Uhr vormittags von seiner Ehefrau, der auch früher württembergischen Staatsangehörigen Emilie, geborenen Schillinger, wohnhaft in Sarona in seiner Wohnung zu Sarona,

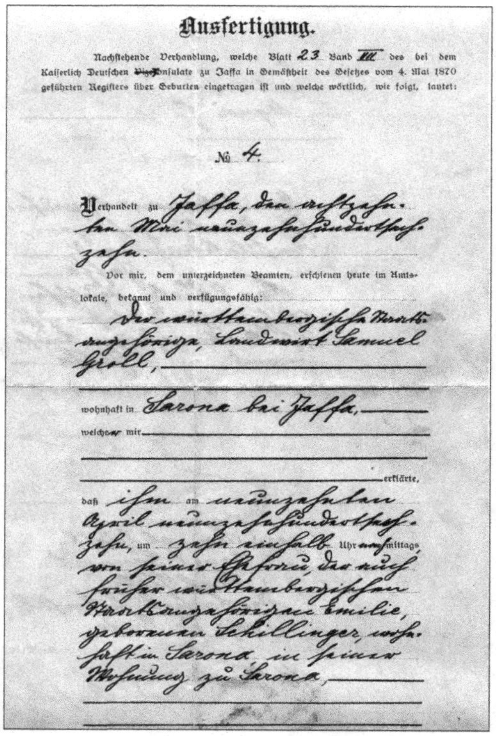

248) Extract of the marriage register of the Sarona Templer community

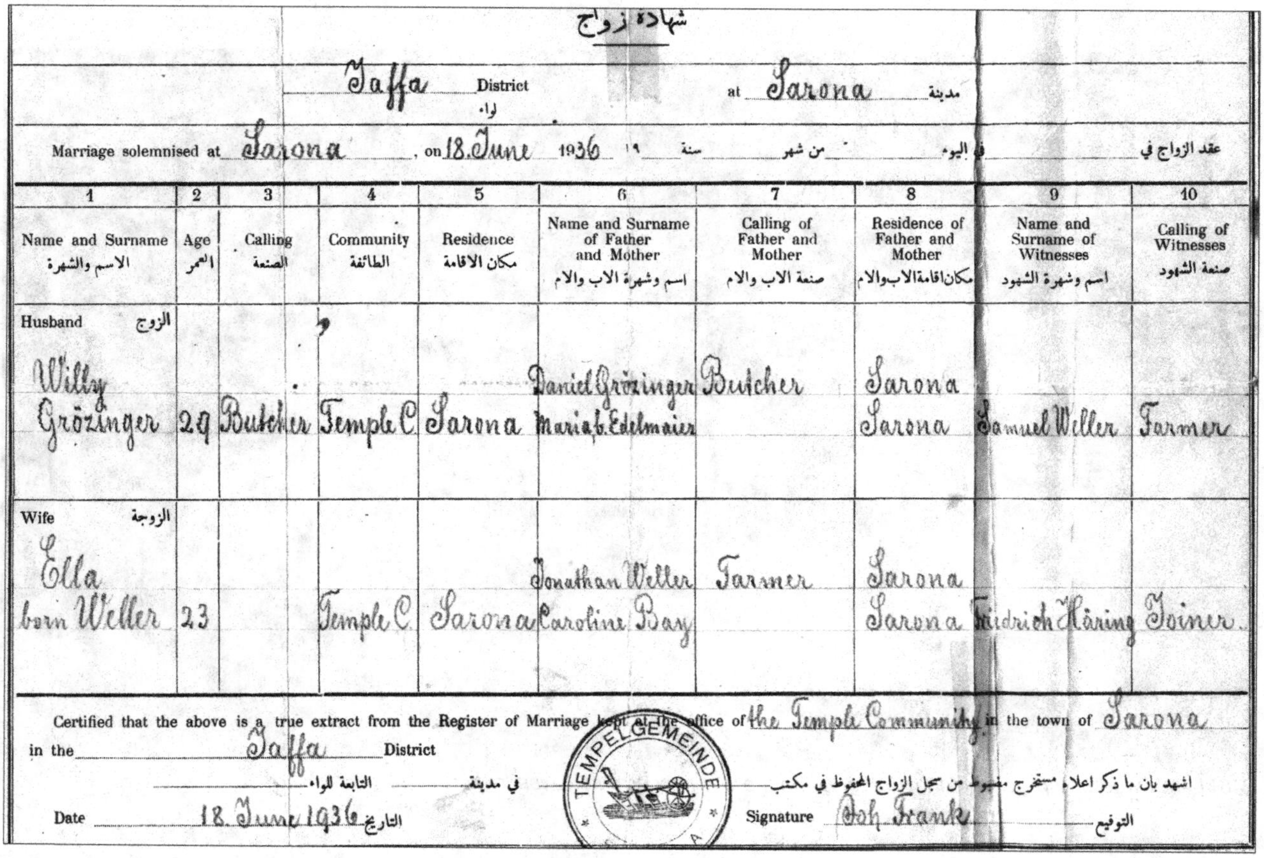

شهادة زواج

Jaffa District لواء at Sarona مدينة

Marriage solemnised at Sarona, on 18. June 1936 ١٩ سنة من شهر في اليوم عقد الزواج في

1	2	3	4	5	6	7	8	9	10
Name and Surname الاسم والشهرة	Age العمر	Calling الصنعة	Community الطائفة	Residence مكان الاقامة	Name and Surname of Father and Mother اسم وشهرة الاب والام	Calling of Father and Mother صنعة الاب والام	Residence of Father and Mother مكان اقامة الاب والام	Name and Surname of Witnesses اسم وشهرة الشهود	Calling of Witnesses صنعة الشهود
Husband الزوج Willy Grözinger	29	Butcher	Temple C.	Sarona	Daniel Grözinger Maria b. Edelmaier	Butcher	Sarona Sarona	Samuel Weller	Farmer
Wife الزوجة Ella born Weller	23		Temple C.	Sarona	Jonathan Weller Caroline Bay	Farmer	Sarona Sarona	Friedrich Häring	Joiner

Certified that the above is a true extract from the Register of Marriage kept at the office of the Temple Community in the town of Sarona in the Jaffa District

اشهد بان ما ذكر اعلاه مستخرج مضبوط من سجل الزواج المحفوظ في مكتب في مدينة التابعة للواء

Date 18. June 1936 التاريخ Signature Joh. Frank التوقيع

TEMPELGEMEINDE

Losungskalender der Tempelgesellschaft für das Jahr 1936

Siebenter Jahrgang der Bibelabschnitte zum täglichen Gebrauch nach den neu durchgesehenen Tabellen von Chr. Hoffmann

249) Biblical text calender (table of lessons) for the Temple Society in 1936

Todesanzeige.

Allen Verwandten, Freunden und Bekannten geben wir die schmerzliche Nachricht, daß unsere liebe, treubesorgte Mutter, Großmutter und Schwiegermutter

Frau Maria Kübler
geb. Weeber

am 25. März d. J. im Alter von nahezu 76 Jahren in die Ewige Heimat abberufen wurde.

Wir danken auf diesem Wege Allen für die herzliche Teilnahme, sowie für die vielen Blumenspenden bei der Beerdigung unserer lieben Mutter.

In tiefer Trauer:
Familie Chr. Kübler,
Klara Kübler,
Albert Kübler,
Familie Ernst Kübler,
Walter Kübler.

Sarona bei Jaffa,
26. März 1938.

250) Death notices were published in the Templer Sentinel (Warte)

Funerals were a time of sadness amongst the tightly knit community of Sarona. There was no undertaker in Sarona. Whenever a bereavement occurred, the community would be notified by a written notice being circulated. A death notice was also placed in the Warte (Sentinel newspaper) for notification to the wider Templer community.

The corpse was kept at home, usually moved to a cool area in the house and covered with a sheet, until the funeral service was held—usually within 24-48 hours of death. A coffin was made at the Venus joinery or by Dosters in Jaffa, and often lined with palm fronds. An Arab worker was employed to dig the grave in the cemetery. The coffin was draped in black cloth and taken from the home of the deceased, or from the Jaffa Hospital if the person had died there, to the cemetery on a two-horse-carriage, owned by the Streckers in Walhalla. The mourners would gather there and an Elder would conduct a graveside service. The community bell would be tolled at 10 second intervals until the cortege had left the confines of the Sarona settlement and entered the cemetery. After the service, the settlers would return home or go back to work. Many graves did not have headstones. If a headstone was placed on the grave, it would be ordered from and made by Josef and Hugo Wennagel. Hugo Wennagel described how the name and details of the deceased were first carefully

251) View of Sarona cemetery with World War I memorial

252) A list of the fallen in WW I

PAUL REINHARDT		ALFRED WOLFER	
HANS FABER		HERMANN EPPINGER	
KARL WAGNER		PETER von USTINOW	
PHILIPP WAGNER		HUGO WIELAND	
JOH. WENNAGEL		DANIEL GROZINGER	
WILHELM UHLHERR		JOH. LAMMLE	
JOH. BALDENHOFER		WILHELM SPOHN	
SAMUEL SCHEERLE		FRIEDRICH JUNG	
CHRISTIAN ORTH		WILLY FABER	
GEORG KAPPUS		HERMANN UHLHERR	
SAMUEL SICKINGER		PAUL GUNTHNER	
THEODOR WAGNER		JAKOB MAYER	

chiselled into the concrete slab and then the chiselled out lettering filled with molten lead. After the lead had cooled the surface was smoothed.

253) War memorial with wreaths on Remembrance Day

254) Floral wreaths for laying in the cemetery

The Sarona **Cemetery** was located 1-2 kilometres from the settlement near the "Model Farm" and not far from the electricity works. The cemetery had been established in the early 1890s in conjunction with the Templer Jaffa community. The first cemetery used by the early Sarona settlers was at "Mount Hope", a foundation of the Steinbeck family[281]. A cemetery was later established by the community in the 1870s near the Roehmshof. That cemetery was used until the 1890s when the main Sarona/Jaffa cemetery was developed just outside the Sarona settlement. The human remains of the early graves were transferred from the "old" cemetery to the Sarona cemetery during WW I.

The cemetery was enclosed with a barbed wire fence and cypress trees. It had a locked gate and the very large key was kept at Guenthners. The graves were cared for by the family or by volunteers if the deceased had no immediate family. Girls would sometimes be sent to tend the graves of their relatives.

191

255) Community hall decorated for Rembrance Day Service

A service was held each year to mark **"Heldengedenktag" (Remembrance Day).** Families, relatives and members of the community would gather at the war memorial in the Sarona cemetery. Garlands were made and draped over the memorial and wreaths were also laid there to commemorate the fallen of World War I. On some occasions a divine service was conducted in the community house.

Christmas was a time of joyous celebration. It was celebrated at home as a family occasion on Christmas Eve. People used local cypress trees or bought imported spruce trees for Christmas. These were decorated and the candles were lit on Christmas Eve. Christmas carols were sung and presents given. Everyone baked their own Christmas "Gutsle" (cookies), usually at home, although some families baked their cookies and bread in the community oven. It was customary to give Christmas cookies to the Arab workers and helpers. On Christmas Day a religious service was held and relatives were visited.

At the Christmas service all school children would be involved in singing carols on stage, reciting poems or performing in a nativity play. A big Christmas tree was erected in the community hall to provide a festive atmosphere. After the service, "Father Christmas" appeared and each child was given a small gift and some Christmas cookies.

Easter—At Easter time, there was a religious service on Good Friday. Eggs were hard boiled and dyed in various colours. On Easter Sunday, the eggs were hidden in the garden around the homes and the children would then search for them. Often the families would visit relatives and the children were able to look for more eggs there. The loyal Arab house workers would also be given coloured Easter eggs.

Children's birthday parties were held in the homes of the children. Friends were invited—girls only at girls' parties and boys only at boys' parties. Mothers would bake birthday cakes and lemonade from Friedrich Orth's factory would be served. Small presents, often home-made items, would be given as gifts. At the parties children played party games.

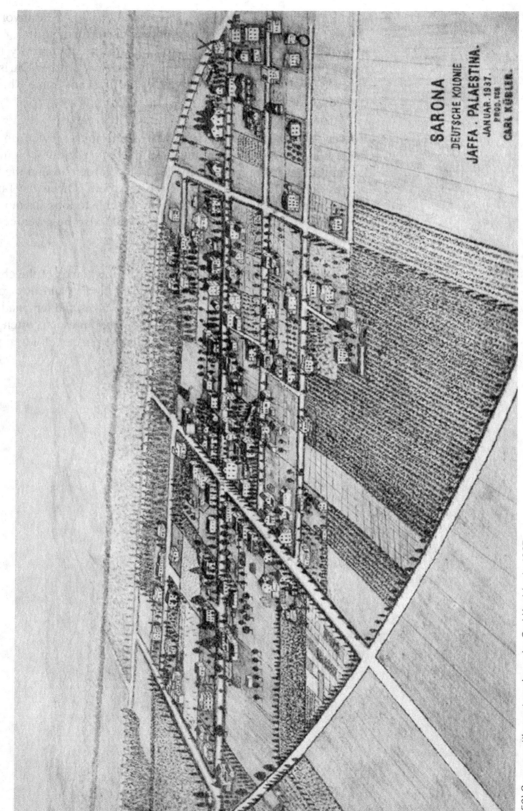

SARONA
DEUTSCHE KOLONIE
JAFFA . PALAESTINA.
JANUAR. 1937.
PROD.026
CARL KUEBLER.

256) Sarona settlement as drawn by Carl Kuebler in 1937

CHAPTER NINE

Special Characters

As in all communities, there were some special individuals from outside the Templer community in Sarona who nevertheless were known to all Saronians. They were real characters and well liked by the local community. They included:—

Dahar, an Arab who rode his small donkey from a bakery in Jaffa every Saturday afternoon. He was employed there by a German baker named Kaiser. He brought pretzels and other homemade cakes for sale in two wooden chests tied to the donkey's saddle. He was often teased by the children of Sarona who would call out:

> "Fauler Dahar, schlag 'naus
> Esele schlag 'naus
> Esele scheisst 'naus
> Ich sags 'em Vater, Steckele"

A broad translation of this saying is "Lazy Dahar, kick out, the donkey will kick out, the donkey will "poop", I'll tell father, little stick!"

The Schacherjud (the bartering Jew) was a tall man who went from house to house selling mainly dress cloth material. One always haggled with him before buying anything. When haggling, he would say "Madam, es ist 'geschinkt'". (Madam, it is a gift).

258) Group of settlers and Arab workers

(The details of the following chapter are mainly based on personal interviews conducted with persons who lived and grew up in Sarona. In other instances individuals sent letters or other written material of their recollections and experiences in Sarona. Care was taken so that the information provided by one individual was wherever possible corroborated by someone else. A copy of the notes of the interviews, other printed material and in some cases tape recordings was given to the Temple Society of Australia archives by M Haering and H Glenk.)[282]

257) Arab lady in traditional dress (background)

The Eselesmann (the donkey man) was an Arab named Yusuf. He rode a well kept, strong donkey with a large carry saddle known as a "khurutch" in which he carried a variety of household needs (flour, rice, beans and lentils). He called on each house to sell goods and if he did not have them, he would buy them and bring them at a later time. He could neither read nor write but remembered everything and would deliver items correctly up to a week later.[283]

Madam Leah was a Polish/Russian Jewess who called regularly with a big basket, asking "Haben Sie ein Schmalzhuhn?" (Have you got a fat hen?). She would buy these and then sell them at the Tel Aviv market.

Frau Mueller was a Jewess who lived in Montefiore near Sarona. She was a tiny lady who pushed a heavy trolley with food stuffs and other household needs from house to house in Sarona. She would also set up a display of her wares in Sarona and one could buy things there. Buying and selling was never done without haggling.

Arab Boys called by and sold sesame rings (known as "Simsimringe") which came with a mixture of sesame, cumin and thyme, served on a piece of tissue paper. They also sold flat cakes which would rise when cooked to form a hollow inside, with a crisp thin outside crust (known as "drums") with mixed spices. These were cooked on a small charcoal fire. Small bundles of green chick peas on their stems were also roasted on the hot plate by the Arab boys.

Jakarine, an Arab beggar, visited the settlement regularly, pretending that he was disabled and could not walk.

An elderly **Armenian Lady** came regularly to Sarona selling fine lace work.

Habibi was a well known Jewish musician who taught a number of children from Sarona to play the piano and the cello.

CHAPTER TEN

PRE WORLD WAR II SARONA - AN OVERVIEW

I N THE MID 1930s, although Sarona had been rebuilt and was a flourishing community, it was faced with very real and significant issues as to its immediate and long term viability and existence as a German Templer settlement.

The overall situation facing all the German Templer settlements in the late 1930s is eloquently described in the publication *100 Jahre Tempelgesellschaft* (100 Years Temple Society) where reference is made to the beginning of Philipp Wurst's term of office as President of the Temple Society in 1935.

"He started his term in difficult times. As a small, independent, German religious group in Palestine, the Temple Society found itself in a critical situation. The newly arrived Zionists regarded them (the German settlers) with suspicion; pressured unsuccessfully by the Arabs to join their cause against their struggle with the Jews; under constant surveillance by the Mandate authorities; and regarded suspiciously by the totalitarian regime in Germany as being patriotic, but nevertheless having a religious attachment to Palestine. The Society could therefore only tediously extricate itself from these presumptions, with varying success. At the same time, the pressures from the political situation with the increasing immigration only heightened the Arab-Jewish conflict which in turn impacted on the economics of individual Templers, as well as the financial institutions of the Society. These were very sound financial institutions, but at that time, the Temple Society was considering financing the development of new settlements in Lebanon, without any prospect of an early return of capital."[284]

Land prices in Palestine had reached exorbitant levels and were out of reach of prospective young settlers

The land purchase in Lebanon was aimed at providing an area for future Templer settlements outside of Palestine, as land prices in Palestine had reached exorbitant levels and were out of reach of prospective young settlers.

The publication gives a further insight into the situation just prior to World War II.

The time between the world wars [. . .] covers the period of the greatest economical blossoming of our settlements but also the collapse of our settlement work in the Holy Land. The settlements recovered surprisingly quickly from the ravages of World War I, trade and commerce flourished, however the cultivated land around our agricultural settlements became too confined. Further new farming land was bought around Sarona, Wilhelma and Akko, however it soon became obvious that the establishment of a new settlement was desirable [. . .]

This blossoming also bore a seed which later led to the great turbulences in the country and finally the collapse. The first local skirmishes between the Arabs and the British on one hand and between the Arabs and the Jews on the other did not have much influence (effect) on our settlements. However, the anti-Jewish policies of the Third Reich, created hatred against the Germans by the Jews."[285]

The tensions referred to above had direct effects on Sarona. The prosperity of the Sarona community was generated to a large extent by the sale of agricultural products to the Jewish population. Although the settlers as a whole were trying to keep good relations with their Jewish neighbours, they were powerless against the wider political forces in Germany. In the 1930s (1933 and 1935), there were two partial boycotts of German products by the Jewish population. In Sarona this had an immediate impact on the sale of vegetables and milk. The continuing anti-Semitic policies of National Socialist Germany started tensions and animosity between the Germans and the Jews in Palestine.[286]

In 1933 when the National Socialists came to power in Germany, many of the Templer settlers, who were ardent patriots, were drawn by the nationalistic fervour of the period—just like millions of their own fellow citizens in Germany and elsewhere. They hoped that a German resurgence would possibly strengthen their own position as a German minority in a foreign land.[287]

The NSDAP (National Socialist German Labour Party) gradually increased its influence within the German communities in Palestine. From a small beginning in 1933, the number of persons joining the party increased steadily over the next five years. The NSDAP was able to develop a structure with local district groups (Ortsgruppen). One such group covered the Jaffa/Walhalla/Sarona area. That group had a membership of 113 in 1938. Within this group further units were formed with a particular focus on the younger generation. These units included Bund deutscher Maedel (League of German Girls) and Hitler Jugend (Hitler Youth) etc. and they organised a range of activities for their members.[288]

The increasing influence of the new political ideology and its developments amongst the German settlers created internal problems for the Temple Society. It had to grapple with both challenges to its

259) Invoice for purchase of motor car being offset against a shipment of citrus fruit. The details on the invoice state: "I hereby advise, that I have, through the Faig Bros., Jaffa, agents for the Auto Union Ag Chemnitz/Berlin, ordered for my own personal use, one Horch Innensteuer Limousine 930V mit Lederpolsterung (a Horch car with undivided cabin and leather upholstery) for RM5050 (five thousand and fifty Reichs Mark). This amount will be paid through a shipment of citrus fruit to Germany. I await your confirmation to this arrangement. signed W. Groll"

ideology and its community way of life as well as realising that the NS activities would heighten tensions between Germans and Jews in Palestine. The settlers remained strictly neutral in the Arab/Jewish conflict in the 1930s. The economic wellbeing of the settlers was very dependent on the local non German population. The settlers had co-existed with both Arabs and Jews for decades. Close ties had been developed with both groups.[289]

Another economic consequence of the political situation in Germany was that the sale of produce for German Reichsmarks (RM) became valueless due to the non recognition of the RM in Palestine. The settlers therefore opted, in many instances, to exchange their produce for imported goods. For example, a Mercedes car could be acquired in exchange for 50 cases of oranges.[290]

Jews were particularly interested in buying this land for a good price, the policy of the Sarona community council was that no land was to be sold

In the 1930s, the Sarona settlement itself was nearly encircled by the city of Tel Aviv which was growing and expanding rapidly. Hundreds of new homes were being built in Tel Aviv. This created further deep tensions within the Sarona community as many residents owned land outside the confines of Sarona proper. Jews were particularly interested in buying this land for a good price, and although some landowners were willing to sell, the policy of the Sarona community council was that no land was to be sold.[291]

260) Identity card for Gottlob Graze as issued by the British authorities during the 1930s

The German settlers were concerned for their safety. Arab snipers were shooting at Europeans, not knowing whether they were German or Jewish. Leaving Sarona and travelling became a dangerous venture. In order to show that they were German, the settlers put small German pennants on their cars, motor cycles and other modes of transport whenever they left Sarona, particularly when they had to go through Arab towns or settlements. These pennants with the swastika were resented by the Jews who assumed that all the Germans settlers were Nazis. The British authorities issued everyone with identity cards. With the continual unrest between the Jews and the Arabs escalating, there were shooting skirmishes around Sarona and in the orange groves. Venturing outside Sarona after dark was risky and the British imposed curfews in an attempt to reduce the violence and shooting that was occurring.[292]

Every year from the mid 1930s onwards, the young men of military age were called up for two years of military training in Germany. Those born in 1914/15 were the first ones called up. They went to Germany by ship for their training.[293]

For the younger generation in Sarona, the future employment opportunities were bleak. Already a number of persons had left for Germany because they simply could not find work in Sarona nor, for that matter in Palestine. Due to no further land being available, and with escalating land prices, purchase of land for farming, even elsewhere in Palestine, was out of the question. Employment in other occupations was limited as few new enterprises were being started and those in trade or other positions were well established and unlikely to move on. There were practically no openings for professional employment within the Templer settlements or businesses such as engineering.[294]

The population of the Sarona/Jaffa community in 1939 was 574 Templers (428 in Sarona and 146 in Jaffa), and 75 other Germans (10 in Sarona and 65 in Jaffa) a total of 649. It was estimated that there were 104 residences in Sarona and 36 in Jaffa, as well as over 100 out buildings.[295]

Just prior to the outbreak of WW II the German Consulate General in Palestine advised the men of military age to leave and go to Germany. The young men who had completed their military service previously, were told to leave for Germany at once. 41 men from Jaffa/Sarona left for Germany in August 1939, some were accompanied by their families.[296]

CHAPTER ELEVEN

WORLD WAR II AND INTERNMENT

THE OUTBREAK OF WAR

On 1 September 1939 Germany invaded Poland and two days later, on 3 September, Great Britain and France declared war on Germany. This was a major turning point for the Templers in Palestine (a British Mandate Territory). It marked the beginning of the end of their settlements in Palestine.

261) Badly damaged Heinrich Jung house (No.10) after bomb blast in Sarona

(The details of the following chapter are mainly based on personal interviews conducted with persons who lived in Sarona at that time. In other instances individuals sent letters or other material of their recollections and experiences during their internment. Care was taken so that the information provided by one individual was wherever possible corroborated by someone else. A copy of the interviews, other printed material and in some cases tape recordings was given to the Temple Society of Australia archives by Manfred Haering and Helmut Glenk)[297]

Cleaning up after a bomb blast which badly damaged several houses (background)

The people of Sarona knew that war was likely but had no inkling that they would be interned as soon as war broke out

In response to the German Consulate's earlier request that all men of military age and their families prepare themselves for departure to Germany, a number of families assembled in front of the community house (No. 09a) on the morning of 3 September 1939. Suddenly, Mrs Maria Haering who had been listening to the radio, called out from the balcony of the Geschwister Haering house (No. 26) that they should quickly go home as war had been declared by Great Britain. Within a couple of hours of Mr Chamberlain's announcement that Britain was at war, the British police and military encircled Sarona without warning. They quickly erected a high barbed wire fence around and through Sarona. (see pages 290-291) The people of Sarona had known that war was likely but had no inkling that they would be interned as soon as war broke out.

By negotiating with the British, the President of the Temple Society, Philipp Wurst, was able to persuade the authorities not to deport the German settlers as had been done in WW I. The British had originally planned to intern the settlers in a camp (former military barracks) in Amman, Jordan. The four agricultural settlements— Sarona, Wilhelma, Bethlehem and Waldheim—became "perimeter" settlements instead.[298]

The people in the houses on the outside of the perimeter fence were told to pack as their houses were to be vacated. The British police ordered the women to go to their homes and all men to assemble in the community hall. All men of military age were told to get their basic possessions as they were going to be interned away from Sarona. They were taken to Acre (Akko) by bus the next day, approximately 100 kilometres away.

All houses were searched, all firearms and ammunition had to be given up and the road passes which had been issued for travel in Palestine by the British authorities just before the war, were confiscated.

The families living outside the wire perimeter were moved to the inside of the compound. Wherever possible, families from outside the compound with relatives inside were put together to share a house.

However, the British had also rounded up all non-Templer Germans living outside and near Sarona. They were brought into the enclosed Sarona compound. The British authorities placed these people in any home that had a spare room. The home owners were given no choice in this—the persons, often total strangers, were just allocated to a house by the police.

On 12 September 1939, the British High Commissioner gave an order under the Banking Emergency Orders, directing the winding up of the Bank der Tempelgesellschaft (Bank of the Temple Society). The Bank was put into liquidation and a separate trust account established with, and administered by the Barclays Bank. The account was known as the German Community Fund Account (GCF). The credit balances of all the settlers were transferred into the GCF and the settlers had to deposit all their income into the GCF. Monthly withdrawals from the GCF were allowed up to a certain limit to pay for ongoing living expenses. These transactions were monitored by the Custodian of Enemy Property.[299]

INTERNMENT IN ACRE

The men were taken to Acre, where a former prison was used to hold the men not only from Sarona but from the other Templer settlements as well. Some additional barracks had been built and the internees were housed in these with approximately thirty men to a barrack. The authorities tried to keep the men from each settlement together as best they could. The camp was close to the coast. It was surrounded by a four metre high barbed wire fence. The internees were treated fairly well, although the rations were small initially. The meat was often goat meat and tough—luckily they had a chef amongst them who helped prepare some better meals.

The men were often bored as there was little they could do except read, walk around and talk. There were occasional excursions to the beach. On these trips, the beach would be scoured for bits of wood or, more importantly, shells—large and small. These would be taken back to camp and then carved or made into brooches or other ornaments. The internees had no tools other than pocket knives or eating utensils.

The internees were permitted to write one letter per week to their family and they could obtain the Palestine Post newspaper.

The families in Sarona were allowed to send food parcels to the interned men. These parcels, especially those with fruit and vegetables, were much appreciated by the internees as this food supplemented the camp rations.[300] The men spent Christmas 1939 in camp away from families and friends.

In October 1939, a few men with special skills were allowed to leave Acre and return to the settlements. They were needed to help in the settlements to maintain and repair equipment and machinery needed for the production of primary produce.

The authorities tried to keep the men from each settlement together as best they could

The men spent Christmas 1939 in camp away from families and friends

In February 1940 a further 108 men were transferred back to the settlements to help with running the agricultural enterprises, especially milk and dairy production, which was proving to be too much work for the women, children and elderly men. A number of these men returned to Sarona.

The remaining internees were finally transferred from Acre to Jaffa in November 1940 to continue their internment there. This camp was known as Camp XIII.[301]

INTERNMENT IN SARONA UP TO JULY 1941

Sarona was now surrounded by a four metre high barbed wire fence, and guarded day and night, like the other perimeter camps at Wilhelma, Betlehem and Waldheim. Life had to continue as best it could without the men, who had either left for Germany just before the war, or were now interned at Acre.

In 1940, it was estimated that up to 1000 persons were interned in the Sarona perimeter camp.[302]

Petrol rationing coupons were introduced and diesel fuel to run motors became very scarce. Blackouts were imposed throughout Palestine and even Bedouins were not permitted to light camp fires.[303]

The interned settlers had no control over the activities and work that was being done outside the compound

Arab workers were not allowed to enter the compound. All work inside the compound had to be done by the people inside. Stables and horses cleaned and cared for, dairy cows milked and fed, vegetable gardens cultivated etc. Arabs had to be employed for work in the orange groves and vineyards outside the compound, as well as for cutting maize or Lucerne for cow feed, cultivating or any other work. This was done by arranging for the Arab foremen to come to the gate—here instructions would be given as to what had to be done. If the work required horses or mules, these would also be brought to and handed over at the gate under the close supervision of the Jewish guards. The interned settlers had no control over the activities and work that was being done outside the compound—they had to rely on the honesty and goodwill of their Arab workers.

In cases of serious illness, a special pass was issued to allow the person to seek medical attention outside the compound. Mamlok, the chemist, was permitted to enter the camp and sell medical goods or bring in prescribed medicine. The veterinarians Faerber and Glauber, were also permitted to come in to attend to livestock.

Direct communication with the outside world was difficult. Only one letter per month with 25 words in a set format was allowed to be sent overseas via the Red Cross. Similarly, letters from overseas relatives,

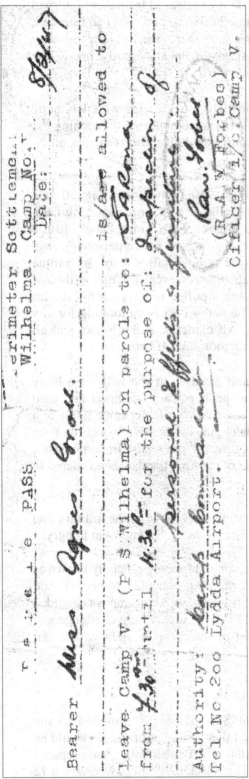

262) Land pass issued to Agnes Groll to allow her to leave the Sarona internment camp

263) Agnes Groll inspecting in Sarona with two Arab workers, 1947

mainly in Germany, were bound by these restrictions. These letters, all of which were censored, went via Switzerland, and took months to reach their destinations. The censored letters often had segments cut out and were known as "Fensterbriefe" (window letters). Incoming mail for the internees had to be addressed—"Name", Internment Camp, Sarona, c/o Inspector General C.I.D. Jerusalem, Palestine. Even letters from the Sarona camp to the Wilhelma camp took three weeks to reach their destination.[304] News from overseas could still be obtained by the short wave radios which people had and from the Palestine Post newspaper (an English language newspaper from Jaffa).

The women and elderly men struggled to maintain the agricultural production. The British military and many of the Palestine population were dependent on the food products that had been produced by Templer agricultural settlements. As production fell, the impact was soon apparent in the wider outside community.

Nobody inside the compound was paid for their work

In February 1940, some of the 108 men released from Acre returned "home" to Sarona. For those whose husbands and sons had returned, this was a joyous occasion; for others there was sadness that they were still separated from their loved ones. Nobody inside the compound was paid for their work.

News of German war victories in 1940 were greeted with delight by the internees. To stop the news reports from Germany reaching the compound, the British Police confiscated all radio receivers on 24 May 1940.

A few days later at the end of May 1940, without warning, all men were ordered to immediately assemble on the Sarona sporting field. The women and children were ordered to go immediately to the main community hall. Then several groups of police personnel, each group was accompanied by a male representative from the Sarona community, conducted thorough house searches. Cupboards and drawers were emptied and bed linen pulled up as each house was searched from top to bottom. The authorities were looking for any weapons or radios/transmitters. All cameras, many books and all maps were confiscated. The search took several hours.

During this time, the women and children at the hall were body searched. Children's prams and pushers were stripped and also searched. After the house searches, many residents came home to a very messy home—goods and belongings were strewn over the floor and pictures and wall hangings torn off the walls. In some cases, the ladies had been in the middle of cooking meals when ordered to leave.

During internment, some rations were received from the military and supplemented by the internees' own products. No one went hungry.

In November 1940, the Sarona compound became officially known as Camp IV.[305] A strict curfew was imposed, lights had to be switched off at 9.00 pm and windows were blacked out. The camp was guarded at all times and patrolled at night. The guards would challenge any movements around the perimeter of the camp at night with a call "Halt! Who goes there?"

DEPORTATION TO AUSTRALIA

It was announced that a number of people would be deported to an unnamed destination

In July 1941, all the people of Sarona were summoned to the community hall. It was announced that a number of people would be deported to an unnamed destination. The British Police had prepared a list of those who had to leave. The selected internees were given 72 hours to pack. Each adult was allowed 40 kilograms and each child 30 kilograms of luggage plus what they could carry as personal hand luggage and a specified amount of money per person.[306] The selected internees were advised that if their luggage was overweight it would be left behind. They did not know where their journey would take them except that they would be going to a place where it would be springtime and to take some summer clothing and a few woollen (warmer) garments. From that the settlers deduced that it was likely to be somewhere in the southern hemisphere.

The authorities permitted some personal sewing machines and a few kerosene heaters to be taken. In addition, some educational material and books from the school were taken to allow the children's education to be continued.[307] These books formed the basis for the school that was later established in the Tatura Camp III in Australia.

The logic underlying the selection is unclear—why some were chosen and others were not. In some cases, some members of families had to go and others stayed behind. Even husbands and fathers were separated from their wives and children. Two criteria for selection appear to have been: firstly, those men (and their families) capable of bearing arms; and secondly, that the selected internee had to be in good health. All people were checked for trachoma (an eye disease) before departure. At that time persons with trachoma were treated with Hoellenstein (silver nitrate) eye-drops. Some children's eyes, possibly with ailments other than trachoma, were treated with these drops anyway, even though they may have had nothing more than sore eyes. These children had to stay behind with their mothers, while their fathers had to go—the authorities were taking no chances. The settlers had not expected that the British authorities would actually separate families for deportation.

Husbands and fathers were split from their wives and children

The settlers did not expect that the British authorities would separate actual families for deportation

A difficult time began for those who had to leave. People had a hard time deciding what to take. They had to go through all their possessions and choose what to pack. They packed and weighed and reweighed their luggage to ensure that they were within the imposed weight limits. It was a heartbreaking task. Clothing was a problem as no light-weight garments, as are known today, were available in the 1940s.

Another difficult matter was what to do with personal jewellery and valuables. In a number of cases these items were hidden in secret locations or buried.

Finally, on 31 July 1941, the settlers about to be deported had to assemble and leave their luggage at the community hall. There were scenes of heartbreaking farewells as families were separated. The

And so the journey to the unknown commenced. For this group of Saronians it was a farewell from their settlement forever

deportees, 198 from Sarona, were put on buses, the luggage was loaded on trucks, and taken to the railway station at Lydda. And so the journey into the unknown commenced. For this group of Saronians it was a farewell from their settlement forever—although they did not know this in July 1941. All those who had to leave are listed in Appendix 6.

Their journey took them by bus to Lydda, onto a special train with the settlers from the other German Templer settlements and camps in Palestine. A total of 665 persons were deported from the various German Templer settlements in Palestine on that day. The special train, guarded mainly by Jewish police, took them from Lydda to Kantara in Egypt. They were ferried across the Suez Canal and continued their journey by rail through Ismailia to Suez. From Suez they were ferried out into the Red Sea where the liner *Queen Elizabeth* lay at anchor out of range of the German Luftwaffe. They boarded the *Queen Elizabeth* which had been converted and used as a troop carrier between Australia and the Middle East. Their journey continued to Sydney, Australia where they disembarked on 24 August 1941 and transferred by train to internment camps at Tatura in central Victoria, Australia.[308] There they remained interned until 1946-47 unable to return to Sarona again. (Details of their journey into the "unknown", internment in Australia and starting their lives after the war are not covered in this book).

264) The liner Queen Elizabeth was used as a troop carrier during World War II and brought some of the interned Templer settlers to Australia

INTERNMENT IN SARONA JULY 1941 TO 1944.

After the deportation of many of their fellow settlers in July 1941, those remaining had to adjust to the changes that had been forced upon them. The Spanish Government agreed that the Spanish Consulate General in Jerusalem be authorised to safeguard the interests of the remaining Germans in Palestine.

Many of the empty houses were requisitioned and occupied by the military and camp authorities. For example, Wilhelm Aberle's house (No. 29) became the District Commissioner's house, Froeschle's house cellar (No.23) was converted into the camp canteen; Graze's house (No. 24) became the German Camp Office; Annelies Lippmann's house (no. 46) was used as a medical facility ("hospital"), Glenk's house (No.61) was occupied by the Camp Commandant; John's (No.77), Otto Weller's (No. 78), Krafft's (No. 80), Hoffmann's (both Sam (No.83) and Walter (No. 82) houses were occupied by British personnel. The Sarona school building (No.84) was used to house Jewish police, and the former office of the Sarona community (No.09a) became the British Police administration centre. In 1944, the British High Commissioner moved into Albrecht Aberle's house (No. 43). Kuebler's Bar and home (No.69) were turned into a general store where many items were sold. The homes had to be cleared of furniture before they were occupied. Siegfried Hahn, an internee, was in charge of this operation. He, together with four or five Arab labourers (who were given special permission to enter the camp) and several other internees, would load the furniture on trucks (formerly owned by Lippmanns and Wagners) and take the furniture to the wine cellar for storage.

Schooling for the remaining children continued in Jakob Weiss's house. The children were taught by Propst Johannes and Mrs Doering (they belonged to the German Protestant Church), Mr Fast, Mr Bamberg, Hedwig Aberle and Mrs Theodora Wieland. These people were not qualified teachers but ensured that the children received some education.

All produce from Sarona was sold and recorded in the German Community Fund with the Barclays Bank. Similarly, any expenses or income derived from the occupied houses were recorded there. In summary, the Fund provided the reference point for all commercial transactions. On a monthly basis, the books would be examined by an inspector from the British Finance Department.[309]

Strict military regulations and directions for anything and everything were proclaimed. An example of one of the more intriguing directions was "The Defence (Control of Containers) (Glass) Direction 1943".

265) A Direction issued by the Controller of Salvage in 1943. Such directives were issued for a range of matters by the British authorities during the settlers internment during World War II

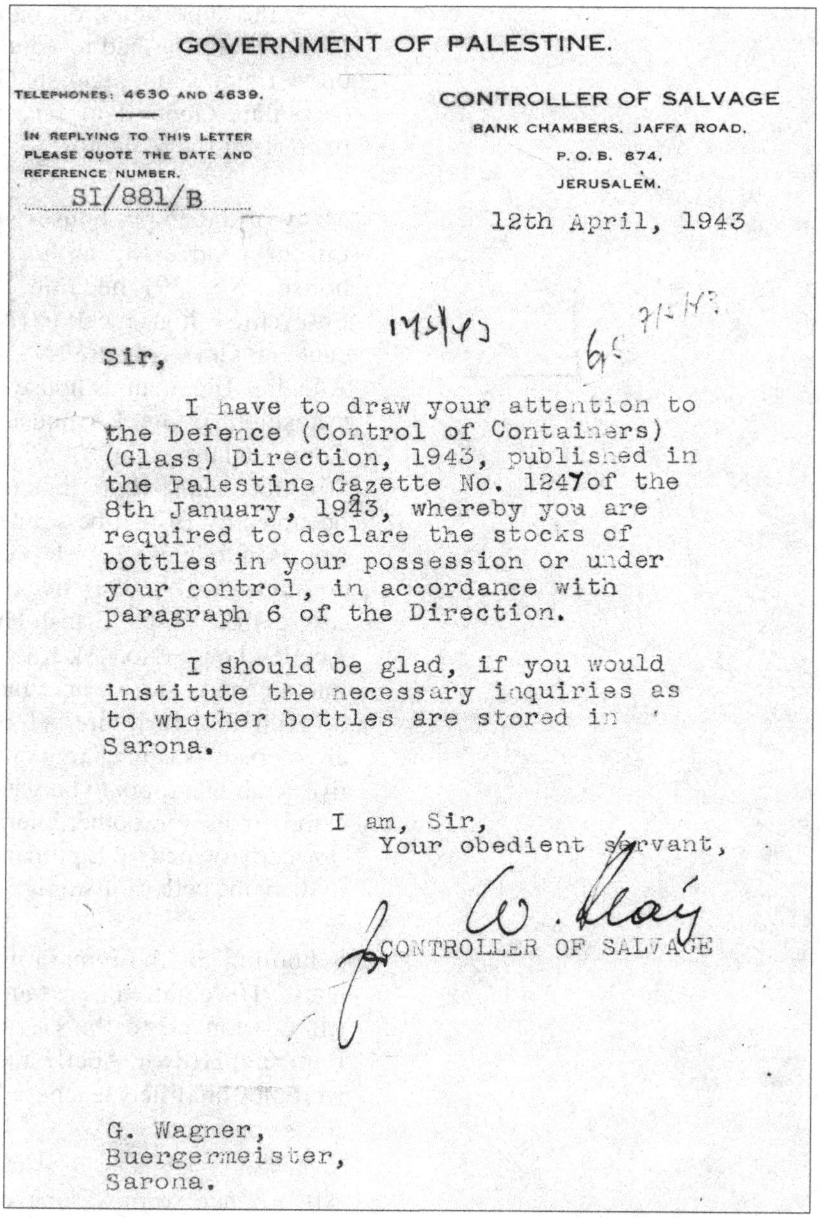

GOVERNMENT OF PALESTINE.

TELEPHONES: 4630 AND 4639.

IN REPLYING TO THIS LETTER
PLEASE QUOTE THE DATE AND
REFERENCE NUMBER.

SI/881/B

CONTROLLER OF SALVAGE

BANK CHAMBERS, JAFFA ROAD.

P. O. B. 874.

JERUSALEM.

12th April, 1943

Sir,

I have to draw your attention to the Defence (Control of Containers) (Glass) Direction, 1943, published in the Palestine Gazette No. 1247 of the 8th January, 1943, whereby you are required to declare the stocks of bottles in your possession or under your control, in accordance with paragraph 6 of the Direction.

I should be glad, if you would institute the necessary inquiries as to whether bottles are stored in Sarona.

I am, Sir,
Your obedient servant,

W. Clay
CONTROLLER OF SALVAGE

G. Wagner,
Buergermeister,
Sarona.

This was published in the *Palestine Gazette No. 1247* of 8 January 1943 and required persons or bodies to declare stocks of bottles in their possession. Such a direction was issued to Gotthilf Wagner, Buergermeister, Sarona in April 1943. Mr Wagner replied:—
"The following stocks are notified to you:

Wine Cellar
About 3500 ¾ litre bottles empty
500 1 litre bottles (or smaller filled with wine, spirits (liquors)
(correct counting was difficult due to limited access to the cellar)

Camp Canteen
About 500 empty ¾ litre bottles
About 1350 ¾ litre bottles filled with wine, spirits and other substances

Aerated Water Establishment
About 2000 empty bottles of less than ¾ litre
About 200 ¾ litre bottles empty

266) Request on behalf of the Sarona Local Council to allow vaccination of stock to prevent the spread of African horse sickness

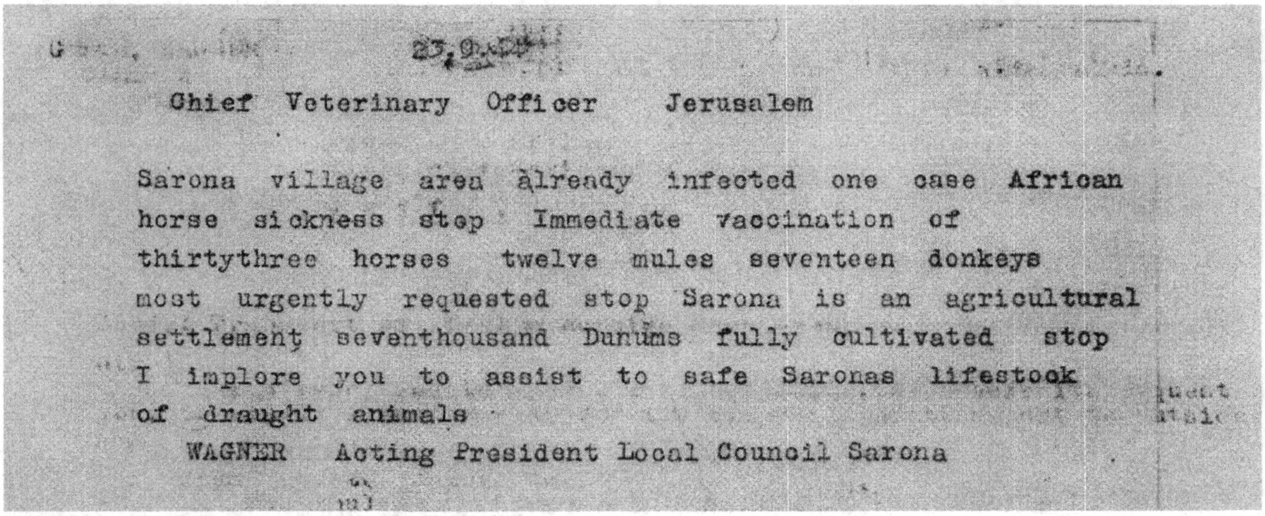

Individuals
About 850 bottles in all of ¾ litres and less have been notified."[310]

Chief Veterinary Officer   Jerusalem

Sarona village area already infected one case **African horse sickness** step Immediate vaccination of thirtythree horses   twelve mules   seventeen donkeys most urgently requested stop Sarona is an agricultural settlement seventhousand Dunums fully cultivated   stop I implore you to assist to safe Saronas lifestock of draught animals
    WAGNER   Acting President Local Council Sarona

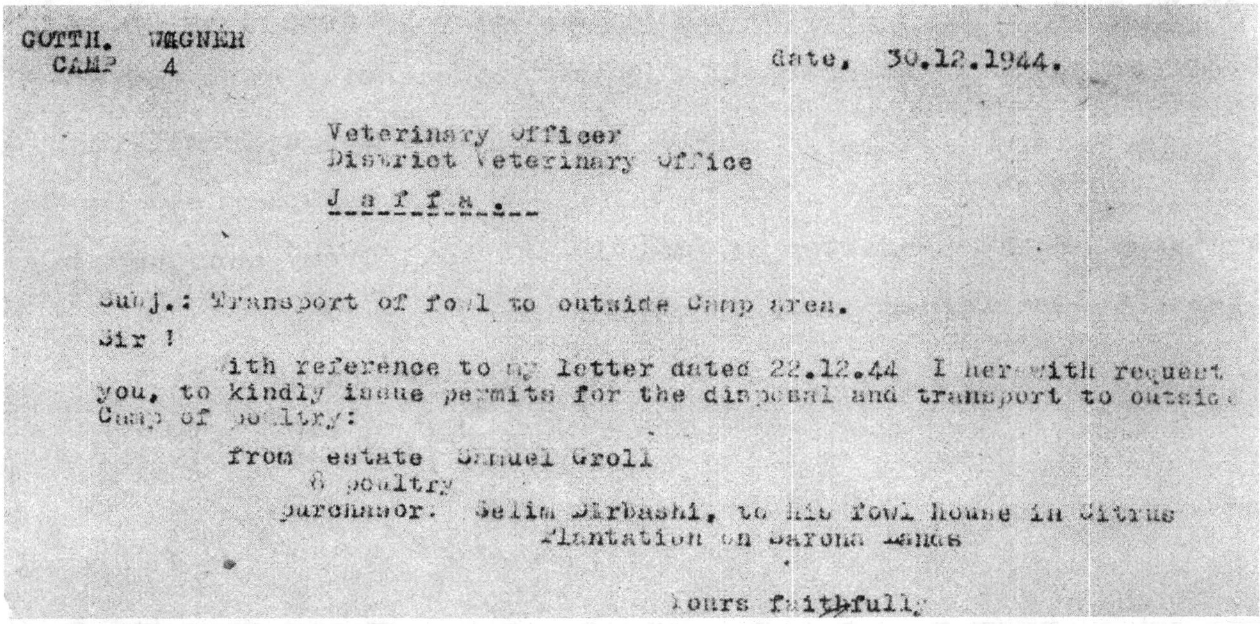

GOTTH. WAGNER
CAMP   4   date, 30.12.1944.

        Veterinary Officer
        District Veterinary Office
        J a f f a .

Subj.: Transport of fowl to outside Camp area.
Sir !
        with reference to my letter dated 22.12.44 I herewith request you, to kindly issue permits for the disposal and transport to outside Camp of poultry:

        from estate Samuel Groll
                6 poultry
        purchaser: Selim Jirbashi, to his fowl house in Citrus
                Plantation on Sarona Lands

                                        Yours faithfully

267) Request for the sale of six chickens and their transport and disposal outside the Sarona perimeter settlement. The British authorities' approval was required for the most trivial transactions

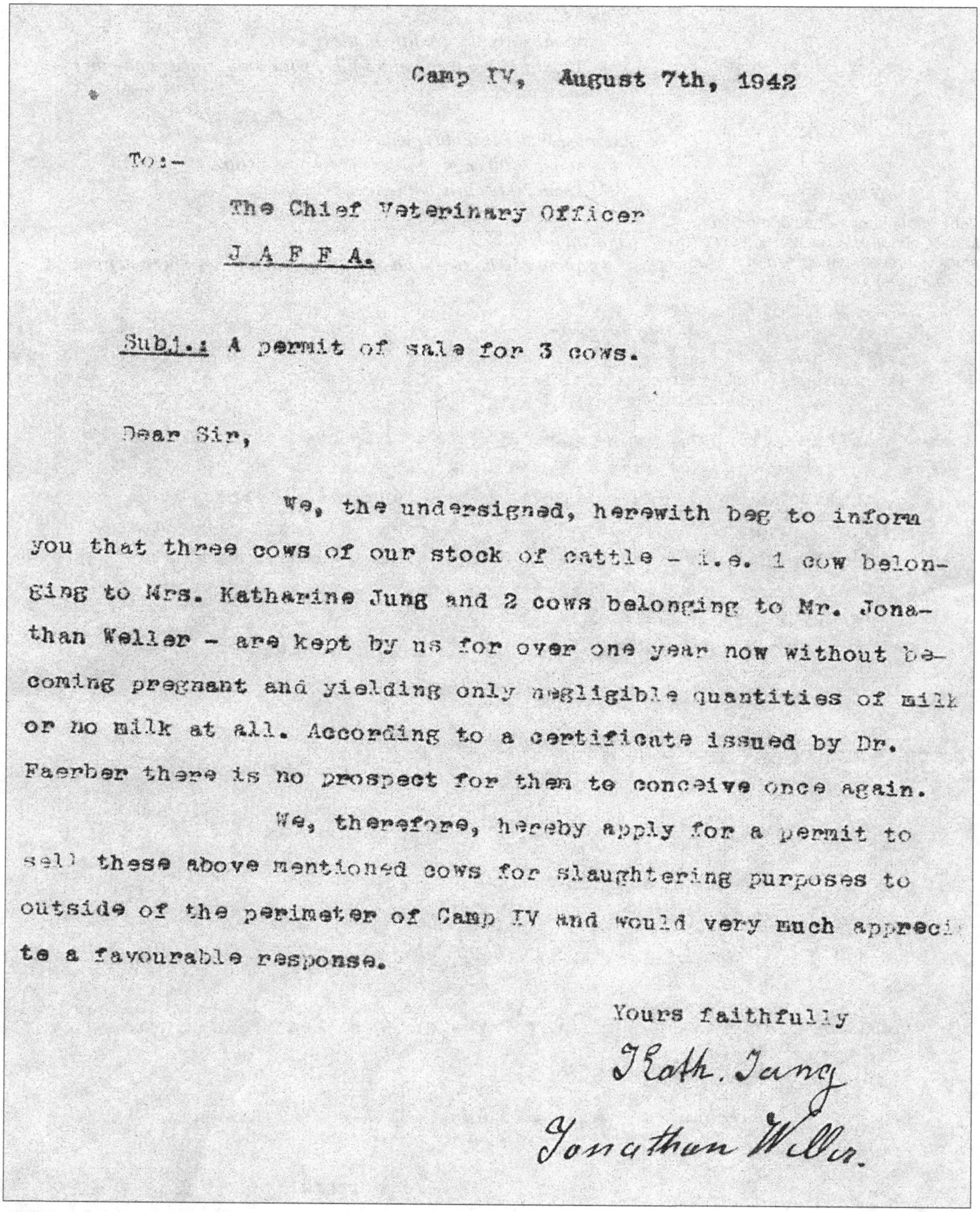

Camp IV, August 7th, 1942

To:-

The Chief Veterinary Officer
J A F F A.

Subj.: A permit of sale for 3 cows.

Dear Sir,

We, the undersigned, herewith beg to inform
you that three cows of our stock of cattle - i.e. 1 cow belonging to Mrs. Katharine Jung and 2 cows belonging to Mr. Jonathan Weller - are kept by us for over one year now without becoming pregnant and yielding only negligible quantities of milk
or no milk at all. According to a certificate issued by Dr.
Faerber there is no prospect for them to conceive once again.

We, therefore, hereby apply for a permit to
sell these above mentioned cows for slaughtering purposes to
outside of the perimeter of Camp IV and would very much appreci-
te a favourable response.

Yours faithfully

Kath. Jung

Jonathan Weller.

268) *Request for the sale of three cows*

Looking after the remaining livestock, especially the dairy cows and their daily milking requirements was a problem

Pets such as dogs and cats were put down

Other regulations required the Chief Veterinary Officer, Veterinary District, Jaffa to approve the sale of livestock including poultry. The Chief Veterinary Officer also had to be asked to allow the vaccination of any sick stock.

Even before the 1941 deportation, the settlers had sold some of their livestock. Looking after the remaining livestock, especially the dairy cows and their daily milking requirements was a problem. The livestock, mainly cows, horses and chickens, was sold as quickly as possible. Some of these transactions were arranged through the Jewish veterinarian who still visited the camp to look after the livestock. Pets such as dogs and cats were put down.

Some contact was maintained with the Arab workers and some cultivation and harvesting work was still being done in the orchards, vineyards, gardens and fields of the settlers outside the camp—albeit on a much reduced scale. Passes were issued for "land inspection" outside the camp perimeter. However, the fields, orchards, vineyards and crops were no longer being cared for properly. The effect of this drop in care was that pests—lice, fruit flies, rodents etc became more prevalent especially as crops were not fully harvested and the fruits etc dropped to the ground and rotted.

The British authorities continued to treat the internees well.[311]

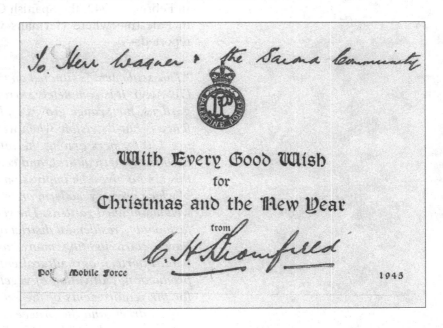

269) Christmas and New Year greetings card received by the Sarona community from the British Mobile Police Force, 1943

The authorities allowed the internees to visit family and friends in the other camps on a rotational basis. These visits were usually short but served a very useful purpose in that settlers were able to stay in touch and exchange experiences with each other.

The male internees had to assemble each day between the old community house (No. 25) and Graze's house (No. 24) for roll call. Female and child internees had to present themselves at the front door of their homes each afternoon. Several male internees checked off the female and child internees and then reported back to the British authorities. On a monthly basis, a representative from the British Police Criminal Investigation Department would visit the camp and inspect the internees. The Sarona Camp IV was guarded by Jewish police under the supervision of British police officers.

The deportation of family and friends cause sadness amongst the remaining internees

The deportation of family and friends caused sadness amongst the remaining internees. This sadness was increased as reports of war casualties were received in the Sarona compound. The German Templers in Palestine knew most of the families in the other settlements, in fact they were often related to families in these other settlements. The news therefore of deaths in combat was felt by all. A list of war casualties from Sarona in WW II is shown in Appendix 4.

The news of deaths in combat was felt by all

REPORT BY THE SPANISH CONSUL GENERAL 1942

The Spanish Consulate in Palestine had several staff involved in looking after the interests and wellbeing of the German internees. The camps were visited by these staff members on a regular basis. In February 1942, the Spanish Consul General visited all the camps in Palestine where Germans were held. In regard to Sarona he reported:—

"This settlement is situated on the periphery of a very important city (Tel Aviv). It is completely surrounded by barbed wire, including the gardens, the orange groves and the grazing land. Incidentally, this fence is hardly visible when walking through the settlement. There are 120 farmers among the internees . . . Settlement No. 4 is not exclusively agricultural, and compared with the other settlements of this kind it gives the impression of great diversity. The houses, some of which are very modern, are generally surrounded by beautiful and well maintained gardens. The visitor has the impression of being in a fashionable residential district of a Mediterranean city. All buildings have electric lighting, many have very modern installations of this kind. Fourteen agricultural enterprises are being operated; dairy production, cultivation of vegetables, oranges, bananas and grain for the requirements of the settlement. The surplus is sold on the open market, and the proceeds are used for operating the various enterprises and to aid the families deported to Australia . . . ."[312]

BOMB BLASTS

The internees in the camp felt quite secure in their confined area. The camp which with its guards provided a barrier against the outside unrest between Arabs and Jews, which continued unabated. The British were hard pressed to contain the fighting and were subject to hostile attacks themselves. However, several incidents occurred in the camp in 1943 which created a significant amount of unease amongst the Sarona internees.

As mentioned previously, there was a roll call twice a day when people had to assemble in front of Graze's house (No. 24) (the German camp office). There was a small bench seat near the assembly area where people often sat. On 16 June 1943, just after the internees had left the morning roll call, a bomb which had been planted there, exploded. Fortunately, everyone had left and no-one was seriously injured or killed but the bomb caused considerable damage to the nearby buildings. If it had gone off whilst the internees were all assembled, it would have caused mayhem and death.[313]

Further incidents occurred in August 1943, the first at the Sarona cemetery when a bomb exploded and another one was found unexploded; and the second, the explosion of a device at the new Sarona school building, which was occupied by the Police. Fortunately again, no one was killed or badly injured by these blasts. The blasts, however, created anxiety amongst the internees who realised how vulnerable they actually were.[314]

A further serious bomb blast happened in Sarona after the German settlers had left and only British police and military personnel were still occupying the homes and buildings. In April 1947 a postal van loaded with explosives was driven into the compound and left parked between Heinrich Jung (No.10) and Jakob Weiss's (No.11) houses. When the van exploded, several British policemen were killed and nearby buildings badly damaged.[315]

INTERNEE EXCHANGES

Since early in the war, negotiations had taken place between the German and British governments regarding the possible exchange of German citizens living in Palestine with Jews who had Palestinian passports but were interned in German concentration camps.[316] This resulted in several exchanges taking place.

Three persons involved with the German Consulate had left earlier in the war and were exchanged for British personnel.[317]

270) Jakob Weiss' house (No 11) was badly damaged by a bomb blast, 1947

The blasts however created anxiety among the internees who realised how vulnerable they actually were

The first internee exchange took place in December 1941. The persons who were considered for this exchange were Consular staff and those who had immediate family in Germany, as well as some members of the Kaiserswerth Diakonissen (a Lutheran religious order). A number of women and children from Sarona were included in the exchange. The internees had to assemble at the community house.

271) Members of the first exchange group in 1941

They were allowed to take a limited amount of luggage, similar to the internees who had been deported earlier in July 1941. They travelled to Germany via Lebanon and Turkey.

The next exchange occurred in October/November 1942 and involved over 300 internees from Palestine, including 130 from the Sarona camp. This exchange only came about after lengthy negotiations between the German and British government authorities, via the Swiss Protecting Power. The persons eligible to apply for exchange included those whose husbands or other relatives who were in Germany.

In October 1942, the internees to be exchanged were taken from the various internment camps in Palestine to a transit camp in Atlit, near Haifa. They had to wait for the negotiations of their exchange to be finalised. The conditions in the camps were poor. The barracks, particularly the mattresses, were infested by bedbugs. Many mattresses were burnt, and kerosene was used to clean the barracks. The food at the camp was of poor quality and with winter approaching many of the internees became ill. Finally, on 6 November 1942 their journey back to Germany began—first by bus and then by train, via Syria and Turkey. At the Turkish/Bulgarian border the exchange of internees took place. Their journey continued until 14 November 1942 when they arrived in Vienna. From there they travelled to various destinations in Germany.

A third and final exchange was made in 1944, when a further 42 internees from Palestine, including a number of Saronians, were exchanged. This exchange had a very sad ending for several families from Sarona. The exchanged settlers arrived in Stuttgart, Germany on 13 July 1944. On 26 July 1944, ten former Palestine settlers (including some from the Baldenhofer and Heselschwerdt families) were killed in an air raid whilst still at the repatriation centre in Stuttgart.[318]

The people who were part of the internee exchanges are listed in Appendix 7. It should be noted that not only former residents of Sarona were interned in the Sarona camp. German nationals from outside Sarona as well as settlers from the Jerusalem Templer settlement also passed through the Sarona camp. Therefore the list in Appendix 7 contains the names of these additional persons.

FINAL DAYS IN SARONA AND TRANSFER TO WILHELMA

Following the internee exchanges, Sarona was largely devoid of its original inhabitants. Those remaining continued to move most of their furniture to the wine cellar for storage. Nearly all the remaining livestock was sold off. The British authorities warned about the viability of staying on in Sarona. Personal possessions and goods were sold mainly to Arabs at give-away prices.

For those settlers remaining in Sarona a most difficult and heart-breaking period of uncertainty began to unfold

For those settlers remaining in Sarona a most difficult and heartbreaking period of uncertainty began to unfold. They had experienced the anguish of the departure of most of their friends, relatives and loved ones; and witnessed the demise of a flourishing and happy community. Many of the settlers who were deported or left in 1941 and 1942, although sad and reluctant to leave, still hoped that one day they would return to Sarona when the war was over; many had in those early years expected Germany to win the war. However, for those now remaining, it became increasingly clear that the future of the Sarona settlement was very tenuous.

For those now remaining it became increasingly clear that the future of the Sarona settlement was very tenuous

In October/November 1944, the British authorities had most of the remaining internees from the Sarona compound moved to the Wilhelma settlement (Camp V).[319] Only a handful of internees were allowed to stay to provide basic agricultural products to the British military. There were many tears of sadness as the people left their homes—the places where they and their forefathers had grown up. Many realised it would be a good-bye forever!

Many realised it would be a good-bye forever

The remaining settlers were allowed to occupy only six houses—the homes of Samuel Groll (No. 28), Jakob Weller (No.27), Geschwister Haering (No.26), Jakob Sickinger (No.33), Jonathan Weller (No.34) and Johannes Orth (No.35). The settlers arranged accommodation in the houses and continued their work practices which were limited by many restrictions. Geschwister Haering's house was also used as the office for the community. The remaining internees, included Samuel, Emilie, Roesle, Adelheid and Agnes Groll, Carl and Pauline Kuebler, Immanuel and Bertha Knoll, Katherine and Luise Jung, Annchen Kruegler, Elly Wennagel, Maria Orth, Jakob Sickinger, Jakob, Elisabeth, Irmgard and Gerda Weiss, Karoline and Ruth Weller, Gotthilf and Frida Wagner. They moved together into six houses and stayed there until after the war in Europe had ended.

In the last years of Sarona when many of the landowners were no longer in Sarona nor Palestine, Gotthilf Wagner assumed the responsibility for carrying out the various administrative tasks required to keep the settlement's agricultural and business activities going and in order. He was supported by a small team of workers— Annchen Kruegler, Elly Wennagel, Irmgard Weiss and Frida Wagner (Gotthilf's sister). Gotthilf Wagner was greatly respected by the Sarona settlers for his dedication, diligence and accuracy of his work.

He also continued to nurture the religious practices of the remaining settlers by conducting a regular Sunday church service. This was held each week in Groll's lounge room.

In August /September 1945 the British authorities ordered the transfer of the last settlers to Wilhelma. When the final order to leave was given, the few remaining animals were sold (given away) and the pets poisoned. The families were able to take their personal possessions and some bedding with them.

They were the last of the German Templers to leave Sarona

They were the last of the German Templers to leave Sarona.

INTERNMENT IN WILHELMA (CAMP V)

The internment in Wilhelma Camp V continued for another two and a half years until April 1948.

When the Sarona internees came to Wilhelma, they were moved into homes with other families. The Wilhelma camp was guarded by Jewish police and under an early night curfew. Some schooling was provided by Propst Johannes Doering (Pastor at the Erloeserkirche in Jerusalem) and Luise Dreher. Day passes for land inspection and other business outside the camp were issued on application to eligible persons.

Boredom, especially for young people, was a real problem—there was little to do and no entertainment

Boredom, especially for young people, was a real problem—there was little to do and no entertainment. Time was spent walking and talking. A concrete tennis court was built by the internees. If someone wanted to go to Tel Aviv. they were usually accompanied by a Jewish policeman/woman. The internees at Wilhelma received far more military rations than those of the Sarona camp had received.

For many adult Sarona settlers the period of internment at Wilhelma was particularly frustrating and difficult

For many adult Sarona settlers the period of internment at Wilhelma was particularly frustrating and difficult. They were living in strange homes; the war was over, but they were still interned—it had been a long 8½ years (September 1939 - April 1948); their land was being expropriated and they could not stop the sale of Sarona, against their wishes, by the British; they became aware that the internees in Australia were being released from captivity, but not allowed to return to Palestine; these internees were able to start a new life whilst those interned in Wilhelma just had to wait, not knowing their future fate; and their loved ones in Germany were experiencing very difficult times and hunger in war-ravaged Germany. People reacted differently to these circumstances and the psychological effects of stress and loss affected their wellbeing. Strokes and serious illness were noted among the elderly during this period. Burials were no longer permitted at the Sarona cemetery and the deceased were laid to rest at Wilhelma. Many of the elderly were reluctant to leave and give up their (and their forefathers') possessions which had been acquired through diligence and hard work. Others, especially younger persons, just wanted to be released from internment so that they would be free to start a new life.

Despite the hardship, the settlers still bonded together, supported each other and continued community practices that were still possible

The following is an account written by Adelheid Groll of the **last Dankfest on 12 October 1947,** in the Wilhelma compound:—
"At 10 o'clock a church service was conducted by Mr Hermann Imberger in the splendidly decorated "Stiftshuette" (entertainment enclosure) . . . . In the afternoon around 3.30 we continued our thanksgiving in the wooded area behind the Stiftshuette. First we sang the hymn "Praise to the Lord, the Almighty" which was followed by a speech from Mr Imberger, then the mixed choir and the school choir sang beautifully.[. . .] Many people were present and it was a pleasant and entertaining afternoon, enhanced with songs and folk dancing by the young ladies . . . .

In the evening around 7.30, we watched some movies. Frieder Thuma obtained the films from Jerusalem and because they were German films, many came to watch them [. . .]. However, whilst chatting and talking we regretted that we were not able to celebrate the beautiful Dankfest with the ones that were not here. May it be God's will that one day soon this will be possible again."[320]

Between 1946 and 1948, the internees were able to send both food parcels and parcels with personal effects to friends and relatives in Germany. Many such "Care" and "Gift" parcels were sent by mail via the Red Cross or via Switzerland to Germany (British, French and US zones only). These parcels were welcomed by the starving people in Germany. (Similar parcels were also sent by the former internees in Australia to relatives and friends in Germany.) With permission of the authorities the Sarona internees in Wilhelma were allowed to return to the wine cellar to get some of their personal effects. It soon became noticeable that items had been "disappearing" from the wine cellar as other people had apparently broken in or obtained unauthorised access to the goods and furniture that were stored there. Suit cases, wardrobes, chests of drawers were forced open by the thieves and personal goods and clothing strewn on the floor.[321]

Returning to Sarona to retrieve goods was not an easy undertaking. Firstly, they were at great personal risk whilst being out of the Wilhelma compound, and secondly, they saw first hand as road construction and other development was engulfing the former beautiful and fertile orange groves, vineyards and fields around Sarona. In Sarona itself the neglect around the homes and gardens was also obvious.

The last eyewitness account of Sarona is from Agnes Laemmle (nee Groll). She visited Sarona twice whilst out on a "land inspection" pass. She recalls that only one policeman was on duty at the gate of the perimeter fence and she had no problem entering the deserted compound—even the British authorities had left. She was able to walk through the settlement unchallenged. It was an eerie feeling walking along the quiet streets that had once been a hive of activity and vitality in her younger days—not a soul to be seen, no animals, empty houses, some with open doors, untended gardens and no sign of life. She was able to enter her family home—to her dismay persons unknown had chopped wood on the tiled kitchen floor and the house was stripped of anything that could be moved.

The end of Sarona was rapidly approaching.

To return to Sarona for the former settlers was not an easy undertaking

In Sarona itself the neglect around the homes and gardens was also obvious

220

CHAPTER TWELVE

THE END OF SARONA

UNSAFE LIVING CONDITIONS

On 8 May 1945 the war ended in Europe—Germany signed an unconditional surrender. The war had left Germany a devastated country and the full extent of the atrocities that had happened to the Jews in Europe became known. In Palestine, there was understandably widespread hatred by the Jews towards the Germans still interned there. The barbed wire camps guarded by Jewish policemen, under the supervision of British police officers, provided some protection but on several occasions the internees were subject to spasmodic gun fire from passing cars outside the compound. No one was hurt but the unease about their safety and welfare started to impact on the remaining internees.[322]

On 22 March 1946, Gotthilf Wagner, aged 59, the last Mayor of Sarona, was assassinated. He was murdered in Tel Aviv whilst driving a car to pay some Arab workmen who had completed work for the Sarona settlers. His car was forced to stop and two gunmen rushed to his car and shot him in the head. Although there were several passengers in the car none of them was harmed.[323]

Later in November 1946, the British Mandatory Government informed the Templer and Lutheran Church leaders that it was proposing to deport all remaining Germans to Germany. This decision made it clear to the Temple Society leaders that there was no future for the Temple Society in Palestine.[324]

272) Boarding buses on departure from Wilhelma in 1948

Watch tower at the Wilhelma Perimeter Camp (Background)

In 1946, several other incidents occurred—a the slaying of two young Germans and the detention of two elderly Templer ladies in Tel Aviv for several days. The daily lives of the remaining settlers had become difficult as the violence between the Arabs and Jews continued to escalate in the lead up to the United Nations vote on the partition of Palestine and the establishment of the State of Israel. There were instances where the German settlers were harassed by the Haganah, the Jewish Underground, when homes were raided by armed Jewish personnel. The British were powerless to stop this. A raid on the settlement of Waldheim, in April 1948, left two people dead and another seriously wounded, having been shot at point blank range. This raid convinced the British forces to compulsorily move most of the remaining German internees out of Palestine.[325]

This raid convinced the British forces to compulsorily move most of the remaining German internees out of Palestine

It also became apparent to the majority of the remaining settlers that staying on in Palestine would be futile. There were however several, headed by Nikolai Schmidt, who were determined to stay on and hoped that maybe some of the settlements could be saved and the settlers return to them at a later time.[326]

LEAVING PALESTINE

Overseas representations were made by the Templers to be allowed to return to their former settlements. These proved to be unsuccessful.

In Australia, the Templers in the internment camps were given the option of either going to Germany or starting a new life in Australia. The Templers in Germany were looking at a new start there after the war or, once it became apparent that return to Palestine was no longer an option, emigrating to join their family and friends in Australia.[327]

By 1947 and 1948 the settlements had become run down due to the loss of most of the younger manpower. The population was largely made up of the elderly, women, children and ailing persons. They of course struggled on as best they could to keep the basic activities going.

During March 1948 the internees were advised that they could no longer stay in Palestine

During March 1948 the internees were advised that they could no longer stay in Palestine and that they should decide where in the long term they wanted to go—either to Australia or Germany. They were further advised that the British could not offer any protection after 15 May 1948 and that they may have to pay for their own fares. Most of the internees chose to go to Australia to join their families who were already there. The time for departure from Palestine was coming closer but there was still uncertainty as to when, and some were hoping, that somehow things might change and that they would be allowed to stay.[328]

273) Boarding buses on the departure from Wilhelma on 20 April 1948

274) A final view of Wilhelma taken from a bus as the settlers were leaving Palestine in 1948

275) Camp leader Richard O. Eppinger, Brigadier White and Sergeant Walker in Cyprus 1948

276a) The Golden Sands tent camp in Cyprus where the settlers from Palestine were housed during 1948/49

The internees were notified that they had to be ready to leave Palestine on 20 April 1948

In the late evening of 17 April 1948, the internees were notified that they had to be ready to leave Palestine on 20 April 1948. When the transfer to Cyprus was announced, it was time to pack once more. With only three days notice (the settlers had hoped for eight) frantic efforts were made to pack everything. People worked long into the night to sort out items and pack. Everything that was considered necessary was packed—there were no restrictions on what could be taken. Arab labourers were employed to make packing cases (boxes). The packing cases had to be left outside the houses with the owners' names clearly marked and were then taken by truck to Jaffa. All remaining livestock and furniture was left behind.[329]

On 20 April 1948, the internees of Wilhelma, including those who were taken there from Sarona a few years earlier, were moved by bus under British military protection to Jaffa. The next day, in Jaffa, they boarded a ship, the *Empire Comfort,* under the protection of a British warship, bound for Haifa. The elderly and invalids had great difficulty in boarding the ship which lay at anchor off Jaffa. In Haifa, more German internees were taken on board. Heavy fighting was taking place at Haifa at that time and bullets were flying over the ship. On 22 April 1948 approximately 320 internees from the various Templer settlements in Palestine disembarked in Cyprus. They were taken by military buses to a tent camp on the foreshore near Famagusta. The camp was called "Golden Sands"![330]

On 22 April 1948 approximately 320 internees from the various Templer settlements in Palestine disembarked in Cyprus

Some 50 former settlers were still in Palestine. They were predominately the sick who could not join the rushed exodus to Cyprus. Another seven internees also stayed behind to finalise the sale of stock and some furniture. Under the leadership of Gottlob Loebert they tried to sell 300 head of livestock and then they were required to concentrate on the transport and dispatch of the large luggage items of the departed settlers.[331] This latter group was flown to Cyprus at a later date. Some settlers however remained in Palestine. This was of their own choosing. All these persons were moved to the German Hospice in Jerusalem, where they were looked after by the Sisters of St Charles Borromeo. The people who chose to stay are listed in Appendix 9.[332]

After seven to ten months of living in tents and internment in Cyprus, the majority of Templers left for Australia. A small number returned to Germany.

The last Templers left Israel in the autumn (northern hemisphere) of 1950.

276b) Disembarkment in Cyprus

277) The "Empire Comfort" which took the Templers from Palestine to Cyprus in 1948

278) The "Partizanka" brought many of the Templers from Cyprus to Australia in 1949

CHAPTER THIRTEEN

SALE OF SARONA

WHEN GREAT BRITAIN became the Mandatory power, the sale of land was regulated in Palestine. All transfers of land were made subject to administrative consent which was given as a matter of course.[333]

Sarona and the surrounding land owned by the Templers had become a target for purchase by Jewish individuals and organisations involved in the rapid growth of Tel Aviv well before World War II. By 1939 Jewish settlements were bordering right onto Sarona—Montefiore (a Jewish settlement) was separated only by a road from the Sarona settlement. During the latter 1930s, the Templer Council of Sarona urged its members not to sell their land to neither Arab nor Jews.[334]

279) Palestinian currency coin

When war started in 1939, the British Mandatory Government interned all German nationals. Their assets (real estate, businesses, money, livestock etc) were frozen and could only be sold with the express permission of the British authorities. In relation to land sales, this measure, subject to Government approval, was implemented to prevent undesired land sales to Arabs and Jews in certain areas of Palestine.[335]

During the war, land prices in Palestine were high and there continued to be much interest in purchasing "Templer owned" land around Sarona. Offers were received, especially from Jewish interests to buy the land in $US or £Sterling, with payment being made outside of Palestine. The Sarona settlers resisted these offers as they were still hopeful, at that stage, of returning to their homes and land after the war. The British authorities did approve of the sale of a few small lots in some cases to extinguish debt.[336]

In 1943 the British authorities promulgated the *Land (Acquisition for Public Purposes) Ordinance 1943*. This ordinance enabled the Government to acquire land compulsorily for another party if deemed desirable. In accordance with the ordinance, public notice had to be given (usually in the Palestine Gazette) and the land owner informed of the notice of acquisition. The land owner was given two months in which to lodge a claim for compensation with the Director, Department of Land Settlement. In lodging a claim, the land owner had to show his/her right or interest in the land as well as providing a statement giving details of the compensation claimed, including details under categories (accounts) how the amount of compensation was calculated. The British had categorised the Sarona settlers into two groups—"enemy" for those living in Germany and "enemy subjects" those interned in Palestine and Australia. It appears that only "enemy subjects" would receive any compensation.[337]

The time frame of the ordinance in itself created enormous administrative problems. Many of the landowners on whom the Notices of Acquisition were issued were interned in Australia, without access to the documents required to lodge compensation claims. Others were in Germany and their claim may not have been considered valid, in other instances, land was owned jointly, by companies and partnerships and in some cases by an estate of a deceased person or a combination of the above. To overcome some of the time frame and logistical problems between Australia and Palestine the internees in Australia nominated representatives still in Palestine to deal with this issue on their behalf.[338]

From 1944 onwards, the British expropriated more and more land around Sarona in favour of the Tel Aviv City Council. Although

The Sarona settlers resisted these offers as they were still hopeful, at that stage, of returning to their homes and land after the war

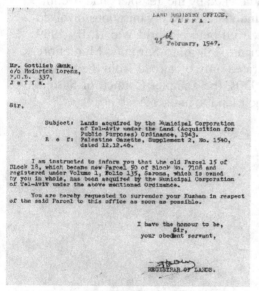

280a) A typical land ordinance order as issued by the British authorities to compulsorily acquire land

From 1944 onwards the British expropriated more and more land around Sarona for the Tel Aviv City Council

claims for compensation were lodged by the affected landowners, no compensation was paid. The settlers in 1946 engaged legal counsel to pursue their claims through the courts if necessary. The legal counsel proposed to seek compensation for both "enemy" claimants and other claimants. The Sarona settlers still in Palestine were reluctant to take this step because they were in an awkward situation, being the plaintiffs against the British Mandatory Government (the expropriating authority) and the Jewish Tel Aviv City Council (the recipient of the expropriated land).[339]

In 1946, several factors had a marked effect on the future of Sarona. One of these was the assassination of Gotthilf Wagner, the last

LAND (ACQUISITION FOR PUBLIC PURPOSES) ORDINANCE, 1943.
NOTICE UNDER SECTIONS 5 AND 7.

IN EXERCISE of the authority vested in the Municipal Corporation of Tel Aviv by virtue of the notice by the High Commissioner under section 22(2) of No.24 of 1943, the Land (Acquisition for Public Purposes) Ordinance, 1943 published in Gazette No.1526 of the 3rd October, 1946, at page 1183, authorising the Municipal Corporation of Tel Aviv to exercise all the powers and rights and perform all the obligations conferred or imposed on ;the High Commissioner or the Attorney General under the provisions of the said Ordinance;

NOTICE IS HEREBY GIVEN that the land specified in the Schedule hereto is required by the Municipal Corporation of Tel Aviv absolutely and that the Municipal Corporation of Tel Aviv is willing to treat for the acquisition of the said land.

Any person claiming to have any right or interest in the said land who desires to receive compensation in respect of the said land is required within two months from the date or the publication of this notice in the Gazette to send to the Director, Department of Land Settlement, a statement of his right or interest in the said land together with evidence in support, which evidence shall include particulars of the registration, if any, in the land registers, and a statement of any claim to compensation made by him, giving details of the compensation claimed, distinguishing the amounts under separate and showing how the amount claimed under each head is calculated.

AND NOTICE IS ALSO HEAREBY GIVEN that the Municipal Corporation of Tel Aviv intends to enter into possession of the said land forthwith as it is urgently required for the purpose for which it is to be acquired, and that the Municipal Corporation of Tel Aviv has directed, and it is hereby directed that any persons having possession of the said land shall yield up possession thereof forthwith.

SCHEDULE

A piece of land having a total area of 30 metric dunums, or thereabout comprising Parcels Nos. 80, 81, 82, 99, 100, 102 and 132 of Land Registration Block No. 6161, Salame, and part of Parcels Nos. 9, 16, 18 and 20 of Land Registration Block No. 6160, and such shares as are not registered in the name of the Municipal Corporation of Tel Aviv in part of Parcels Nos. 6, 10,11 and 12 of Land Registration Block No. 6160, Salame, and coloured light brown and edged with dark brown, on a plan entitled "Plan of Land for Water Supply Reservoirs for Tel Aviv"; a copy of which may be inspected during the usual office hours, at the offices of the Municipal Corporation of Tel Aviv.

This 7th day of October, 1946   I. ROKACH
                                                                Mayor of Tel Aviv.

280b) A typical land ordinance order as issued by the British authorities to compulsorily acquire land

Mayor of Sarona, who was against the sale of Sarona land. Shortly before Mr Wagner's death, Nikolai Schmidt reported on a discussion between Mr Wagner and the Camp Commandant just prior to leaving Sarona. Schmidt writes *"Shortly before our departure, he (Wagner) spoke with the Camp Commandant, who had tried to console him by telling him that if Sarona could not be retained then compensation would be made, to which he (Wagner) replied that Sarona has now existed for 75 years, it is one of the most beautiful settlements, we want it back and not be paid for it, that's why I'm fighting for it."*[340]

Sauer reports in *The Holy Land Called* that:—

"The motives behind the crime were presumably to dispose of an inconvenient man, to intimidate the Templers and, at last, to bring about the sale of Sarona which Wagner had steadfastly refused."[341]

Other factors included the advice of the non-return to Palestine of the internees in Australia; the announcement to the remaining Templers in Palestine that they would not be allowed to remain there; and the worsening political situation between the Arabs and the Jews which was likely to result in civil war. Prices for land were also starting to fall because of these uncertainties.[342]

Many Sarona settlers realised that the only viable option was to dispose of their properties in Palestine

Many Sarona settlers, both in Australia and Palestine realised that the only viable option was to dispose of their properties in Palestine. To this end the Australian internees forwarded power of attorney to the settlers in Palestine so that they had the authority to negotiate. These powers of attorney were signed in May 1946.[343]

On 12 November 1946 a special meeting was called at the Wilhelma compound to consider the sale of land around Sarona. Nikolai Schmidt, who chaired the meeting, outlined the situation regarding expropriated land, the desire to part on good terms with the British and Jewish authorities, the inability to negotiate a realistic price for the land, (much of the land near Tel Aviv was virtually "frozen" by the City of Tel Aviv—there were no individual buyers). He posed the question whether negotiations should be entered into with the representatives from Tel Aviv who had made offers for certain land allotments. After discussion, it was agreed to sell the land for the price offered.[344]

After discussion it was agreed to sell the land for the price offered

At a further meeting on 5 December 1946, the settlers were advised of the progress of the negotiations and that an average price of £P410.00 per dunum (1000square metres) had been offered. This was in the settlers' view a very low price but they realised that the authorities had the power to force a sale at that price. (A paltry price of only £P100 per dunum was discussed for "enemy" property). In any case the final price and sale had to be approved by the Public Custodian. The meeting was further advised that time was critical and a decision needed to be made. At resumption of the meeting two days later, it was agreed that negotiations for the sale continue.[345]

Shortly after, on 11 December 1946, the Central Board of the Temple Society in Palestine made a written offer to sell all land surrounding Sarona, except the actual central settlement (township), to the Mayor of the City of Tel Aviv, for £P420 per dunum payable in Australia subject to, inter alia, that the City of Tel Aviv obtain the necessary consent from the Government by 31 January 1947; that standing crops belong to the vendor; that fixtures and fittings on the land be valued independently; that rates and taxes from 1 April 1946 be paid by the purchaser; and that the Templers be given assistance to leave Palestine on good terms with Arabs and Jews alike. After some further negotiations, a preliminary contract was prepared. At the time of the proposed sale a separate letter was written by the Templer Board to the Lord Mayor of Tel Aviv. In the letter the Board pointed out that the Sarona settlers had made a great sacrifice in selling their land at such a low price and that this should be taken into account to assist them to leave Palestine and settle in Australia. The letter went on to say that the Templers were most anxious to depart with a feeling of friendship towards both Arabs and Jews.[346]

In the letter the Board pointed out that the Sarona settlers had made a great sacrifice in selling their land at such a low price

the Templers were most anxious to depart with a feeling of friendship to both the Arabs and Jews

The contract for the sale was prepared and signed by the parties on 24 March 1947 but not endorsed by the British authorities.

Months of frustration followed as the British Mandatory Government would not ratify the contract. In June 1947 Nikolai Schmidt noted that land prices were going down and that they were now only a third of what they had been 12 months previously.[347]

In November 1947, the Mandatory Government issued a Vesting Order which in effect stopped the Templer internees in both Australia and Palestine from selling their property in Palestine.[348]

On 13 April 1948, the British authorities called the Templer representatives (Messrs. Schmidt, Imberger, Steller and Hahn) to a meeting in Jerusalem. In the presence of the representatives from the City of Tel Aviv, the Templers were advised that the land of the Sarona settlement and adjoining land owned by the settlers had been sold to the City of Tel Aviv for £P3,095,260. The settlers had no choice but to abide by the decision of the Government.[349]

The amount of £P3.100m was made up of £P2.750m for land and £P 0.400m for the actual Sarona settlement, less expenses of

£P0.050m. An initial payment of £P1.300m was made at the time of sale and the balance was to be paid later.[350]

Sauer refers to this sale as *"The British administration took the initiative and forced the sale of Sarona, mainly because the Public Custodian required finance for the intended resettlement of the Germans from Palestine, and this could be procured most easily from the land sale of Sarona."*[351]

When the State of Israel was established in May 1948 the payment of the balance £P1.795m was withheld. The British had wanted to use the funds to offset internment and repatriation costs as well as paying some compensation to the former settlers. Only those settlers categorised as "enemy subjects" that is those in Australia, would receive a small amount of compensation for their real estate. Those settlers classified as "enemy", that is those who had gone to Germany, would not receive anything.[352]

The Sarona settlers knew that Sarona and its surrounding lands had been officially valued at £P4.775m on 1 May 1947 and that the Public Custodian was aware of its true value. This valuation was £P1.675m more than what the British sold Sarona for. In a note prepared by the British Government Colonial Office in 1952, reference is made to the lower amount paid and it shows that the Public Custodian in Palestine believed in 1947 that he could obtain a better price for Sarona than the Templers could on their own during their negotiations with the City of Tel Aviv.[353]

The Public Custodian in Palestine believed that he could obtain a better price for Sarona than the Templers could on their own during their negotiations with the City of Tel Aviv

After the sale of Sarona in 1948, the British authorities retained £P233,890 of the £P1.3m initial payment. Debts accrued and owed by the Sarona settlers were deducted and the balance of £P968,370, was agreed in July 1948 to be sent to Australia. The Australian Minister of Immigration advised the High Commissioner that the assets belonging to Templer "enemy subjects" in Germany would be held in trust until these persons arrived in Australia.[354] In 1949, the Australian Government established the "Temple Society Trust Fund", by statute, to facilitate the disbursement of compensation payments in Australia.[355]

A long and protracted period followed during the late 1940s, 1950s and early 1960s, in which compensation claims by the settlers were contested and negotiated. During that period compensation claims by settlers from the other German settlements were also included. The arduous and complex negotiations concerning the German assets in Israel involved the Australian, British, German and Israeli Governments; valuation of property and arbitration of disputes by international and independent officials; goodwill by the negotiating parties; and patience by the former German Templer settlers of Palestine (many of whom passed away during the process). Throughout this period some compensation payments were made. The payments were made basically for real estate and businesses. No compensation was made for personal belongings, furniture or other valuables. The final payments were made in March 1969 in Germany and in the early 1970s in Australia. The Temple Society Trust Fund was dissolved in 1981.[356]

Thus ended the German Templer settlement of Sarona which had been founded 76 years earlier in 1871 with so much optimism and devotion, and endured so much suffering and hardship, as well as joyous, prosperous and happy times in its short history.

The settlers of Sarona did however leave a proud heritage of their work in the Holy Land, Palestine and Israel—their buildings, their enterprises and agricultural ventures will forever be remembered as having contributed significantly to the modernisation of Palestine and, ultimately, to the benefit of Israel.

The payments were made basically for real estate and businesses. No compensation was made for personal belongings, furniture or other valuables

CHAPTER FOURTEEN

21ST CENTURY RESTORATION OF HISTORIC BUILDINGS

IN 1948 THE BRITISH LEFT SARONA and it was taken over by the Israeli Government, renamed Hakirya (Kirya in Hebrew means "Government Complex")[357] now the heart of the city of Tel Aviv. Part of the former settlement became a centre for government administrative and military agencies and another part was designated for civilian purposes. Access to a significant part of Hakirya became a restricted zone because of the location of the government agencies.

281) The highrise buildings of Tel Aviv towering over the former (No 1) house.

Sarona an agricultural viillage at the turn of the 20th century (background)

235

Immediately after the British left, in 1948, numerous former Sarona homes were used by the Israeli Government as offices and the school was converted to a maternity hospital for the Ministry of Health. Many babies were born there. The hospital was demolished in 2000. The wine cellar was initially used by the Israeli Air Force to assemble aeroplanes—probably some of the first aircraft of the Israeli Air Force.[358]

A description by Maria Weiberle of the former settlement of Sarona portrays the neglect that occurred in the late 1940s but also the beginning of some new roadworks and changes to homes.

"The roadside to Sarona from the cemetery and Guenthner's former café was littered with old cars, tyres, spare parts and general rubbish. The cemetery was still surrounded with a green hedge but the gate was missing and a low stone wall had been built across the opening [. . .] Inside the cemetery, however, all but three of the gravestones had been smashed and removed; many trees had been cut down and rose bushes removed; high grass and nettles were growing over the whole area; the war memorial and the "trees of life" approaching the memorial were still standing."[359] In 1952, the remains of all the dead buried in the Sarona cemetery were transferred to their final resting place in a collective grave in the Jerusalem cemetery, marked by a memorial stone.[360]

"Just after the cemetery the road had been widened with footpaths and was busy with traffic. Near the Ehnis house (No 16) there were boards over excavations for a new pipeline. This was the only access into the actual former Sarona settlement. To enter the settlement proper permission was still required from the police, who were located near the new wine cellar (No 03).[361]

The wine cellar had been painted white and an entrance built from the street. The land between the cellar and Wieland's house (No 67) had been ploughed. An area there had been levelled and rolled and appeared as if it had been used as a small bus terminal at one stage. In Sarona itself, some of the roads had been realigned, asphalted and footpaths built. Some homes still had their front gardens, but in many instances front fences were missing. An old shed near Laemmle's house (No 07) had been demolished and the area turned into lawn with a nice garden [. . .] Due to the realigned streets, some houses, gardens and buildings, especially near the main cross-road, appeared high above the new street levels. Some houses had had extra rooms or extensions built onto them."[362]

In the mid-1950s when Dr Karl Brandt, Professor of Agricultural Economics, was appraising and reporting on the value of secular

real estate in Israel owned by former residents of German nationality
he commented that in Sarona:—*"A very substantial number of the
newer buildings of the Templers belong up to this day to the finest
buildings in Israel. This is best illustrated by the fact that Prime
Minister Ben Gurion lives in one of the former Templer homes and
that many Israeli government offices, government officials, foreign
consulates and wealthy Israeli citizens are housed in them.*

*The German buildings were often of a type of construction designed
to last for a century. The measurements of rooms, the great height
of ceilings, and the additional conveniences ranged from European
housing standards of well-to-do upper-middle class up to people
of considerable wealth. The buildings were kept neat and trim.
Practically all of them were surrounded by gardens or courts with
old shade trees—a particular convenience in a hot climate."*[363]

In the 51 years that elapsed between 1948 and 1999, some of
the former homes and other buildings were either demolished or
renovated. The surrounding orange groves and market gardens
disappeared and were built on as Tel Aviv grew into a large and
important metropolis. Major roads were constructed and highrise
buildings encroached where former Sarona homes and gardens had
been. But more importantly, many of the former houses remained
because they were (still are) occupied by government agencies. It
virtually became an oasis in the midst of city development.

*It virtually became an oasis in the midst
of city development*

*282) Damaged Entrance to the former
Sarona/Jaffa cemetery in early 1950s*

283) Desecrated graves n the former Sarona/Jaffa cemetery in the early 1950s

284) Removal of remains from Sarona/Jaffa cemetery

*285) Removing the signage from the
former Sarona winery*

In the 1970s, preliminary plans for redevelopment of the southern Kirya area were first mooted. It was not until the late 1970s and early 1980s, when an architectural competition was instigated by the Israel Land Administration (ILA) and the City of Tel Aviv for the redevelopment of south Kirya. The very high land values of the Kirya area prompted its owners the ILA and City of Tel Aviv to proceed with the development of the area. The winners of the competition submitted a proposal to preserve only eleven buildings. These buildings were chosen at random by the Council of Preservation and by the municipality without any real consideration of their historical significance and apparently without regard to the heritage importance of other buildings or of the area as a whole. The proposed redevelopment envisaged two rows of towers (highrise buildings), as well as some other towers and an underground public car park for the whole area. It would have meant that all the old historic trees and other plants in former Sarona would be removed, as well as most of the other structures. This plan was approved by the ILA and City of Tel Aviv. However, there was also significant opposition to the plan and negotiations commenced as to its suitability for the area.[364]

286) Aerial view of Sarona before Tel Aviv was established. Top left is part of Jaffa next to the white sands near the sea, 1917

In 1995 Nitza Metzger Szmuk, then head of the Conservation Team, City of Tel Aviv, became responsible for all the conservation work in Tel Aviv and after closer examination she was convinced of the historical importance of the Kirya precinct and the need to preserve a large proportion of it

Between 1990 and 1995 Nitza Metzger—Szmuk, had been appointed by the City of Tel Aviv to be responsible for Modern Style Architecture in the City which included Jaffa. She met with Dr Ejal Jakob Eisler who briefed her on the background of the former Sarona settlement and the Templers. He also provided her with historical photographs, maps and other information. Professor Yossi Ben-Artzi, then Head of Land of Israel Studies, University of Haifa, as well as Professor Dr Alex Carmel, Schumacher Institute, University of Haifa, were consulted as to the significance of various buildings in Kirya. In the meantime, the ILA and City were still proposing to proceed with the planned redevelopment.

In 1995 Nitza Metzger Szmuk, then head of the Conservation Team, City of Tel Aviv, became responsible for all the conservation work in Tel Aviv (excluding Jaffa). As Dr Ejal Jakob Eisler had written his Doctorate dissertation in 1997 about the Templers at Jaffa she contacted him for his knowledge on the area. After closer examination she was convinced of the historical importance of the Kirya precinct and the need to preserve a large proportion of it. The Preservation

Committee, which is a consultative body to the Local Council (consisting of five persons, all but one being members of the City Council with the fifth person an expert on Planning and Construction Law, usually the City Engineer or his deputy) persuaded the City Engineer of Tel Aviv, Mr Baruch Yoskovitch and the conservation committee to visit and view several of the historic buildings. After their visit they also supported the addition of more buildings to the former list. The number of structures to be preserved was increased to 18.[365]

In 1998 Dr Eisler conducted a tour through Sarona with representatives of the Council for Preservation of Buildings and Historic Sites, architects and other interested persons

In 1998, Dr Eisler conducted a tour of Sarona with representatives of the Council for Preservation of Buildings and Historic Sites, architects and other interested persons. In the same year, the Council for Preservation of Buildings and Historic Sites published a brochure in which it featured various aspects of Sarona—the vineyards of Sarona (Thalmann), Aerial Photographs of Sarona (Garwisch) etc.[366]

287) Former Sarona settlement area in 2003 with the trees in the foreground and highrise buildings of Tel Aviv towering behind. Note the Sarona water tower at front right, a wellknown landmark.

289) Above: Original community house Saeulensaal (No 25)—depicting 1870s architectural style of 1870s

288) Left: Old Laemmle house (No 19)—depicting 1870s architectural style

THREE DISTINCT ARCHITECTURAL BUILDING STYLES USED IN THE SARONA SETTLEMENT

291) The new community house (No 9a)—built with Wieland cement bricks in 1911—depicting the early 20th century architectural style

290) Glenk house (No 61)—built with Wieland bricks depicting the early 20th century architectural style

292) Friedrich Haering's house (No 52)—built in the 1930s—depicting the modern 1930s architectural style

293) The new school and community complex (No 84) built in the 1930s—depicting the modern 1930s architectural design

As the Israeli military was stationed in Sarona when the State of Israel was established in 1948, and early Israeli aircraft were built in the wine cellar of Sarona. The Israeli President, Ezer Weizmann, Israel's first fighter pilot, was approached to support the preservation.[367]

In July 1999, the TSA received an email from Ilan Flint, an architect in Israel and also a member of the Israeli Sites and Building Preservation Society—Tel Aviv Branch. In his email Mr Flint advised that a new town planning scheme was being developed which intended to demolish all the remaining former Sarona buildings, except the 18 buildings already listed. His society wanted to preserve the old buildings for their architectural significance as well as for the "unique mixture of trees and plants dating back to the beginning of the Templer settlements". The Society was hoping to preserve up to 40 buildings. He was hopeful that Sarona could be kept alive and no further damage be done to the existing homes.[368]

An article entitled *"The Quiet Houses and Secret Gardens—an Oasis in the Heart of a Grey City"*, written by Michal Kucik, architect, and published in *"Architecture of Israel—Architecture and Interior Design Quarterly" (No.34-1998)* made specific reference to the historical and architectural value of Sarona and its influence and contribution to the development of modern Israel. Reference is made in the article to the trees planted by the early Sarona settlers. They are credited with introducing both ornamental as well as fruit trees which were new to that part of the world and even now are quite rare. Cypress trees were used to mark boundaries, and Washingtonia palms were planted along streets, eucalyptus trees were planted to provide protection against malaria and shade and other ornamental trees contributed to the beauty of the settlement.[369]

Finally in 1999, due to the diligence and perseverance of the project's architects and the Council for Preservation, together with the election of a new Mayor and the appointment of a new City Engineer, Israel Gudovitch, the redevelopment plan was changed to what it is today

Finally in 1999, due to the diligence and perseverance of the project's architects and the Council for Preservation, together with the election of a new Mayor and the appointment of a new City Engineer, Israel Gudovitch, the redevelopment plan was changed to what it is today.[370]

Although nothing is finalised at the time of this book going to press, 19 former homes and buildings in the Civilian Area have been identified for possible restoration and preservation and another five homes and buildings are proposed to be relocated and restored. These buildings are all on the south side of Kaplan Street (formerly Seestrasse). The homes and buildings in the Military Area (north of the Kaplan Street) are not included in the restoration project. It is hoped that possibly up to 12 of the identified buildings will be handed over to the City of Tel Aviv. It is likely that the remaining structures will probably be sold or leased by the ILA. The plan provides that these buildings should not be offices or residences but should be open to the public, even if used by private organisations. In effect they will become buildings for public purposes such as art galleries, coffee shops, museums etc.[371] At this stage one house has been restored.

294) Restored Immanuel Steller house (No 55), 2003

Dr Dan Goldman in the 2003 manuscript of his Ph.D. dissertation "The Architecture of the Templers in their Colonies in *Eretz-Israel*, 1868-1948, and their Settlements in the U.S., 1860-1925" summarises the architectural qualities of the Sarona houses and buildings. He writes *"Sarona shows some of the aspects particular to Templer architecture. It gave Sandel, a young architect at the time (he was 26 years old in 1871), an opportunity to stand out as a capable settlement designer, and it is possible he designed some of Sarona's first buildings. Those houses were based on the Haifa type, with local adaptations: the material was soft local limestone, but the design characteristics were similar: four levels, including the basement and the attic, with the same functional distribution, symmetry in plan and façade, clay tiles roofs, no ornamentation[. . .].*
The appearance of prefab concrete products created a change in house design approach, providing opportunities for the use of more sophisticated construction details, with a general look that is more decorated and more representative and influencing also wall thickness and accuracy of construction [. . .].

The most architecturally noteworthy houses in Sarona were built between the two World Wars. [. . .].They express two faces of Templer architecture: on the one hand, the outstanding designs and superb craftsmanship, on the other the assimilation into the general consensus of the International Style, in a sense, losing the uniqueness of Templer traditional style and merging with the regional mainstream."[372]

In late 2003, the preservation of former Sarona is being administered by a preservation team of the City of Tel Aviv headed by Peera Goldman, a senior architect. Nitza Metzger-Szmuk was engaged as a consultant to the City Engineer's Office for the conservation plan (not including Sarona).[373]

295) With the restoration and preservation of so many of the former homes and buildings an ongoing legacy will remain of the former German Templer settlement of Sarona

With the restoration and preservation of so many of the former homes and buildings an ongoing legacy will remain of the former German Templer settlement of Sarona. The buildings which range from some of the very first ones built in 1870s to the more modern ones of the 1930s enshrine the architectural styles adopted over the settlement's history.

296) Model of proposed redevelopment of Hakirya. Former Sarona settlement will be an oasis in the midst of highrise buildings

CHAPTER FIFTEEN

SARONA IN SONG AND VERSE

S ARONA WAS FORTUNATE to have a person of musical and artistic talent in its midst. Carl Kuebler (1880-1963) was a musically gifted person who wrote and composed two songs about Sarona. Carl Kuebler not only wrote music but he also conducted the Sarona mixed choir for a number of years. He was renowned for his drawings of the Sarona settlement in 1920 and 1937, and the Sidi Bishr internment camp. As well as writing and composing songs about Sarona he also wrote songs for some of the other German Templer settlements.

297) A piano or pianola was in almost every home for entertainment. Hermann Kuebler at the piano

298) Choir with conductor Carl Kuebler, 1925
Standing left to right: Selma Frank, Magda Weeber, Maria Haering, Cecilie Baldenhofer, Hermann Kuebler
(partly obscured), Helene Orth, Hanna Frank, Carl Kuebler (conductor), Heinrich Steller, Hildegard Jung, Paul Frank,
Else Froeschle, Rosa Bacher, Samuel Weller
Seated left to right: Gertrud Kuebler, Elly Weller, Erni Groll

First Sarona Lied—Wo des Audsche Wellen fliessen

Carl Kuebler wrote the words and music of the first Sarona Lied (Sarona Song) whilst held as a prisoner of war in the camp at Sidi Bishr. This song, arranged for a mixed choir, was sung many times in Sarona.[374]

Wo des Audsche Wellen fliessen
Liegt mein Heim mein Elternhaus
Wie ein Wundergarten Gottes
Wie ein goldnes Paradies
(Chorus)

Where the Audsche waves are flowing
Is my home, my parent's house
Like God's wonder garden
Like a golden paradise
(Chorus)

O Du Heimat meiner Jugend
Dein gedenk ich alle Zeit
All mein Sehnen, all mein Hoffen
O wie liegst Du so weit, so weit.

Oh you home of my youth
My thoughts are with you all the time
All my longing, all my aspirations
You are so far, so far away

Durch der Blaetter gruenes Funkeln
Gluehn Orangen traumverloren
Durch die Luefte suess berauschend
Zieht der Rosen Zauberduft
(Chorus)

Through the sparkling green leaves
Dreaming oranges are glowing
Through the sweet air overwhelming
Flows the magical blossom scent
(Chorus)

Moechte Dich noch einmal schauen
Mich an deiner Pracht erbauen
Unter deiner Sonne wandeln
Ruhen in deiner Erde Schoss
(Chorus)

Would like to see you one more time
To enjoy myself on your splendour
To wander under your sun
To rest only in your soil's lap
(Chorus)

(A broad translation by Helmut Glenk)

299) Right: Original music sheet "Wo des Audsche Wellen fliessen" by Carl Kuebler

Second Sarona Lied—Heimat
This song called "Heimat" was a second song written and composed for a mixed choir by Carl Kuebler in 1942 whilst interned in the Sarona Compound (Camp IV).[375]

He called the song "Heimat" (Home). In the song he expressed a deep sense of love and feeling of farewell from the place he called home.

Auf Sarona's gruenen Fluren	*On Sarona's green fields*
Liegt ein Doerflein nett und klein	*Lays a small friendly village*
Goldorangen, Obstkulturen	*Golden oranges, fruit orchards*
Blumengaerten laden ein	*Flower gardens invite one in*
O, du Heimat deutscher Jugend	*Oh, you home of my German youth*
Dich vergess' ich nimmer mehr	*I'll always remember you*
Frohe Arbeit, schoene Tugend	*Happy work, beautiful virtues*
Die lieb ich so sehr so sehr.	*I love you so much, so much*
Freunde sind in dir willkommen	*Friends are welcomed in your midst*
Fremde fuehlen sich auch wohl	*Strangers are made comfortable there*
Jedes Herz ist hier benommen	*Every heart beats faster here*
Von dem Bild das eindrucksvoll	*Due to your impressive portrayal*
O, Du Heimat deutscher Lieder	*Oh, you home of German songs*
Und erklingen sie dann rein	*They resound so very clear*
Leid durch Freude wechselt wieder	*As sorrow and joy alternate*
Im Gesang, wie fein, wie fein	*In song so fine, so fine*
Und wenn ich muss von dir scheiden,	*And when I have to leave you*
Die Erinn'rung bleibet mir,	*The memories will remain*
Und ich kann es nicht vermeiden,	*I am unable to change events*
Wegzugehen dann von Dir	*As I have to leave from here*
O, Du Heimat deutsches Leben,	*Oh, you home of German living*
Und ist dann das Herz so voll	*And my whole heart's so full*
Dankerfuellt fuer's reiche Geben	*Of thanks for your rich giving*
Sag ich Dir, leb wohl, leb wohl.	*As I say good bye, good bye.*

(A broad translation by Helmut Glenk)

300) Music sheet "Heimat" by Carl Kuebler, (sheet 1)

301) Music sheet "Heimat" by Carl Kuebler, (sheet 2)

In August 1940 a German civilian internee, Dr Josef Gorbach, (Internee Number 128) wrote a poem about Sarona.[376]

The poem is entitled **Sarona:**

Sarona, dich gruess ich mit Herz und Hand,
Ich gruesse das Volk, das dort schafft,
Du trautes Stueck Heimat im Heiligen Land,
Du Zierde germanischer Kraft.

Sarona I greet you with heart and hand
I greet the citizens that live there
You beloved piece of home in the Holy Land
You ornament of Germanic strength

Ich wandle so gerne von Haus zu Haus
In der goldenen Sonne Schein
Die Haeuser, die blicken aus Gaerten heraus,
Ich glaub, in der Heimat zu sein!

I love to stroll from house to house
In the golden sunshine
The homes radiate out of the gardens
I imagine that I'm home again

Die Palmen, die Foehren, die Pfefferbaeum',
Gepflanzt von deutscher Hand,
Sie schuetzen vor Stuermen das deutsche Heim
Und gegen der Sonne Brand.

The palms, the pines, the peppercorn trees
Planted by German hands
Protecting the German homes from storms
And against the scorching sun

Oft steh ich am Fenster zu naechtlicher Stund,
Ganz nahe, da rauschet das Meer,
Der Mond macht ueber Sarona die Rund',
Giesst silbernes Licht drueber her.

I often stand by the window at night
Quite near the sounds of the sea
Above Sarona the moon does its round
Pouring silver light over this town

Schakale sich naehern am Waldessaum,
Ihr Heulen gellt wild durch die Nacht,
Die Kinder Saronas, die laecheln im Traum,
Von liebenden Muettern bewacht.

Jackals come closer at the forest's edge
Their howling shrills wildly thru' the night
Sarona's children are smiling in their dreams
Watched over by their loving mothers

Auf Wiesen und Wegen der deutsche Gruss,
Und lachender Kinder Lust!
Wer hier seine Tage verbringen muss,
Dem lacht das Herz in der Brust.

In fields and roads the German greeting
And laughing children's delight
Whoever can spend their days here
Will have a happy heart in their breast

(A broad translation by H Glenk)

APPENDICES

APPENDIX 1—MAYORS OF SARONA[377]

Philipp Dreher
Christian M Jung
Johannes Dreher
Friedrich Laemmle
Heinrich Weeber (snr)
Philipp Groll
Reinhardt Lippmann
Wilhelm Aberle
Max Frank
Gotthilf Wagner

APPENDX 2 THE PIONEERS WHO DIED DURING THE EARLY YEARS 1871-1874[378]

1871
12 October	Christine Sickinger
29 October	Ulrich Lutz

1872
5 January	Sophie Weinmann (child)
11 January	Daniel Weinmann (14 Year Old)
30 March	Christine Roehm
31 March	Conrad Roehm
19 June	Seth Bernhard
22 June	Wilhelm Roehm
29 June	Jonathan Pflugfelder (child)
26 June	Wilhelmine Laemmle (child)
28 September	Friedrich Mann
14 October	Jonathan Maier (child)
22 October	Wilhelmine Laemmle (adult)
12 November	Tabea Dieterle
12 November	Dorothea Heuschele
14 November	Georg Dieterle
14 November	Pauline Maier
22 November	Christine Wennagel (child)
24 November	Wilhelm Besserer (child)
24 November	Johannes Edelmaier
27 November	Katharina Stiefel
28 November	Johannes Meier
30 November	Adam Dreher
1 December	Gottliebin Dreher (child)
1 December	Johann Martin Wennagel
28 December	Johann Georg Edelmaier
30 December	Friedrich Weinmann

1873
8 January	Friedrich Dieterle
10 February	Johann Georg Neber
31 March	Ernst Besserer (child)
7 May	Elisabeth Weinmann
14 October	Gottfried Pflugfelder
14 October	Elisabeth Wennagel
27 December	Maria Magdalena Dreher

1874
25 January	Gottlieb Stiefel (jnr)
27 January	Anna Maria Lutz
2 February	Philippine Kopp (child)
10 August	Maria Knoll (child)
10 August	Jakob Jenner
18 August	Maria Christine Weiberle
31 August	Philipp Dreher
9 September	Anna Knoll
17 September	Gottlieb Stiefel (child)
4 November	Philippine Guenthner
28 December	Christian Wennagel (child)
29 December	Johanna Kuebler (child)

APPENDIX 3—BUILDINGS AND HOUSES BUILT BEFORE WORLD WAR I

The homes and buildings listed below were identified from Carl Kuebler's 1920 drawing of Sarona.

Carl Kuebler (08)	Samuel Groll (28)
Johannes Weiss (31)	Carl Baldenhofer (60)
Philipp Groll (12)	Johnathan Weller (34)
Jakob Jung (11)	Geschwister Haering (26)
Jakob Sickinger (33)	Johannes Orth (35)
Otto Jung (36)	Willi Groezinger (38)
Samuel Weller (39)	Karl Steller (40)
Karl Kuebler (13)	Fritz, Otto and Lina Laemmle (07)
Heinrich Hasenpflug (06)	Immanuel Knoll (71)
Heinrich Weeber (snr) (04)	Gottlob Graze (40)
Christian Pflugfelder (20)	Immanuel Steller (55)
Ida Lange (57)	Willi Guenthner (21)
Johann Wennagel (68)	Lydia Weller (58)
Georg Weller (22a)	Gottlieb Glenk (61)
Reinhardt Lippmann (46)	Reinhardt Lippmann (47)
Otto Venus (59)	Johannes Frank (54)
Jakob Weller (27)	Jenner (later converted to Altersheim) (53)
Heinrich Jung (10)	Jakob Weiss (11)
Fritz Kuebler (14)	Georg Weinmann (15)
Jakob Jung (32)	Karl Froeschle (23)
Wilhelmine Laemmle (19)	Karl Knoll (05)
Old (1873) comm. house (25)	New (1911) community house (09a)
Winery caretaker house (03)	Winery (2a)
Wine cellar (18)	Knoll old barn (73)

APPENDIX 4—WAR CASUALTIES[379]

World War I Casualties (Jaffa/Sarona)

Johannes Baldenhofer	9/11/6/1915 Arras, France
Hermann Johannes Eppinger	17/4/1917 Bouchain, France
Johann Jacob Daniel Groezinger	20/9/1920 Nazareth, Palestine
Friedrich Jung	1/11/1918 Hayder-Pascha, Turkey
Johannes Laemmle	5/10/1918 Aleppo, Syria
Jakob Mayer/Maier (non Templer)	13/1/1918 Nazareth, Palestine
Christian Orth	29/8/1915 Ostrow, Poland

Samuel Scheerle .... 30/6/1915 Serbia
Samuel Sickinger .... 16/8/1916 Karabaden, France
Peter von Ustinov ....13/7/1917 Ypres, France
Karl Wagner .... 31/10/1914 Messines, France
Philipp Hermann Wagner .... 31/10/1914 Messines, France
Theodor Wagner .... 24/8/1916 Somme, France
Christian Weiss
Johannes Wennagel(jnr) .... 31/10/1914 Messines, France
Karl Alfred Theodor Wolfer .... 27/8/1916 Beaumonte, France

World War II Casualities (Jaffa/Sarona)
Volker Baumkamp
Friedrich Blaich .... January 1945, Silesia, Germany
Friedrich Franz Blanckert .... Russia
Rudolf Friedrich Gollmer.. 13/11/1943
Heinrich Hasenpflug
Oskar Hugo Hoffmann .... 14/11/1943 Leros, Greece
Erich Knoll ....1941 Rostov, Russia
Oswald Knoll .... 1944, Russia
Helmuth Georg Reinhardt 16/8/44
Fritz Sickinger .... 1942 Stalingrad, Russia
Rolf Uhlherr
Kurt Wagner .... 1942 North Africa
Hermann Weigold
Theodor Weller...8/4/1945
Heinrich Wurst 1945

APPENDIX 5—SARONA STATISTICAL INFORMATION[380]

Population
1872	63
1877	138
1884	256
1892	226
1904	250
1914	190
1918	140
1920	80
1921	190
1926	212
1930	236
1935	348
1939	428

Births
1878-82	51
1883-87	54
1888-92	36
1893-97	39
1898-02	36
1903-05	8
1906-20	unknown
1921-25	19
1926-30	23
1931-35	35

Deaths
1873-77	83
1878-82	42
1883-87	48
1888-92	40
1893-97	23
1898-02	30
1903-05	21
1906-20	unknown
1921-25	10
1926-30	14
1931-35	19

School Pupils
1874	20
1884	37
1894	57
1914	60
1924	40
1934	114

APPENDIX 6—THE 1941 DEPORTEES FROM SARONA TO AUSTRALIA[381]

Albrecht Aberle
Julius Aberle
Julie Aberle
Gerd Aberle
Helmuth Bacher
Grete Bacher
Guenther Bacher
Arnold Bacher
Rosa Bacher
Werner Bacher
Irmgard Bacher
Friedrich Baldenhofer
Lina Baldenhofer
Hans-Karl Baldenhofer
Erich Baldenhofer
Werner Baldenhofer
Erhard Baldenhofer
Ilse Baldenhofer
Klaus Baldenhofer
Helga Baldenhofer
Wilhelm Baumert
Elise Baumert
Emma Baumert
Helmuth Baumert
Gottlob Beck
Bertha Beck
Hannelore Beck
Gudrun Beck
Urban Beck
Helene Beck
Isolde Beck
Brigitte Beck
Gunther Beck
Ludwig Beck
Lina Beck
Kurt Beck
Hartmut Beck
Hans Beck
Bernhard Blaich
Hermann Doh
Max Frank
Thea Frank
Ilse Frank
Walter Frank
Eberhard Frank
Friedrich Froeschle

Gunda Froeschle
Ruediger Froeschle
Ewald Glenk
Anne Glenk
Dieter Glenk
Gottlieb Glenk
Paula Glenk
Hermann Graze
Marta Graze
Richard Graze
Gertrud Graze
Theodor Graze
Harald Graze
Ingeborg Graze
Oskar Groll
Willi Groezinger
Ella Groezinger
Ilse Groezinger
Brunhilde Groezinger
Albert Guenthner
Johanna Guenthner
Waldtraut Guenthner
Eberhard Gunthner
Friedrich Haering
Maria Haering
Erich Haering
Manfred Haering
Otto Hennig
Elisabeth Hennig
Elfriede Hennig
Gisela Hennig
Theodor Sam Hoffmann
Luise Hoffmann
Klaus Hoffmann
Ernst Hoffmann
Max Hoffmann
Hermann Hoersch
Olga Hoersch
Heinz Hoersch
Walter Hoersch
Wilhelm Kahlow
Bertha Kahlow
Edgar Knoll
Hermann Krafft
Gertrud Krafft
Bertha Krafft

Ulrich Krafft
Irene Krafft
Walter Krafft
Albert Kuebler
Fritz Kuebler
Johanna Kuebler
Heinz Kuebler
Luise Kuebler
Hermann Kuebler
Betty Kuebler
Ernst Kuebler
Annchen Kuebler
Willi Kuebler
Gretel Kuebler
Wilhelm Kuebler
Maria Kuebler
Egon Kuebler
Christian Kuebler
Maria Kuebler
Gerda Kuebler
Hilda Kuebler
Anni Kuebler
Albert Kugler
Fritz Laemmle
Erni Laemmle
Helmut Laemmle
Waldtraut Laemmle
Erika Laemmle
Friedrich Lippmann
Mathilde Lippmann
Lotte Lippmann
Friedel Lippmann
Agnes Lorenz
Roland Neef
Edith Neef
Helmut Neef
Herbert Neef
Manfred Neef
Friedrich Orth
Auguste Orth
Manfred Orth
Hetty Orth
Horst Orth
Johannes Orth
Reinhold Orth
Theodor Richter
Lotte Richter
Edda Richter
Rosa Roller
Georg Roller
Gotthold Schnerring
Hedwig Schnerring
Helga Schnerring
Guenther Schnerring
Nicolai Schmidt
Eugen Sickinger
Eugenie Steller
Immanuel Steller**
Gotthold Steller
Emilie Steller
Liselotte Steller
Gretel Steller
Renate Steller

Eugen Steller
Elli Steller
Anni Steller
Inge Steller
Reiner Steller
Erich Steller
Emma Steller
Bernd Steller
Friedrich Trefz
Wilhelm Trefz
Anna Trefz
Annemarie Trefz
Hartmann Trefz
Fritz Weiberle
Selma Weiberle
Georg Weinmann
Luise Weinmann
Leni Weinmann
Kurt Weinmann
Theo Weinmann
Christian Weiss
Bertha Weiss
Ingeborg Weiss
Johannes Weiss
Pauline Weiss
Gertrud Weiss
Gretel Weiss
Otto Weller
Samuel Weller
Paula Weller
Rolf Weller
Hugo Weller
Guenther Weller
Gerhard Weller
Hugo Wennagel
Johanna Wennagel
Peter Wennagel
Hermann Wied
Rosa Wied
Irene Wied
Karl Wied
Nelly Wied
Gisela Wied

** Immanuel Steller died of a cardiac arrest on the voyage to Australia. He was buried at sea on 10 August 1941.

APPENDIX 7—THE EXCHANGE INTERNEES FROM SARONA 1941-1944[382]

First Exchange—December 1941
Anna Luise Faig
Auguste Faig
Lothar Faig
Rita Faig
Juergen Faig
Elisabeth Faig
Lydia Gude
Hildegard Keller

Monika Keller
Lina Antonia Kruegler
Martha Dorethea Kuhnle
Ingeborg Martha Kuhnle
Anna Margarete Rohrer
Hellmut Christian Rohrer
Brigitte Rohrer
Hertha Weller
Ingrid Weller
Irene Weller
Kuno Weller
Elenore Wenz
Paul Wieland

**There were 71 persons exchanged on the first exchange including 21 from Sarona (Camp IV). The list of names may include other than Sarona settlers as persons from other areas outside Sarona were interned in Camp IV.

Second Exchange—November 1942
Erna Aberle
Erich Aberle
Heinz Aberle
Hedwig Aberle
Maria Aberle
Hanna Aberle
Frieda Appinger
Klaus Appinger
Klara Bez
Eckhard Bez
Selma Bitzer
Ernstine Bitzer
Anna Bulach
Thekla Ehmann
Annemarie Ehmann
Linda Eppinger

Barbara Faig
Maria Feubel
Margot Feubel
Regina Feubel
Lydia Froeschle
Otto Froeschle
Walter Froeschle
Manfred Froeschle
Tabea Gollmer
Ida Gollmer
Sarah Guenthner
Anni Haar
Felix Haar
Ruth Haar
Hedwig Haar
Traute Haar
Maria Haar
Gisela Haar
Guenther Haar
Rosa Haering
Erich Hahn
Selma Hasenpflug

Elsa Hasenpflug
Rosemarie Hasenpflug
Siegfried Hasenpflug
Else Hermann
Rosine Heselschwerdt
Ingeborg Heselschwerdt
Frieda Heselschwerdt
Liselotte Heselschwerdt
Heinz Heselschwerdt
Uta Heselschwerdt
Maria Hess
Anna Hirschmann
Theodora Imberger
Gertrud John
Charlotte Joite
Margarethe Katz
Kurt Katz
Helmut Katz
Waldtraut Katz
Elisabeth Kell
Elfriede Kell
Linda Kleinknecht
Manfred Kleinknecht
Karl Knoll
Lydia Knoll
Anni Kruegler
Traude Kruegler
Rolf Kruegler
Helga Kruegler
Dorothea Kruegler
Else Kruegler
Paula Kuebler
Siegfried Kuebler
Gisela Kuebler
Alfred Lange
Emma Lange
Grete Lange
Peter Lange
Else Lange
Dieter Lange
Ingrid Lange
Hulda Lange
Gisela Lange
Werner Lange
Ida Lange
Helene Mainhard
Margarethe Mainhard
Frieda Mueller
Mathilde Nuss
Gisela Nuss
Bertfried Nuss
Emma Plesse
Meta Rohde
Laura Roehler
Johanna Schnerring
Ottilie Schulz
Ingrid Schulz
Anna Seeger
Wilhelma Steller
Kuno Steller
Werner Steller
Uta Steller
Hertha Struve

Herbert Struve
Hans Jurgen Struve
Robert Stuetz
Elfriede Stuetz
Ilse Stuetz
Hanna Walther
Gertrud Weberruss
Lydia Weidemann
Erika Weidemann
Helga Weidemann
Ilse Weller
Ursula Weller
Ulf Weller
Ulrich Weller
Martha Weller
Nella Weller
Gunther Weller
Heinz Weller
Hertha Wennagel
Krista Wennagel
Theodora Wieland
Dora Wurster
Elfriede Wurster
Erich Wurster
Hulda Wurster
Nelly Wurster
Peter Wurster
Hans Karl Wurster
Helene Zieschank

** This listing of names refers not only to the Sarona settlers but may include the names of persons exchanged through Sarona (Camp IV). Persons from outside the pre-war Sarona settlement were interned in the camp during the war. There were 302 persons exchanged on the second exchange including 130 from Sarona (Camp IV).

Third Exchange—July 1944
Johanna Baldenhofer†
Dieter Baldenhofer†
Helene Freihofer
Emil Gollmer
Frieda Gollmer
Johannes Heselschwerdt†
Katherine Heselschwerdt†
Olga Heselschwerdt†
Cornelia Heselschwerdt†
Ernst Klink
Dorothea Klink
Sophie Kuebler†
Elly Uhlmann
Karoline Wahl

There were 42 persons in the July 1944 exchange including 14 from the Sarona Camp IV. Some of the names appearing above may

not have been Sarona residents before the war.

"†" denotes those who died in the air raid on Stuttgart on 13 July 1944.

APPENDIX 8—INTERNEES TRANSFERRED FROM SARONA (CAMP IV) TO WILHELMA (CAMP V)[383]

Julie Aberle
Mathilde Aberle
Kaethe Aberle
Inge Aberle
Erika Aberle
Elisabeth Bacher
Carl Baldenhofer
Cecilie Baldenhofer
Dorothea Baldenhofer
Adolf Bamberg
Ludwig Biehler
Else Beck
Ingrid Beck
Rolf Beck
Martha Beyer
Horst Ulrich Beyer
Marie Bienzle
Ernstine Bleyer
Friedericke Blaich
Ilse Blaich
Fritz Buchhalter
Maria Buchhalter
Ida Buchhalter
Leopoldine Dauberger
Fritz Doh
Ilse Doh
Marie Eppinger
Barbara Faig
Dora Faig
Samuel Faig
Johanna Faig
Stephanus Frank
Charlotte Frank
Elisabeth Frank
Johannes Frank
Wega Frank
Wilhelm Froeschle
Maria Froeschle
Mina Froeschle
Helene Froeschle
Gottlob Graze
Cornelia Graze
Marie Graze
Samuel Groll
Emilie Groll
Agnes Groll
Rosine Groll
Adelheid Groll
Wilhelm Groll
Elsa Groll

Loni Groll
Walter Groll
Lina Ground
Johann Griemann
August Haar
Hulda Haar
Charlotte Haar
Siegfried Hahn
Barbara Hagenlocher
Martha Hoffmann
Wilhelm Hoffmann
Sophie Imberger
Emma Imberger
Hermann Imberger
Edith Imberger
Christian Imberger
Elisabeth Imberger
Horst Rainer Imberger
Josef Janush
Eugen John
Emilie John
Heinrich Jung
Luise Jung
Katherine Jung
Jakob Jung
Karoline Jung
Walter Jung
Traude Jung
Gisela Jung
Eckhardt Jung
Karl Kaiser
Karoline Kaiser
Miriam Keilberg
Reginald Keilberg
Ruth Keilberg
Anna Maria Kloz
Josef Kloz
Paula Kloz
Immanuel Knoll
Bertha Knoll
Horst Kolb
Christian Kruegler
Tabitha Kruegler
Anna Kruegler
Maria Kruegler
Klara Kruegler
Heinrich Lorenz
Karl Kuebler
Pauline Kuebler
Klara Kuebler
Timotheus Lange
Irma Lange
Anneliese Lippmann
Anna Moll
Lydia Neef
Martha Noz
Brunhilde Noz
Emma Noz
Maria Orth
Paula Paulus
Herbert Petrick
Lydia Reinhardt

Anna Rohrer
Gottlieb Ruff
Pauline Ruff
Maria Ruff
Julie Scheerer
Theodor Scheerer
Frieda Schmalzried
Martha Schmalzried
Nikolai Schmidt
Rosa Schmidt
Wera Schmidt
Gisela Schmidt
Carl (snr) Schnerring
Carl (jnr) Schnerring
Luise Schnerring
Amalie Schnerring
Theodora Schnerring
Maria Schnerring
Frieda Seerling
Jakob Sickinger
Roesle Sickinger
Rosine Steller
Karl Steller
Martha Steller
Hans Thuma
Irene Thuma
Alfred Thuma
Adolf Wagner
Gotthilf Wagner
Luise Wagner
Maria Wagner
Frida Wagner
Lina Wagner
Daniel Weinmann
Katherina Weinmann
Karoline Weeber
Hilde Weeber
Katherine Weigold
Jakob Weiss
Elisabeth Weiss
Gerda Weiss
Irmgard Weiss
Gottliebin Weller
Jakob Weller
Pauline Weller
Inge Weller
Karoline Weller
Ruth Weller
Lydia Weller
Maria Weller
Elly Wennagel
Gertrud Zeipert

The above list of names of the internees transferred to Wilhelma. It may also include persons who were interned in Sarona (Camp IV) but were not residents of Sarona before the war.

Other Internees—Sarona Camp IV

Other internees from Sarona Camp IV whose future location/destination is unknown. Included in the listing below are the names of the Kaiserswerth Sisters (or Lutheran Sisters) but they have not be able to be identified individually. These Sisters were also transferred to Wilhelma. (In 1943 a number of German speaking East African families were interned in the Sarona compound. They were included in the third exchange in 1944.[384]

Maria Baeuerle
Theodora Barkhausen
Leonhard Bauer
Marie Bauer
Irmela Bauer
Alfred Berler
Ottilie Berler
Donald Berler
Herbert Berler
Franz Billy
Margarethe Bieda
Helene Freihofer
Edward Hanauer
Sophia Heidheus
Klara Kleinknecht
Jamila Kleinknecht
Anita Kleinknecht
Paola Kleinknecht
Hilda Kleinknecht
Wolfgang Kleinknecht
Joachim, Graf von Luettichau
Maria Maass
Bernhard Nienhaus
Maria Orleans
Helene Orleans
Anna Pentinghaus
Rosine Prinz
Anna Prisseka
Rosalie Posluschny
Meta Rohde
Carl Schaaf
Ursula Sachs
Katherine Seeger
Christine Speidel
Emilie Steinberg
Gabrielle Orfan, Graefin von Tornau
Julie Uhlmann
Karl Ludwig Uhlmann
Lina Uhlmann
Erich Weinzinger
Martha Wimmer
Siegfried Zwillinger

APPENDIX 9—INTERNEES WHO CHOSE TO REMAIN IN PALESTINE[385]

Nikolai Schmidt
Babette Schmidt
Agathe Lange
Repha Franz
Hermann Imberger
Edith Imberger
Christian Imberger
Elisabeth Imberger
Horst Rainer Imberger
Anna Rohrer
Jakob Imberger
Rosa Imberger
Bertha Knoll
Maria Weller
Heinrich Lorenz
Karoline Dreher
Heinrich Jung
Dorothea Specker
Hans Bulach
Marie Bienzle
Julie Aberle
Mathilde Aberle
Maria Weiberle
Selma Hasenpflug
Karl Schnerring (snr)
Luise Schnerring
Karl Schnerring (jnr)
Samuel Faig
Dora Faig
Johanna Faig
Sophie Schanz
Lydia Weller
Maria Ruff
Pauline Ruff
Mathilde Weigold and her mother
Emma Imberger
Frieda Schmalzried
Martha Schmalzried
The Kaiserswerth Sisters (orLutheran Sisters)

The above all moved to Jerusalem after the departure of the internees to Cyprus.

ACKNOWLEDGEMENTS

We acknowledge the help, encouragement and information provided by the following persons. Without their wonderful recollections, photographs and items of interest, as well as assisting us in our research, this historic documentation could not have been compiled in such detail. In many instances they opened their hearts to share with us happy and joyous memories as well as sad ones and hardship. We thank each and everyone of them.

In Australia
Gerd Aberle
Anni Beck
Vera Bieg
Erich Baldenhofer
Renate Beilharz
Dr Rolf Beilharz
Gertrud Blessing
Hans Blessing
Charlotte Dravenicks
Ingrid Edelmaier
Rolf Edelmaier
Kurt Ehnis
Albrecht Frank
Andrew Glenk
Brendon Glenk
Dieter Glenk
Traude Glenk
Theo Graze
Brunhilde Groezinger
Felix Haar
Siegfried Hahn
Ilse Heinrich
Else Hermann
Mark Herrmann
Renate Herrmann
Olga Hoersch
Gisela Hoffmann
Klaus Peter Hoffmann
Peter Hornung
Lurline Knee
Gretel Krockenberger
Oskar Krockenberger
Olga Kroh
Anni Kuebler
Helene Kuebler
Otto Kuebler
Agnes Laemmle
Dr Charlotte Laemmle
Lina Laemmle
Manfred Loebert
Otto Loebert
Kristine McAree
Siegfried Messner
Hedwig Meyer
Lieselotte Minzenmay

Luise Minzenmay
Ilse Nicholson
Cecil O'Brien
Reinhold Orth
Gretel Ottenhoff
Hans Pisch
Ernst Ruff
Helmut Ruff
Irene Ruff
Manfred Schnerring
Erika Schulz
Guenther Schulz
Elly (Eugen) Steller
Elly (Hugo) Steller
Gisela Steller
Herbert Steller
Elisabeth Venus
Inge Vitols
Gerhard Wagner
Hugo Weller
Gunter Weller
Hartmut Weller
Rolf Weller
Hedwig Wennagel
Hugo Wennagel
Loni Wilke

In Germany
Wolfgang Blaich
Erna Brenner
Peter Bruessel
Hildegard Groezinger
Brigitte Hoffmann
Karin Klingbeil
Brigitte Kneher
Peter Lange
Lore Paulus

In England
Martin Higgins

In Israel
Yoel Amir
Dr Jakob Eisler
Dr Danny Goldman
Benny Kenan
Nitza Metzger-Szmuk
Dr Yaron Perry

ABOUT THE AUTHORS

Helmut Glenk

Helmut was born in 1943 at Tatura, Victoria, Australia where his parents were interned. He is a descendant of the Glenks who emigrated to Palestine in 1876 and who settled in Sarona. His paternal grandfather and grandmother, Gottlieb and Paula (nee Knoll) were both born in Sarona, Palestine in the 1880s. His father Ewald was born there in 1909. His mother Anne (nee Schurr), came from Geislingen, Germany and went to Palestine in the 1930s. Helmut's brother, Dieter, was born in Jaffa, Palestine in 1938. The Glenks were part of the contingent of deportees who were brought to Australia in 1941.

After the war the Glenks settled in Bayswater, Victoria, Australia. They were the first Templers from Camp in Tatura to settle in Bayswater in November 1946. Helmut grew up there and finished his primary and secondary education in the local area.

On completion of secondary schooling he joined the Victorian Public Service and studied Public Administration at the Royal Melbourne Institute of Technology graduating with a Diploma. After a career spanning nearly 40 years with the Victorian Public Service, during which he held a number of senior positions as well as being Chief Executive Officer of a Statutory Authority, he left the service in 2000 to pursue other interests. On leaving the VPS he was awarded Life Membership of the Institute of Public Administration for *"outstanding contribution to the achievement of the Institute's objectives and for exemplary service to the Victorian Community"*.

In 2001 he was a member of the group which organised the 60th anniversary get together of the Templer internees who had been interned at Tatura in 1941.

He has co-authored a short history of the Glenk family in Bayswater (published in "The Fruits of Bayswater/Wantirna" as well as contributing other articles for Bayswater Inside Out (a local newsletter). He was a contributor to "Ringwood Recalls" (a history of the first 50 years of Ringwood High School/Ringwood Secondary College). He has been interviewed on the local Community Radio on some of his childhood experiences in Bayswater.

After extensive research of archival material and written texts as well as personal interviewing, he wrote the text for this publication and the captions for the illustrations.

Helmut lives in the Eastern suburbs of Melbourne with his wife Lorraine. They have three children and five grandchildren.

His interests are his family, history, travelling and reading. He is a keen vegetable gardener and likes the outdoors, especially fishing and hunting.

Manfred Haering

Manfred, was born in Jaffa/Sarona in 1938. He is the second son of Friedrich and Maria (nee Loehmann) Haering. The Haering family had lived in Sarona since 1873. Manfred's mother came from Oberjesingen near Herrenberg, in Germany. His older brother, Erich, was born in Jaffa/Sarona in 1934.

In 1941 Manfred, and his family, were part of the group of Templers that were deported to Australia. He spent the next 6½ years interned with his family in Camp III at Tatura, Victoria, Australia. His sister, Resi, was born there in 1944. The Haering family were the last internees to leave camp on 7 January 1948 after nearly 6½ years internment.

After leaving Camp the family first settled in Mount Macedon for just over a year before settling in Boronia. Manfred has continued to live in the Boronia/Bayswater area all his life. After schooling he completed an Electrical Mechanics apprenticeship and then started his own successful electrical contracting business until he retired in 2002.

Manfred is married to Jacomina (Minnie) and they have two children and three grandchildren. He is an active member of the Bayswater/Boronia Temple Community—currently President of the Bayswater Kegel Club.

Manfred has videoed several functions involving the Templers in Australia—in August 1991, he video recorded the 50 year celebrations at Tatura of the arrival and subsequent internment of the 1941 contingent of Germans from Palestine, and in 2002 the official opening of the Templer Chapel in Bayswater. In 2001 he was the instigator and a member of the organising group for the 60 years commemorative celebrations of the former internees and their families at Tatura. He also videoed the celebrations.

In April 1999, Manfred joined a tour to Israel which had been organised by the Temple Society in Germany. A highlight of the tour was a visit to Hakirya a suburb of Tel Aviv and the site of the former German Templer Settlement of Sarona. Manfred was able to gain access to his parent's house—the house of his early childhood. This left a huge personal impression on him. Therefore when the opportunity arose to help with the restoration of the buildings designated for preservation in Hakirya he became the main mover to gather support in Australia for this project. He has worked tirelessly to seek out information and speak with persons who could provide relative details and photographs for the restoration work and this publication.

His interests are his family, travelling, fishing, hunting, playing tennis and snow skiing.

Horst Blaich

Horst was born in 1932 in Haifa, Palestine. His parents Albert and Hertha nee Katz were both born in Palestine. During WW II Horst, his mother and brother were interned in the Waldheim Camp and exchanged to Germany in November 1942. After the war Horst completed an apprenticeship as a colour-photo lithographer and emigrated with his family to Australia and settled in Bayswater.

In the early 1950s he was very active in the Templer Jugendgruppe (Younger set) publishing the early JG newsletters and helping organise the annual Templer Sommerfest.

Horst furthered his education and skills by completing an advanced Printing Technology Course and then proceeding to study management and Industrial Engineering. As a member of the Institute of Industrial Engineers he served on their committee for a number of years.

Horst developed an interest in Quality and Productivity, and in particular the Quality Circle concept after he undertook a comprehensive study in 1978 of Japan's phenomenal productivity boom. In 1982 Horst successfully installed Quality Circles at W D & H O Wills (Australia), a major company of the AMATIL group of companies.

As an Industrial Engineer, with long standing production management experience, Horst continued to demonstrate the benefits of Quality Circles-group problem solving through employee participation. Horst was one of the "pioneers" in the Quality Circles concept in Australia. In 1982 he was instrumental in forming the Melbourne Chapter of the IQAC (now the Australian Quality Production) the first such chapter outside the continental USA. As President of the Chapter he organised the first Quality Circles conferences in Australia. After five years the Chapter became the independent Australian Quality Circle Association with Horst as its inaugural President.

In 1985 Horst formed his own company—Horst Blaich Pty Ltd—Total Quality Management Consultants and Publishers. Horst has worked successfully for and with major organisations in Australia including government authorities, defence forces, the manufacturing sector and service industries. In conjunction with donald dewar, of the usa, horst published "team leader manual" on statistical problem solving techniques for employee participative team work.

Horst has a keen interest in Family History and has lectured and trained people in the sciences of Genealogy. He voluntarily served as the Genealogical adviser to the Church of Jesus Christ of Latter Day Saints for many years and trained the Family History Centres staff throughout Australia. Horst served in many Church Leadership positions and as Bishop for the Church.

Horst is married to Irene and they have five children and ten grandchildren.

He is now retired and writing his family's history and maintains his *"Albert Blaich Family Archive"* with a large Templer Family computer data base. He has been supplying valuable information to the "Sarona Restoration Team" under the control of the Tel Aviv Municipal Council and UNESCO offices in Israel. He supplied many photographs and information about the Templer architecture to Danny Goldman, Architect and University Lecturer. Dr Goldman used this in preparation of his doctorate dissertation and referred to Horst as his "partner in crime".

Horst has initiated the Temple Society Australia Heritage Group and is leading the group into the modern archival and historical research era. The Heritage Group is also developing a photographic database, Templer family genealogical database and the translation and publishing of historical books.

Horst designed the cover and coordinated the book layout and illustrations for this publication.

In recent times Horst has organised and presented photographic exhibitions of the former German Templer Settlements in Sydney, New South Wales, Tanunda, South Australia and Melbourne, Victoria. Horst has researched and written a series of family history booklets

Descendants of Johann Katz, 1660, published 1998;
The Blaich Family of the Black Forest, published 1999;
Descendants of David Unger, 1667, published 2000;
A Visit to the Old Neuweiler—Black Forest, published 2002;
The old Hofstetter Blaich House—Black Forest, published 2002;
A Young Man on the Way to a New World of Hope—Sea Journey From Germany to Australia 1951, published 2002.

BIBLIOGRAPHY

Balke, Ralf 2001, *Hakenkreuz im Heiligen Land—Die NSDAP—Landesgruppe Palaestina (Swastika in the Holy Land—The NSDAP Country Group Palestine).*—Sutton Verlag GmbH, Erfurt, Germany

Bauer, Leonard 1903, *Volksleben im Lande der Bibel (Life in the Land of the Bible)*—Kommission Verlag von H G Wallmann, Leipzig, Germany

Ben-Artzi, Yossi 1992, Religious *Ideology and Landscape Formation in Historical Perspective*, Cambridge University Press

Bitzer, Karl 1968, *Rueckschau ins gelobte Land 1894-1968 (Looking back into the Promised Land)*—Stuttgart, Germany

Brandt, Professor Dr Karl 1957, *Report on the Value of Secular Real Estate in Israel—Owned by Former Residents of German Nationality or Extraction*—Report to the Ministerial Director Wolff, Department of Foreign Affairs, Federal Republic of Germany, Bonn

Brugger, Hans 1908, *Die deutschen Siedlungen in Palaestina (The German Settlements in Palestine)*—published in the New Year Newsletter of the Literary Society Bern, Switzerland, 1909

Bullock, D L 1988, *Allenby's War—The Palestine-Arabian Campaigns 1916-1918*—Blandford, London, England

Carmel, Alex 1973, *Die Siedlungen der wuerttembergischen Templer in Palaestina 1868-1918 (The Settlements of the Templers from Wuerttemberg in Palestine 1868-1918)*—W. Kohlhammer Verlag, Stuttgart, Germany

Carmel, Alex 1978, *Palaestina Chronik 1853-1882 (Palestine Chronicle 1853-1882)*—Vaas Verlag, Ulm, Germany

Carmel, Alex, Eisler, Jakob 1999, *Der Kaiser reist ins Heilige Land, (The Kaiser travels to the Holy Land)*, W. Kohlhammer Verlag, Stuttgart, Germany.

Christliche Pioniere in Palaestina—Der deutsche Beitrag zum Wiederaufbau des Heiligen Landes 1799-1918 (The German Contribution towards the Reconstruction of the Holy Land 1799-1918) 2003. An accompanying booklet at the exhibition held in the Wuerttemberg State Library, Stuttgart on *"The German contribution to the Reconstruction of Palestine in the 19th Century"* by the *"Gottlieb-Schumacher-Institute of Research"* University of Haifa and by the *"Institute for Jewish Studies"* University of Basel

de Haas, Rudolf 1930, *Der Orangenpflanzer von Sarona (The Orange Grower from Sarona)*—Ensslin & Laiblins Verlagsbuchhandlung, Reutlingen, Germany

Eisler, Jakob 1997, *Der deutsche Beitrag zum Aufstieg Jaffas 1850-1914—Zur Geschichte Palaestinas im 19. Jahrhundert (The German Contribution to the Rise of Jaffa 1850-1914—To the History of Palestine in the 19th Century)*—Harrassowitz Verlag, Wiesbaden, Germany

Eisler, Jakob 2001, *"Deutsche Kolonisten im Heiligen Land—Die Familie John Steinbeck in Briefen aus Palaestina und USA (German Colonists in the Holy Land—The John Steinbeck Family, Letters from Palestine and the USA)"*, Hirzel Verlag Stuttgart, Germany

Eisler, Jakob, Haag, Norbert, Holtz, Sabine 2003, *Kultureller Wandel in Palaestina im fruehen 20. Jahrhundert (Cultural Change in Palestine in the early 20th Century)*—bibliotheca academia Verlag, Epfendorf, Germany

Eisler, Jakob 2004, *Die Erkundungsreise der Templer nach Palaestina im Jahre 1858 (The Fact Finding Mission of the Templers in 1858)*, Beilage der Warte des Tempels No. 11

Encyclopaedia Britannica—Volume 17, (1962), William Benton Publisher, Chicago,

Fast, Theodor 1927, *Zur Statisik des Deutschtums in Palaestina (Statistics of German Customs in Palestine)*—published in the "Journal of the German Palestinian Society" of the Palestine Society 50

Freie Tempelgemeinde (Free Templer Community) 1893-1897—*"Mitteilungen aus der Freien Tempelgemeinde" (Communications from the Free Templer Community)*, Newsletters from Dr Ejal Jakob Eisler's Personal Archives

Goldman, Dan 2002, *Sarona—Settlement Design*—Part of documentation dossier prepared by the Tel Aviv Preservation Team

Goldman, Dan 2002, *Sarona, Third Colony*—Part of documentation dossier prepared by the Tel Aviv Preservation Team

Goldman, Dan 2003, *The Architecture of the Templers in their Colonies in Eretz-Israel, 1868-1948, and their Settlements in the U.S., 1860-1925*—Manuscript Ph.D. dissertation at The Union Institute and University, The Graduate College, School of Interdisciplinary Arts and Sciences, Cincinnati, Ohio, USA

Hedin, Sven 1918, *Jerusalem,* F A Brockhaus Verlag, Germany

Hoffmann, Gisela 1998, *South Beach Idyll*—unpublished private manuscript

Imberger, K., 1938, *Die deutschen landwirtschaftlichen Kolonien in Palaestina (The German Agricultural Colonies in Palestine)* including the appendix *Statistik ueber die Berufe in den deutschen Kolonien 1935 (Statistics regarding the Businesses of the German Colonies 1935)*—published in the "Tuebinger geographische und geologische Abhandlungen, Reihe II, Heft 6—Oehringen"

Kucik, Michal 1998, *Die stillen Haeuser und heimlichen Gaerten—eine Oase im Herzen der grauen Stadt (The Quiet Houses and Homely Gardens—an Oasis in the Heart of a City)*—(translated text from "Architecture of Israel—Architecture & Interior Design Quarterly—No.34(1998)")

Laemmle, Charlotte 2002, The *Laemmle House*—unpublished private manuscript

Laemmle, Otto 1980, *Einiges Wichtiges aus meinem Leben (Some Important Matters from my Life)*—unpublished private manuscript

Laemmle, Otto 1980, *Erinnerungen und Erlebnisse eines Landwirtes und Buergers der Tempelgemeinde Sarona bzw. Jaffa-Sarona in Palaestina in der Zeit zwischen den Jahren 1910 und 1948 (Recollections and Events in the Life of a Farmer and Citizen of the Templer Community in Sarona respectively Jaffa/Sarona in Palestine during the Period 1910 and 1948)*—unpublished private manuscript

Laemmle, Otto 1980, *Glocken der Heimat (Bells from Home)*—unpublished private manuscript

Laemmle, Otto 1995, *Fritz (Friedrich) Laemmle—der alte Fritz (the old Fritz)*—unpublished private manuscript

Lange, Friedrich 1899, *Geschichte des Tempels (History of the Templers)*—Verlag von C Hoffmann, Jerusalem, Stuttgart, Germany.

Lange, Peter 1992, *Templer Handbuch (Templer Handbook)*, TGD, Stuttgart, Germany

Lorch, Fritz 1909, *Die deutschen Tempelkolonien in Palaestina—Ein Blick auf ihre Vergangenheit (The German Templer Colonies in Palestine—A Glance into their Past)*—published in the Information and News Journal XXX11 of the Palestine Association (Palaestina Verein)

Ninck, Pastor C 1911, *Auf Biblischen Pfaden—Pilgerreise durch den Orient (On Biblical Paths—Pilgrimage through the Orient)*—publication with the TGD-Reg.Nr. T-686

Paetzig, Max 1967, *Meine Reise nach Palaestina im Jahre 1935 (My Journey to Palestine in the Year 1935)*—Verlag der Evang.-Luth. Mission, Erlangen, Germany

Rubitschung, Otto W A 1956, *Palestine—as I saw it*—unpublished private manuscript

Rubitschung, Otto W A, *Der Werdegang des deutschen Krankenhauses in Jaffa von 1869-1927 (The Formation of the German Hospital in Jaffa 1869-1927)*—Syrisches Waisenhaus Verlag, Jerusalem, Palestine

Ruff, Dieter P 1985, *The Temple Society—An Overview*—Temple Society Australia, Melbourne, Australia

Sauer, Paul 1991, *The Holy Land Called (The Story of the Temple Society)*—Temple Society Australia (TSA), Melbourne, Australia

Sawatzky, Heinrich 1955, *Templer mennonitischer Herkunft (Templers of Mennonitic Origin)*—Echo-Verlag, Winnipeg, Manitoba, Canada

Schneller, Ludwig 1899, *Die Kaiserfahrt durch's Heilige Land (The Kaiser's Journey through the Holy Land)*—Kommission Verlag von H G Wallmann, Leipzig, Germany

Taylor, A J P & Mayer, S L 1974, *History of World War One*—Optus Books, London, England

Gebietsleitung der Tempelgesellschaft in Deutschland (TGD) 1990, *Damals in Palaestina—Templer erzaehlen vom Leben in ihren Gemeinden (Memories of Palestine—Narratives about life in the Templer Communities)*, Stuttgart, Germany

TGD 1961, *100 Jahre Tempelgesellschaft (100 years Temple Society)*, Stuttgart Germany

TGD/TSA 1974, *denen, die uns vorgegangen sind, zum gedenken—Deutsche Friedhoefe Haifa und Jerusalem (In memory, of those who have gone before us—German Cemeteries Haifa and Jerusalem)* Stuttgart, Germany and Melbourne, Australia

TSA—*Templer Handbuch*

Temple Society Periodical Publications
Sueddeutsche Warte (South German Sentinel)—various editions
Jerusalemer Warte (Jerusalem Sentinel)—various editions
Warte des Temples (Temple Sentinel)—various editions
Circulars and Templer Record TSA—various editions

Van Sommers, Tess, in collaboration with religious authorities 1964, *Religions of Australia—No 26—"The Templars"*—*PIX October 24*, pp18, 19

OTHER REFERENCE SOURCES

Albert Blaich Family Archives—Bayswater, Victoria, Australia
Brigitte Kneher Personal Records—Stuttgart, Germany
Brunhilde Groezinger Personal Records—Victoria, Australia
Charlotte Laemmle Personal Records—Brighton, Victoria, Australia
Ejal Jakob Eisler Personal Archives—Stuttgart, Germany
Helmut Glenk Personal Records—Ringwood East, Victoria, Australia
Helmut Ruff Personal Records—Bayswater, Victoria, Australia
Ingrid Edelmaier Personal Records—Beaumaris, Victoria, Australia
Landeskirchliches Archiv;—Stuttgart, Germany
Martin Higgins Personal Records—Cheltenham, Gloucestershire, England
National Archives of Australia—Melbourne, Victoria, Australia
Temple Society Australia Archives—Bentleigh, Victoria, Australia
Tempelgesellschaft Deutschland Archives—Stuttgart, Germany
Theo Graze Personal Records—Doncaster, Victoria, Australia

ABBREVIATIONS

ABFA	Albert Blaich Family Archives—Australia
CLPR	Charlotte Laemmle Personal Records
DIP	*"Damals in Palestina"* (see Bibliography)
DSS	Deutscher Sportverein Sarona (German Sports Club Sarona)
EJEPA	Ejal Jakob Eisler Personal Archives
GCF	German Community Fund
HGPR	Helmut Glenk Personal Records
HRPR	Helmut Ruff Personal Records
Ibid	ibidem, in the same place
IEPR	Ingrid Edelmaier Personal Records
ILA	Israel Land Administration
JW	Jerusalemer Warte (Jerusalem Sentinel) (see Bibliography)
MFT	Mitteilungen aus der Freien Tempelgemeinde
MHPR	Martin Higgins Personal Records
MHaPR	Manfred Haering Personal Records
NAA	National Archives Australia
NS	National Socialist
RM	Reichsmark
SDW	Sueddeutsche Warte (Southern German Sentinel) (see Bibliography)
SG	Siedlungsgenossenschaft (Settlement Co-operative)
TGPR	Theo Graze Personal Records
TSA	Temple Society Australia
TSA-A	Temple Society Australia—Archives
TSA-TH	Temple Society Australia—Templer Handbook
THLC	Sauer, Prof Dr P, *"The Holy Land Called"* (see Bibliography)
TGD	Tempelgesellschaft Deutschland
WAKO	Wiederaufbaukommission (Reconstruction Commission)
WDT	Warte des Tempels (Templer Sentinel) (see Bibliography)
WW I	World War One
WW II	World War Two

ENDNOTES

1 Tempelgesellschaft in Deutschland (TGD), 1961, 100 Jahre Tempelgesellschaft (100 Years Temple Society); Temple Society Australia (TSA), The Temple Society—An Overview; Templer Handbook (TH)

2 Eisler, J., 2004, Die Erkundungsreise der Templer nach Palaestina im Jahre 1858 (The Fact Finding Mission of the Templers in 1858) Beilage der, Warte des "Tempels" (WDT), Nr. 11

3 Lange, Fr., 1899, Geschichte des Tempels (History of the Temple Society), pp 195 & 218; Eisler, J., 1997, Der deutsche Beitrag zum Aufstieg Jaffas 1850-1914 (The German Contribution towards the establishment of Jaffa 1850-1914), p 86

4 TGD, 1961; TSA, 1974, in memory of those who have gone before us; Sauer, P., 1991, The Holy Land Called (THLC), Chapter 1

5 Sueddeutsche Warte (South German Sentinel)—(SDW), No. 11, 18 March 1869

6 Ben-Artzi, Y., 1992, "Religious Ideology and Landscape Formation: The Case of the German Templers in Eretz-Israel", pp 83-106

7 Encyclopaedia Britannica, 1962, Vol. 17, p 132; E. J. Eisler Personal Records (EJEPR)

8 Bitzer, K., 1968, Rueckschau ins Gelobte Land 1894-1968, p 6

9 Eisler, J., 1997, pp 5-17

10 Ibid., pp 94-95

11 Ibid

12 Ibid

13 Carmel, A., 1973, Die Siedlungen der Wuerttembergischen Templer in Palaestina 1868-1918 (The Settlements of the Templers from Wuerttemberg in Palestine), p 41

14 TSA Archives (TSA-A), A07-46, Nikolai Schmidt Speech, 1946, Translated by Glenk, H.

15 Martin Higgins Personal Records (MHPR); Brugger, H., 1908, Die deutschen Siedlungen in Palaestina (The German Settlements in Palestine)

16 MHPR; Imberger, K., 1938, Die deutschen landwirtschaftlichen Kolonien in Palaestina (The German Agricultural Settlements in Palestine); TGD Archives

17 Goldman, D., 2002, Sarona—Settlement Design; Eisler, J., 1997, pp 103-104

18 TSA-A, A07-46, Translated by Glenk, H

19 Ibid

20 SDW, No. 39, 28 September 1871

21 Goldman, D., 2002

22 SDW, No. 39, 28 September 1871

23 Ibid, No. 37, 14 September 1871; TSA-A, A07-46; MHPR

24 SDW, No. 39, 28 September 1871; TGD Archives; Imberger, K., 1938

25 SDW, No. 37, 14 September 1871

26 Ibid, No. 38, 21 September 1871

27 Carmel, A., 1973, p 43

28 SDW, No. 47, 23 November 1871

29 Ibid, No. 5, 1 February 1872

30 Ibid, No. 11, 11 April 1872, Translated by Glenk, H.

31 TSA-A, A07-46

32 SDW, No. 24, 13 June 1872

33 TSA-A, A07-46

34 Ibid

35 SDW, No. 1, 7 January 1875

36 SDW, No. 11, 13 March 1873

37 Sawatzky, H., 1955, Templer mennonitischer Herkunft (The Templers of Mennonitic Origin), p 19

38 TSA, Templer Record, No. 256, June 1968

39 TSA-A, A07-46, Translated by Glenk, H

40 MHPR; Rubitschung, O., 1928, Der Werdegang des deutschen Krankenhauses in Jaffa von 1869-1927 (The Formation of the German Hospital in Jaffa 1869-1927)

41 SDW, No. 1, 2 January 1872

42 Ibid, No. 47, 21 November 1872

43 Ibid, No. 1, 2 January 1873

44 Ibid, No. 31, 31 July 1873

45 Ibid, No. 32, 9 August 1873

46 TSA-A, A07-46

47 SDW, No. 31, 31 July 1873, Translated by Glenk, H

48 Ibid, No. 13, 26 April 1874

49 Goldman, D., 2002a, Sarona, Third Temple Colony

50 Laemmle, O., 1980, Erinnerungen und Erlebnisse eines Landwirtes und Buergers der Tempelgemeinde Sarona bzw. Jaffa in Palaestina in der Zeit zwischen den Jahren 1910 und 1948 (Recollections and Events in the Life of a Farmer of the Sarona Temple Community respectively Jaffa/Sarona in Palestine in the period from 1910 to 1948)

51 HGPR—Hermann, E. interview February 2004

52 Carmel, A., 1973; Eisler, J., 1997, p 100

53 Sauer, P., 1991, THLC

54 HGPR, confirmed by Dravenicks, C., November 2003

55 SDW, No. 27, 2 July 1874

56 MHPR; Imberger, K., 1938

57 SDW, No. 25, 18 June 1874

58 Die Warte des Tempels (Templer Sentinel)-(WDT), No. 24, 14 June 1877

59 Ibid

60 Goldman, D., 2002a

61 Carmel, A., 1973, p 57

62 WDT, No. 31, 30 July 1874

63 MHPR; Brugger, H., 1908

64 WDT, No. 15, 12 April 1877

65 TSA-A, A07-032, Translated by Glenk, H.

66 Charlotte Laemmle Personal Records (CLPR), Fritz Laemmle—Der Alte Fritz (The Old Fritz)

67 WDT, No. 36, 8 September 1881

68 HGPR—Hermann, H. interview February 2004

69 Sauer, P., 1991, THLC, p 63

70 Ibid, p 67

71 Ejal Jakob Eisler Personal Archive (EJEPA)

72 Sauer, P., 1991, THLC, p 63

73 WDT, No. 10, 8 March 1883

74 Goldman, D., 2002a

75 TGD Archives; Ninck, C., 1911, Auf biblischen Pfaden (On Biblical Paths), Translated by Glenk, H

76 TSA-A, A01:11, Schmidt, N., Geschichte des Tempels,

77 Sauer, P., 1991, THLC, p 66

78 Ibid, pp 58-59

79 Ibid, p 71

80 Ibid; Carmel, A., 1973, p 65; EJEPA, "Manuskript-Mitteilungen aus der Freien Tempelgemeinde" (MFT) 1893

81 EJEPA, MFT, No. 2—Dezember 1893

82 Ibid.

83 CLPR, Fritz Laemmle—Der Alte Fritz

84 Ibid, Translated by Glenk, H.

85 EJEPA, MFT, No. 2—December 1893

86 Ibid, No. 7—May 1895; Ibid, No. 12—June 1896

87 Ibid, No. 9—May 1896

88 Ibid, No. 8—April 1896

89 Ibid, No. 7—May 1895

90 CLPR, Fritz Laemmle—Der Alte Fritz

91 TSA-A, TH; TSA-A, The Temple Society—An Overview

92 Carmel, A., 1973

93 Sauer, P., 1991, THLC, p 71

94 TGD, 1961, pp 17-18

95 Sauer, P., 1991, THLC, p 68

96 Ibid, p 69

97 Ibid; EJEPA, MFT, No. 7—May 1895

98 Sauer, p., 1991, THLC, p 70

99 Ibid

100 Ibid, p 67

101 HGPR

102 Sauer, P., 1991, THLC, p 67

103 EJEPA, MFT, No. 15—December 1894

104 Sauer, P., 1991, THLC, p 67

105 Ibid, p 96

106 Goldman, D., 2002a

107 EJEPA

108 Ibid, MFT, No. 17—September 1895; ibid No. 8—April 1896

109 Ibid

110 Ibid, No. 8—April 1896

111 Sauer, P., 1991, THLC, pp 72-74

112 HGPR; Carmel, A./Eisler, E.J., 1999, Der Kaiser reist ins Heilige Land

113 Schneller, Ludwig 1899, Die Kaiserfahrt durch's Heilige Land, (The Kaiser's Journey through the Holy Land), Translated by Glenk, H.

114 Sauer, P., 1991, THLC, p 73; Carmel, A./Eisler, E.J., 1999, p 120

115 Damals in Palaestina—Templer erzaehlen vom Leben in ihren Gemeinden, 1990, (Memories of Palestine—Narratives about Life in the Templer Communities)—(DIP), p 79; Sauer, P., 1991, THLC, p 79; CLPR—The Laemmle House

116 Sauer, P., 1991, THLC, p 96

117 EJEPA, MFT, No. 8—April 1896

118 Ibid

119 Ibid, No. 7—May 1895

120 Sauer, P., 1991, THLC, p 96

121 Carmel, A., 1973, p 57

122 Sauer, P., 1991, THLC, p 96

123 CLPR, Fritz Laemmle—Der Alte Fritz

124 SDW, No. 22, 29 May 1873; ibid, No. 27, 2 July 1874

125 Albert Blaich Family Archives (ABFA)

126 SDW, No. 11, 13 March 1873

127 Goldmann, D., 2003, The Architecture of the Templers in their Colonies in Eretz-Israel, 1868-1948, and their Settlements in the U.S., 1860-1925, (Manuscript for Ph. D); HGPR/MHaPR—Interview notes with Hugo Wennagel

128 Eisler, J., 1997, p 96

129 CLPR

130 MHPR; Imberger, K., 1938; SDW, No. 27, 2 July 1874, HGPR

131 Eisler, J., 1997, p 137

132 ABFA, Paper from Blessing, G., July 2003

133 DIP, 1990, p 15

134 EJEPR

135 HGPR/MHaPR, Interview notes Pisch, H., and Orth, R.

136 Encyclopaedia Britannica, 1962, Vol. 11, p 528; Sauer, P., 1991, THLC, p 74; Carmel, A./Eisler, J., 1999

137 Christliche Pioniere in Palästina, 2003

138 WDT, No. 224, September 1980, Translated by Glenk, H.

139 WDT, No. 10, 6 March 1902

140 Ibid, Translated by Glenk, H.

141 DIP, 1990, p 87, Translated by Glenk, H.

142 SDW, No. 47, 24 November 1904; WDT, No. 8, 30 April 1934

143 Sauer, P., 1991, THLC, p 70

144 EJEPA, MFT, No. 9—May 1896

145 Sauer, P., 1991, THLC, pp 74-79

146 Ibid, pp 76-77, 99, 105

147 Ibid, p 105; HGPR—Glenk, E. Tape recording

148 Sauer, P., 1991, THLC, p 105-106; WDT, February/March, 1911; HGPR, Blaich, W., Email August 2003; Heinrich, I., Interview November 2002 and Glenk, E., Tape recording

149 Eisler, J., 1997, p 138

150 Sauer, P., 1991, THLC, p 106

151 WDT, No. 5, 1 February 1906

152 TSA-A, TH, p 149

153 HGPR, Hermann, E interview

154 WDT, February/March, 1911

155 Eisler/Haag/Holtz, 2003, pp 211, 216-217

156 CLPR, Erinnerungen und Erlebnisse eines Landwirtes . . . (Manuscript)

157 WDT, February/March, 1911

158 Ibid

159 Ibid

160 EJEPA

161 Sauer, P., 1991, THLC, p 106

162 DIP, 1990, p 39

163 Ibid, p 14-15

164 Eisler, J., 1997, p 124-126

165 HGPR/MHaPR, Interview with Wennagel, H.; Eisler, J., 1997, p 123-124

166 HGPR/MHaPR, Interview with Kuebler, H.

167 HGPR, Glenk, E. Tape recording

168 WDT, February/March, 1911

169 ABFA

170 Ibid, 1910 Dedication Report

171 DIP, 1990, p 96

172 WDT, February/March, 1911; Sauer, P., 1991, THLC, p 80

173 Jerusalemer Warte, (JW) No. 48, 30 November 1911

174 WDT, February/March, 1911

175 Sauer, P., 1991, THLC, p 129
176 De Haas, R., 1930, Der Orangenpflanzer von Sarona, (The Orange Grower from Sarona), p 6
177 Ibid
178 JW, No. 7, 17 February 1913, Translated by Glenk, H.
179 Ibid
180 Translated by Blaich, Irene and Laemmle, Charlotte
181 Sauer, P., 1991, THLC, pp 124-127
182 Ibid
183 Ibid; DIP, 1990, pp 40, 163
184 Encyclopaedia Britannica, 1962, Vol. 17, p 139
185 HGPR/MHaPR—Hermann, E. interview and Hahn, S. February 2004
186 Ibid; DIP, 1990, pp 48-49, 135, 202-203; Sauer, P., 1991, THLC, pp 126-127; HGPR, Glenk, E. tape recording and Hermann, E. interview
187 Hedin, S., 1918, Jerusalem, pp 121-123; TAS-A, 07-043, Translated by Glenk, H.
188 Sauer, P. 1991, THLC, p 128
189 Ibid, p 130; Encyclopaedia Britannica, 1962, Vol. 17, pp 139-141; Bullock, D., 1988, Allenby's War, pp 73-81
190 HGPR, Glenk, E. Tape recording
191 Ibid
192 Ibid; Sauer, P., 1991, THLC, p 131
193 HGPR, Glenk, E. Tape recording; Hermann, E. Interview
194 Ibid, Glenk, E. Tape recording
195 Ibid, Hermann, E. Interview
196 Ibid, Glenk, E. Tape recording; Hermann, E. Interview
197 Sauer, P., 1991, THLC, p 132
198 HGPR, Glenk, E. Tape recording
199 Ibid, Glenk, E. Tape recording; Hermann, E. Interview
200 Ibid, Glenk, E. Tape recording
201 Ibid; DIP, 1990, p 41-42; Sauer, P., 1991, THLC, p 134
202 Ibid
203 DIP, 1990, pp 41-42, 206-208; HGPR, Hermann, E. Interview
204 Ibid, Glenk, E. Tape recording
205 Ibid, Hermann, E. Interview
206 Ibid; DIP, 1990, pp 42, 208
207 Encyclopaedia Britannica, 1962, Vol. 17, p 133
208 Ibid
209 Sauer, P., 1991, THLC, pp 136-143
210 Ibid
211 Ibid, pp 141-143
212 Ibid, p 144
213 Ibid, p 140
214 Ingrid Edelmaier Personal Records (IEPR), Translated by Glenk, H.
215 Sauer, P., 1991, THLC, p 140; DIP, 1990, p 56-57; HGPR, Glenk, E. Tape recording
216 Sauer, P., 1991, THLC, pp 144, 148-150
217 Ibid, p 144; MHPR
218 Sauer, P., 1991, THLC, 145; DIP, 1990, p 21-22
219 HGPR, Hermann, E. Interview
220 Sauer, P., 1991, THLC, p 163
221 Museum, Bad Mergentheim
222 Sauer, P., 1991, THLC, p 144-145; DIP, 1990, p 58-59; HGPR, Glenk, E. Tape recording
223 Ibid
224 CLPR, Glocken der Heimat (Bells from Home), Translated by Glenk, H.
225 Ibid, Erinnerungen und Erlebnisse; HGPR, Glenk, E. Tape recording and Hermann, E. Interview
226 Sauer, P., 1991, THLC, p 149; CLPR, Erinnerungen und Erlebnisse
227 Ibid; HGPR, Glenk, E. Tape recording and Hermann, E. Interview
228 TSA-A, TH, p 135
229 Sauer, P., 1991, THLC, p 150; CLPR, Erinnerungen und Erlebnisse; HGPR, Glenk, E. Tape recording and Hermann, E. Interview
230 TSA-A, TH, p 135
231 Sauer, P., 1991, THLC, p 151
232 CLPR, Erinnerungen und Erlebnisse; HGPR, Glenk, E. Tape recording
233 TSA-A, Report on the Value of Secular Real Estate in Israel—owned by Residents of German Nationality or Extraction, p 29
234 Sauer, P., 1991, THLC, p 157
235 TSA-A, TH, p 135
236 Encyclopaedia Britannica, 1962, Vol. 17, p 133
237 CLPR, Erinnerungen und Erlebnisse
238 Bitzer, K., 1968, p. 19; Sauer, P., 1991, THLC, p 160
239 CLPR, Summary of the Report of the Palestine Royal Commission
240 Encyclopaedia Britannica, 1962, Vol. 17, p 134-135; HGPR, Glenk, E. Tape recording
241 Sauer, P., 1991, THLC, pp 79-82; National Archives Australia (NAA), Box TSTF2A, Hoffmann/Aberle Memorandum 11 July 1948
242 Ibid
243 Sauer, P., 1991, THLC, pp 157-159, pp 161-162
244 Ibid
245 Ibid
246 Ibid, pp 161-162
247 CLPR, Erinnerungen und Erlebnisse
248 Sauer, P., 1991, THLC, p 162
249 TSA-A, A07—Satzung der Deutschen Tempelgemeinde Sarona/ Jaffa (Constitution of the Temple Community Sarona/ Jaffa), Translated by Glenk, H.
250 Persons interviewed by HG and MHa, or who provided information—Charlotte Dravenicks (Asenstorfer), Gertrud Blessing (Wennagel), Kurt Ehnis, Albrecht Frank, Theo Graze, Brunhilde Groezinger, Siegfried Hahn, Ilse Heinrich (Blaich), Else Hermann (Froeschle), Renate Herrmann (Steller), Olga Hoersch (Wennagel), Gisela Hoffmann (Rubitschung), Klaus Peter Hoffmann, Brigitte Kneher (Rohrer), Gretel Krockenberger (Weiss), Anni Kuebler, Helene Kuebler (Knoll), Otto Kuebler, Agnes Laemmle (Groll), Hedwig Meyer (Orth), Lieselotte Minzenmay (Kuebler), Reinhold Orth, Gretel Ottenhoff (Steller), Hans Pisch, Irene Ruff (Weller), Manfred Schnerring, Erika Schulz (Aberle), Elly Steller (Lippmann), Gisela Steller, Herbert Steller, Gerhard Wagner, Gunter Weller, Hugo Weller, Rolf Weller, Hugo Wennagel, Loni Wilke (Groll), Inge Vitols (Aberle), HGPR, Glenk, E. tape recording

251 TSA-A, TH, p 136; CLPR, Erinnerungen und Erlebnisse
252 MHPR, Nachrichten aus Palaestina (News from Palestine), No. 59, 1927
253 TAS-A, TH, p 150
254 TSA-A, A07
255 Ibid
256 Ibid
257 HGPR/MHaPR, Vitols letter, 26 October 2003
258 CLPR, Taxation Assessment for Samuel Groll
259 Ibid
260 Sauer, P., 1991, THLC, pp 164-165
261 BKPR
262 Sauer, P., 1991, THLC, pp 164-165
263 DIP, 1990, pp 304-305
264 Sauer, P., 1991, THLC, p 222
265 TSA-A07 "Constitution of the German Co-operative Vine-culture Society Wilhelma-Sarona Ltd"
266 Sauer, P., 1991, THLC, p 160; WDT, No. 13, 15 July 1938
267 Ibid
268 CLPR, The Laemmle House Sarona
269 CLPR, Copy of agreement between Palestinian Electricity Corporation Ltd and landowners
270 TSA-A, Gewerbe (Businesses) Hoffmann, R., 15 May 1968; CLPR, 1937, Nachweis deutscher Geschaefte in Palaestina
271 Sauer, P., 1991, THLC
272 WDT, No. 13, 15 July 1935
273 EJEPA
274 Ibid
275 Eisler, J., 1997, p 121
276 WDT, No. 21, 15 November 1934, p 167; and interviews
277 EJEPA
278 Bitzer, K., 1968; HGPR, and MHa Hoffmann K. P., Email
279 MHa, Hoffmann, G., South Beach Idyll
280 WDT, No. 13, 15 July 1935, Translated by Glenk, H.
281 Eisler, J., 2001, Deutsche Kolonisten im Heiligen Land—Die Familie John Steinbeck in Briefen aus Palästina und USA (German Colonists in the Holy Land—The John Steinbeck Family, Letters from Palestine and USA) pp 1-19
282 Persons interviewed and who provided information—see listing in Endnote 250
283 TGD, DIP, 1990, p 299
284 TGD, 1961, pp 23-24—Translated by Glenk, H.
285 Ibid, pp 26-27
286 Sauer, P, 1991, THLC, pp 220-223
287 Ibid, pp 198-199; TSA-A, A Brief Historical Introduction
288 Sauer, P., 1991, THLC, pp 195-219; s. Balke, R., 2001, Hakenkreuz im Heiligen Land—Die NSDAP Landesgruppe Palaestina (The Swastika in the Holy Land—The NSDAP Palestine Country Group), p 69
289 Sauer, P, 1991, THLC, pp 195-230
290 MHa, Elly Steller letter and interview 14 October 2003
291 CLPR, Glocken der Heimat
292 HGPR, Tape recording Glenk, E.; CLPR, Erinnerungen und Erlebnisse; Sauer, P., 1991, THLC, pp 223-226
293 HGPR, Tape recoding Glenk, E.
294 Sauer, P., 1991, THLC, pp 226-230
295 TSA-A, A01:11
296 TSA-A, TH, p 138; Sauer, P., 1991, THLC, p 231
297 Persons interviewed or who provided information: Hedwig Wennagel (Aberle), Felix Haar, Siegfried Hahn, Ilse Heinrich, Else Hermann, Agnes Laemmle, Helmut Ruff, Erika Schulz, Elly Steller, Loni Wilke, Inge Vitols; HGPR, Tape recording MHPR
298 Sauer, P., 1991, THLC, pp 232-233
299 TSA-A, A07-001, 026, 027, 034, 037; Sauer, P., 1991, THLC, p 265
300 DIP, 1990, p 267
301 Sauer, P., 1991, THLC, p 233
302 Rundschreiben der Gebietsleitung der Tempelgesellschaft No. 1, 2 Dezember 1940 (Circular of the Temple Society (Germany) No 1-2 December 1940)
303 Ibid
304 Ibid, No. 2, 18 December 1940
305 Sauer, P., 1991, THLC, p 233
306 Ibid, p 235
307 Ibid
308 Ibid, pp 235-237
309 TSA-A
310 Ibid
311 Sauer, P., 1991, THLC, p 257
312 Ibid, p 256
313 Ibid, p 258
314 Ibid
315 CLPR, Personal correspondence,
316 Sauer, P., 1991, THLC, p 246
317 Ibid, p 233
318 Ibid, pp 246-250
319 Ibid, p 258
320 CLPR, Personal correspondence, Translated by Glenk, H
321 Ibid
322 Sauer, P., 1991, THLC, p 260
323 Ibid; CLPR, Personal correspondence
324 Sauer, P., 1991, THLC, p 262
325 Ibid, p 268
326 Ibid, pp 261-262
327 Ibid, pp 264-266
328 Ibid, p 267; CLPR, Personal correspondence
329 Ibid; DIP, 1990, pp 417-418
330 Ibid; Sauer, P., 1991, THLC, p 270
331 Ibid
332 Ibid, pp 271-276; CLPR, Personal correspondence
333 NAA, Box 1321, TSTF2A
334 Sauer, P., 1991, THLC, p 238
335 NAA, Box 1321, TSTF2A
336 Ibid
337 TSA-A
338 Ibid
339 TSA-A; NAA, Box 1321, TSTF2A
340 TSA-A, Letter dated 8 September 1946 from Sarona/Jaffa Templer Community, Translated by Glenk, H
341 Sauer, P., 1991, THLC, p 260
342 NAA, Box 1321, TSTF2A
343 Ibid
344 Ibid; TSA-A
345 Ibid

346 Ibid; NAA, Box 1321, TSTF2A
347 Ibid
348 Ibid
349 Ibid; TSA-A
350 Ibid
351 Sauer, P., 1991, THLC, p 263
352 NAA, Box 1321, TSTF2A; TSA-A
353 NAA, Box 1321, TSTF2A
354 Ibid
355 Ibid
356 Ibid; TSA-A; Sauer, P., 1991, THLC, p 298-308
357 Goldman, D., Advice November 2003
358 "Eretz" Magazine, No. 32, February/March 2003
359 WDT, No. 5, May 1950, Translated by Glenk, H
360 TGD/TSA, 1974, pp 26, 47
361 WDT No. 5, May 1950, Translated by Glenk, H
362 Ibid
363 Brandt, K., "Report on the Value of Secular Real Estate in Israel—Owned by Former Residents of Germany Nationality or Extraction", 1957
364 HGPR, Goldman/Metzger-Szmuk interview, Oct. 2003
365 Ibid
366 Ibid
367 HGPR, Email Brigitte Kneher December 2003
368 MHa, Email September 1999
369 Kucik, M., 1998, Architecture of Israel—Architecture and Interior Design Quarterly, No. 34
370 HGPR, Goldman/Metzger-Szmuk interview
371 Ibid
372 Goldman, D., 2003
373 HGPR, Goldman/Metzger-Szmuk interview
374 TGPR
375 HGPR
376 Ibid
377 TSA, Various editions of DWT; HGPR, Various interviews MHa
378 TSA-A, A07-46, Schmidt, N., 1946; MHPR
379 MHPR; "in memory of those who have gone before us", pp 68-69
380 MHPR; TSA-A
381 HRPR
382 MHPR
383 Ibid
384 MHaPR; Interview L. Wilke 11 November 2003
385 MHPR; CLPR, Personal correspondence

LIST OF ILLUSTRATIONS

SOURCES OF ILLUSTRATIONS

The first number refers to the number of the illustration and the second number refers to the page number in this book. Copies of many photos are also found in various family collections and archives.

Archive of the Temple Society Australia, Bentleigh, Victoria, Australia: 2:1, 3:1, 4:1, 8:4, 18:16, 24:24, 53:52, 105:97, 114:109, 250:189, 261:201, 270:215, 272:221, 273:223, 274:223, 283:238, 284:238.

Archive of the Tempelgesellschaft in Deutschland, Degerloch, Germany: 5:2, 6:2, 19:17, 27:28, 33:38, 50:50, 78:69, 124:115, 137:124, 142:128, 193:160, 282:237, 289:242.

Bayerisches Hauptstaatsarchiv, IV Kriegsarchiv, Muenchen, Germany: 286:240.

Blaich, Horst, private collection, Bayswater, Australia: 17:14 (Drawing by Horst Blaich), 56:54, 58:54.

Carmel, Alex, private collection 13:9

Eisler, Jakob, Historian, private collection, Israel: 25:25, 29:23, 46:48, 54:52.

Encyclopaedia Britannica, Inc. 1962 Issue: 20:18.

Eppinger-Blaich, Irene, private collection, Bayswater, Australia: 32:37, 242:186, 275:224, 276:224, 276a:225, 277:226, 278:226.

Evangelisches Landeskirchliches Archiv; Foto-Sammlung des Schneller Nachlasses, Stuttgart, Wuerttemberg, Germany; photos taken by Paul Hommel during several visits to Palestine between 1927 and 1931: 9:5, 97:89, 101:94, 125:116, 146:130, 149:133, 152:134, 155:137, 162:143, 163:143, 219:171, 251:190.

Geographische Anstalt Wagner and Debes, Leipzig, Germany: 12:8, 15:10.

Glenk, Helmut, private collection, Ringwood East, Australia: 280a:228, 280:229, 290:242.

Goldman, Dan, Architect, private collection, Israel: 10:6, 135:122, 160:141, 281:235, 287:241, 294:245, 295:246.

Kaiserin Auguste Victoria-Stiftung, Bericht des Jahres 1910, Berlin, Germany: 59:54.

Katz, Kalmann, and Yaron Katz, Planning Architects, Yahel Engineers, Project Management for the South Hakirya, Tel-Aviv, (computer simulation image): 296: 246.

Kneher, Brigitte, Historian, private collection, Kirchheim a T., Germany: 112:105, 238:183, 217:216.

Laemmle, Charlotte Dr, private collection, Brighton, Australia: 11:7, 22:21, 26:27, 43:46, 44:47, 47:49, 48:49, 49:49, 80:70, 84:74, 86:78, 96:88, 98:91, 102:96, 103:97, 104:97, 106:99, 107:99, 108:100, 110:103, 109:102, 111:104, 115:109, 119:112, 132:120, 133:121, 136:123, 139:126, 141:127, 153:136, 158:140, 167:146, 168:148, 169:149, 170:149, 171:151, 172:151, 173:151, 181:156, 194:160, 197:161, 207:165, 208:166, 243:186, 244:186, 247:188, 259:199, 262:205, 263:205, 265:210, 266:211, 267:211, 268:212, 269:213, 285:239, 288:242.

Preiss, Ludwig—Verlag Julius Hoffmann—Stuttgart, Germany: 7:3.

Tatura War Museum: 264:208.

Verlag Julius Hoffmann—Stuttgart, Germany: 1:ii.

Weiss, Max Dr, Berlin, Germany: 41:44.

The following photographic images are in the 'Albert Blaich Family Archive-Australia' (Bayswater) computer data base, under the specific family name collections:

Amir, Yoel, Israel: 35:38.

Asenstorfer, Charlotte: 199:162.

Beck, Ingrid: 94:87, 279:227.

Blaich, Karl: 39:43, 40:44, 42:45.

Blaich, Bernhard: 249:189, 206:165.

Edelmaier, Ingrid: 68:60, 69:62, 87:79, 120:113, 121:113, 166:145, 196:161, 203:164, 221:171, 222:172, 223:173, 224:175, 225:175, 233:180, 237:182, 303:285.

Eppinger, Richard O. :23:23, 31:35, 76:68, 90:83, 90:82, 99:92, 74:65.

Frank, Andreas: 75:66, 254:191.

Gohl, Erhard: 21:19.

Graze, Theo (Carl Kuebler): 71:63, 77:68, 85:76, 88:81, 114:109, 130:119, 138:126, 140:127, 148:132, 154:136, 161:142, 174:152, 175:152, 176:153, 182:157, 183:157, 184:157, 191:160, 211:167, 212:167, 214:169, 215:169, 236:182, 258:197, 260:200, 297:247, 298:248, 299:251, 300:253, 301:254.

Groezinger, Hildegard, (Germany): 28:30, 34:38, 62:57, 67:60, 93:87, 95:87, 100:93, 190:159.

Groezinger, Brunhilde: 113:106, 177:154, 248:188, 253:191.

SOURCES OF ILLUSTRATIONS

Haering, Manfred: 52:51, 83:73, 92:84, 117:111, 144:129, 145:130, 156:138, 178:154, 213:168, 216:170, 226:176, 229:179, 240:185, 241:185, 246:187, 252:190, 255:192, 257:194, 292:243.

Hermann, Else: 89:82.

Hoffmann, Peter: 61:56, 64:57, 126:116.

Krockenberger, Oskar: 55:53, 291:242.

Kuebler, Otto: 185:158, 186:158, 187:158, 188:158, 189:159, 198:162, 200:163, 201:163, 202:164, 204:164, 205:165.

Lippmann, Lotte: 123:115, 151:133, 164:144, 218:170, 234:181, 235:181.

Loebert, Otto: 179:155, 231:180, 232:180.

Neef, Roland: 165:144.

Orth, Reinhold: 45:48, 116:110.

Paulus, Lore, (Germany): 60:55, 118:112.

Schmidt, Nikolai: 30:35, 143:129.

Schnerring, Irmgard: 57:54.

Steller, Eugen: 79:69, 82:72, 91:83, 122:114, 239:184, 245:187, 159:141,

Strasser/Lutz: 4:9, 131:119.

Venus, Family: 51:51, 72:63, 73:64, 129:118, 134:122, 180:155, 195:161, 217:170, 220:171, 227:178, 228:178, 230:179.

Wagner, Georg: 46:48.

Weller, Hartmut: 70:62.

Wennagel, Hugo: 36:39, 37:39, 38:41, 63:57, 65:58, 66:59, 127:117, 128:118, 147:132, 157:139, 192:160, 209:166, 293:243.

INDEX

Page numbers in italics refer to illustrations.

Ladies who are referred to in different parts of the text by their maiden name and their married name have been entered in the index under their married name with a reference to their maiden name.

Subheadings are arranged alphabetically with the exception of those under the heading Sarona, Templer settlement, which are arranged chronologically.

303) Map of old Jaffa, Tel Aviv and Sarona compiled by Zev Vilnay in the late 1930's

SARONA German Temple Settlement 1937

Original drawn by Carl Kuebler in 1937, and adapted for the Sarona Preservation Team in Tel Aviv by Horst Blaich in 2003

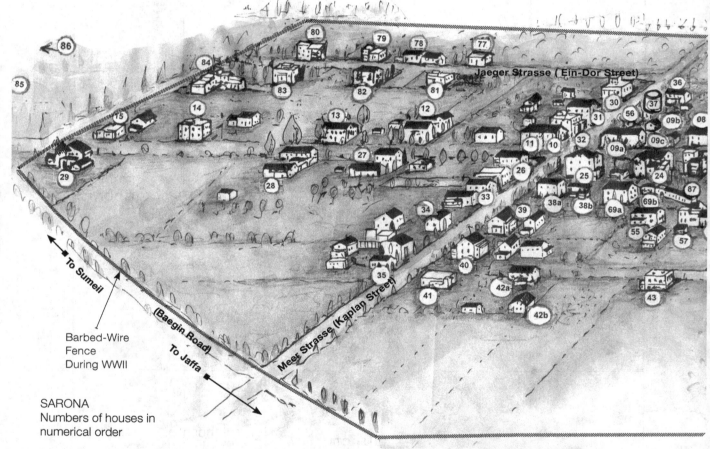

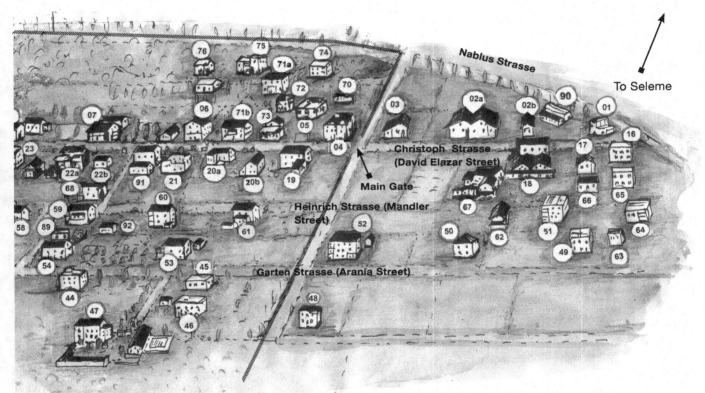

291